Pharmaceutical Economics and Policy

Stuart O. Schweitzer, Ph.D.
Professor of Health Services
UCLA School of Public Health

New York   Oxford
OXFORD UNIVERSITY PRESS
1997

Oxford University Press

Oxford   New York

Athens   Auckland   Bangkok   Bogota   Bombay   Buenos Aires
Calcutta   Cape Town   Dar es Salaam   Delhi   Florence   Hong Kong
Istanbul   Karachi   Kuala Lumpur   Madras   Madrid   Melbourne
Mexico City   Nairobi   Paris   Singapore   Taipei   Tokyo   Toronto

and associated companies in
Berlin   Ibadan

Library of Congress Cataloging-in-Publication Data
Schweitzer, Stuart O.
Pharmaceutical economics and policy /
Stuart O. Schweitzer.
p.   cm.   Includes bibliographical references and index.
ISBN 0-19-510524-9
1. Pharmaceutical industry—United States.
2. Pharmaceutical policy—United States.
3.   Pharmaceutical industry.
I. Title.
HD9666.5.S385   1997   388.4'76151'0973—dc21   96-40855

1 2 3 4 5 6 7 8 9

Printed in the United States of America
on acid-free paper

Preface

Pharmaceuticals constitute only a small share of health expenditures in the United States, but they are a much larger share in other countries, and the proportion is especially large in the developing world. In addition, pharmaceuticals raise the productivity of other health care inputs, such as physician visits and hospitals, so this sector is vitally important in every country. Although topics in pharmaceutical economics and policy are frequently discussed in academic and policy circles, comprehensive examinations of the entire sector are surprisingly rare. This is an especially serious problem because the health care system is complex and its components interact with one another. Policies affecting one segment will have an impact on the others. Therefore, health reforms designed with the best of intentions have frequently had serious unintended consequences. The purpose of this book is to explore the pharmaceutical sector within the context of complete health systems. Concerns such as research and development priorities, cost containment, and quality assurance pertain to both wealthy and developing countries.

This text uses an economic framework to examine separately the supply and demand sides of the pharmaceutical market as well as policies that attempt to alter market performance. Throughout the book, problems are encountered that have no simple solutions because interests and objectives conflict. Solutions do exist, but tradeoffs must be considered and the effects of policy alternatives must be weighed. Economics is the appropriate discipline to guide this inquiry.

The inquiry is divided into five sections. The first is an Introduction, which outlines some of the issues that will be addressed in subsequent chapters. Section I looks at the supply side of pharmaceuticals—the industry.

The two elements that differentiate this industry from most others are the large investment in research and development and the substantial expenditures devoted to promoting the diffusion of new products through marketing. Section II addresses the demand for pharmaceuticals, looking first at consumer behavior but recognizing that in any health care market the consumer is not alone in making consumption decisions. Physicians, pharmacists, and—to an increasing extent—insurers also have a role in determining pharmaceutical use. Pharmaceuticals are shown to be both a "good" and a "service," leading to difficulty in assessing the industry's performance. After both the supply and demand sides of the pharmaceutical market have been examined, four dimensions of market performance are analyzed in Section III: the pricing of drugs, the international structure of the pharmaceutical industry, international price comparisons, and variation in the timing of the adoption of new products in different countries. Observations of this variation, for example, have led some to conclude that the United States suffers from a "drug lag." The last section of the book, Section IV, considers the development of two public policy issues related to the management of new technology in the United States: approval of new drugs and granting of market exclusivity through patent protection.

The book employs the tools of microeconomics, but the analysis requires no more than a minimal exposure to the field. Thus, it will be appropriate for a wide audience, including students of public policy, health economics, health administration, and pharmacy administration. It is also written for those presently working in health policy arenas, in both the public and the private sectors. The book's scope is broad enough to interest readers in a number of settings, including regulatory agencies, industry, health delivery organizations, and insurers.

Acknowledgments

Many of the policy issues presented in this book have been discussed in the UCLA School of Public Health Seminar in Pharmaceutical Economics and Policy, which is directed by my friend and colleague, William Comanor. The seminar is part of the UCLA Research Program in Pharmaceutical Economics and Policy. My fellow codirector of the program, Michael Intriligator, has also provided invaluable guidance. I am grateful to all of the seminar speakers, as well as to the UCLA faculty and student participants, for providing an unending series of challenging and thought-provoking discussions over the past seven years. I also wish to thank Ariel Linden, Xiao-Feng Liu, and Amardeep Singh Thind for their valuable research assistance in preparing the manuscript. Without the inspiration of Arthur and Frances Urwitz; the love, support, and advice of my wife, Suzanne; and the encouragement of my sons, Maurice, Theodore, and Jeremy, this book could not have been written.

Contents

IV. Intervention in the Pharmaceutical Market: Public and Private

Pharmaceutical Economics and Policy

Introduction

The pharmaceutical industry is praised as one of the nation's leading industrial sectors. The fruits of its extensive research and development are sold world wide and have improved the length and quality of life of countless individuals. At the same time, however, the industry is criticized for its marketing and pricing practices—and even for its research and development priorities (see Comanor 1986). This introduction highlights aspects of the pharmaceuticals market that differentiate it from other markets. The approach taken is like that of a standard economic inquiry. First we deal with the pharmaceutical supply—the industry, its research and development and its marketing. Then we turn to the demand side of the marketplace, identifying not one, but four parties involved in the consumption decision: physician, patient, pharmacist, and, increasingly, the insurer. The next topic is market performance, including the pricing of drugs and the multinational character of the market. Then regulatory issues that differentiate the pharmaceutical market from other markets are examined: the drug approval process and patent policy. The chapter concludes with a series of policy questions often asked about the industry, all of which involve balancing conflicting goals and priorities. These questions illustrate the role of economic analysis in formulating policies regarding the pharmaceutical sector.

The study of pharmaceutical economics and policy investigates just one sector of health economics, but it naturally leads to an investigation of the appropriate roles of public and private sectors in managing complex and rapidly changing technology, a question pertaining as well to a broad array of technology-based industries, including electronics, aerospace, and communications. Additionally, the transfer of pharmaceutical knowledge between nations illustrates the spillover effect by which decisions made in the

3

United States, Europe, and Japan, the regions where most new pharmaceuticals are developed, affect other countries.

The US pharmaceutical industry has been singularly successful in developing treatments for many of the nation's leading causes of morbidity and mortality. And this success has been achieved at a relatively low cost. Expenditures on drugs and other medical nondurable products sold outside hospitals and nursing homes constituted only 8.4% of national health expenditures in the United States in 1993 (US Department of Health and Human Services 1995).* The figure for 1994 fell to less than 8.3%. The share of national health expenditures devoted to *prescribed* drugs was only 5.5% (Genuardi et al. 1996).† These numbers are far smaller those of the hospital or physician sectors. At the same time the pharmaceutical industry has, nonetheless, become highly visible as a result of its high-tech successes and its employment growth. It has become an international leader in transforming basic science into readily available consumer goods that are sought all over the world. Scrutiny by consumer groups and both the legislative and executive branches of the federal government no doubt stems from the unusual dual roles of the industry, which is both a manufacturer of health inputs and a producer of health services as a member of the health care team (Comanor and Schweitzer 1994). Furthermore, the demand for its products is both consumer-driven (as is typically the case for other consumer goods) and generated from the decisions of others, such as physicians. It is clear that the pharmaceutical industry is unique in many ways and that the peculiar nature of the industry creates particular dilemmas in public policy. This book studies the pharmaceutical industry in terms of its structure and its performance, both domestically and internationally.

The pharmaceutical sector is, of course, a component of any health *system*; drugs are but one of many inputs, which include physician services and hospital and ambulatory-based capital equipment. In many instances, pharmaceuticals complement these other inputs, as in the case of antibiotics. And there are other examples of a *substitution effect*, in which one input—in this case drugs—replaces other inputs. For instance, in the 1970s psychoactive drugs permitted ambulatory care of patients with mental illness who had previously required hospitalization.

This *systems* view of the health sector is useful in trying to understand health care finance. Insurance systems that differentiate between service categories, paying differentially for hospital care, physician visits, mental health

---

*This includes both prescribed and nonprescribed drugs sold in ambulatory settings. Although this excludes sales of drugs in hospitals and nursing homes, the shift in the locus of care from hospital to ambulatory settings increases the role of ambulatory drugs.

†This figure excludes over-the-counter (OTC) medications. As prescription drugs are "switched" to OTC status over time, the proportion of health expenditures accounted for by prescription drugs will tend to decline.

care, dental procedures, and drugs, create incentives (and disencentives) for particular kinds of care and often shift demand from one sector to another.

Martin and McMillan (1996) have observed that reduced insurance coverage for drugs leads to increased use of hospital care. Health system efficiency will be increased whenever outcomes are produced at minimum cost to society. Society is therefore better off if payment and regulatory decisions are designed to encourage the use of the most cost-effective combination of resources. Piecemeal interventions, ignoring the interrelatedness of health services, are likely to decrease overall health system efficiency and increase costs.

These issues become particularly contentious in health care because technology changes so rapidly, making assessment difficult. Early studies of a new technology may not capture the real potential of a new service. Early studies of computerized axial tomography (now called CT scan), for example, saw it merely as a complement to ordinary x-ray technology and predicted only a cost-increasing effect. These predictions failed to foresee the new uses of these scans in making diagnoses that had previously been impossible. In fact, CT scans ultimately replaced other technologies that were either less accurate or presented higher risks to patients.

In addition, much health technology increases the quality of outcomes, so traditional assessments of cost, assuming the same output, are inappropriate. H_2-antagonist drugs, which allow nonsurgical treatment of ulcers, could be evaluated traditionally. (Is cure of the condition achieved more cheaply by drugs than by surgery?) But what about the intangible costs of surgery, including pain and anxiety? And other technologies such as joint implants and cardiac drugs permit the resumption of normal activities by patients with previously incurable acute or chronic disease. Standard efficiency measures are inadequate to assess these technologies.

The Supply of Pharmaceuticals

The foundation of the pharmaceutical industry is its research and development. Pharmaceuticals are one of the economic and technological success stories of the twentieth century in the United States, where expenditures on drugs have grown nine percent per year since 1960 (United States Department of Health and Human Services 1995).* The Office of Technology

---

*Throughout this book the terms "pharmaceuticals" and "drugs" are used interchangeably. Both terms refer to prescribed and over-the-counter products, but exclude medical sundries such as skin lotions, antacids and analgesics unless they are specifically mentioned. Historically the distinction between prescribed and over-the-counter products was of major importance, because it differentiated between the physician or the patient making the product selection decision. But with the "shifting" of many prominent prescription drugs to over-the-counter status the distinction has become blurred because even powerful drugs are now directly available to consumers.

Assessment of the United States Congress reported that research and development spending by US pharmaceutical companies was between $5.7 billion and $6.6 billion in 1990, having grown at an annual rate of between 7.6 and 9.4% per year since 1976 (US Congress, Office of Technology Assessment 1993). Ninety percent of pharmaceutical research and development (R&D) is done by the private sector. Although the direct government share of R&D expenditures is small, it is targeted to specific needs. For example, where commercial rewards of research are too small to elicit private sector investment, two federal programs attempt to stimulate private sector activity. In 1983 Congress passed the Orphan Drug Act to create incentives for private pharmaceutical companies to engage in research and development into drugs without a large commercial market. And in 1986 Congress enacted the Federal Technology Transfer Act, which established Cooperative Research and Development Agreements (CRADAs) (US Congress, Office of Technology Assessment 1993). Through CRADAs, a federal laboratory directly transfers research resources to a private developer to facilitate cooperative research. These programs subsidizing noncommercially viable research also suggest a model whereby R&D could be directed to problems of developing countries, where incidence and prevalence of diseases infrequently seen in industrialized countries—such as malaria—may be enormous, but incomes of those afflicted are so low that the commercial market is small.

The pharmaceutical industry is also differentiated from other industries by its marketing efforts. Marketing prescription pharmaceuticals is unlike marketing most other products because of the peculiar consumer–agent relationship characterizing health care demand. Traditionally, prescribed drugs are selected by physicians on behalf of their patients, whose role in product selection is passive. By definition, purchase of prescription drugs by patients must be authorized by a physician. Firms compete heavily in many of the more popular therapeutic markets, such as those for cardiovascular, analgesic, and digestive system drugs. Historically, this marketing has taken the form of advertising in medical journals and magazines and visits by sales representatives to physician offices and hospitals. Physicians frequently report that their primary source of information about new drugs is pharmaceutical company representatives (Bowman 1994). But there is considerable concern as to whether this drug marketing has been in the best interest of patients. Wilkes et al. (1992) studied print advertising for drugs and found that over 90% was to some degree misleading and incomplete. On the other hand, those who are exposed to this marketing might be expected to know that advertising is, by its very nature, biased and incomplete, and should not be relied upon for comprehensive information. In either case, it follows that physicians need unbiased information to assist them in selecting the best products for their patients.

In recent years another type of drug marketing has appeared: advertisements aimed directly at the end-user, the patient. These advertisements, in the press and on television, urge patients to tell their physicians that they would like to try a particular product. Will consumers be responsive to such advertising? And will physicians feel unduly pressured to prescribe drugs that they feel are inappropriate? We do not yet know the answers to these questions.

The Demand for Pharmaceuticals

The demand for pharmaceuticals, of course, derives from the demand for health. While most markets have two participants, the producer and the consumer, demand for health care is also determined by so-called "third-party intermediaries," the insurers or other payers who stand behind the patient ready to pay for whatever he or she decides to purchase. But the picture for health care is even more involved because the physician frequently has two roles as decision-maker: as a provider of care and as the consumer's agent. This "agency relationship," in which the professional acts in the consumer's best interest, has been the subject of intense debate for decades, primarily because of the incentives built into fee-for-service medical care, still the predominant form of physician payment in the United States and most other countries. Fee-for-service payment rewards the practitioner for performing additional services. A disquieting, inherent conflict of interest faces the physician who is paid according to the quantity of services performed. Of course, there are many other areas of our lives in which our expertise as consumers is so limited that we must trust others to make decisions for us. We trust our accountant to advise us regarding arcane tax regulations, and we similarly rely upon our architect and contractor when we contemplate a construction project. Similarly, most of us also rely on the advice of our auto mechanic. And then there are our professors, who set the curricula, teach the courses, and may even write and recommend the textbooks! Health insurance creates an odd division between professional advice, service delivery, consumption, and payment. Health services are traditionally selected by the physician, who neither consumes the service nor pays for it. The patient receives the service, but for approximately 80% of expenditures, does not pay for it directly (US Department of Health and Human Services 1995). Payment is left to government or private insurers, acting as "third-party payers." Of course patients ultimately pay, but only indirectly, and as part of a greater pool of insurance beneficiaries and taxpayers. In the pharmaceutical market another professional also participates—the pharmacist. The role of pharmacists is changing rapidly, and we will look particularly at some of the forces shaping the future of this profession.

But the health care picture is becoming even more complicated. Treatment decisions, formerly arrived at jointly between the physician and the patient, are increasingly being made by third-party payers. Both the privately insured and those insured by public programs, such as Medicare and Medicaid, are joining managed-care plans, many of which combine the insurance function with medical-care decision-making. Treatment plans are frequently established by the managed-care plan as a way of improving quality of care while reducing the use of unnecessary care and lowering the cost of necessary care. In the case of pharmaceuticals, these treatment protocols, or guidelines, frequently specify which drugs are to be used or denote when generic versions of a drug are to be prescribed.

But third-party insurance coverage is far less comprehensive for pharmaceuticals than it is for many other health services. While insurance (both government and private) covered 96% of hospital services in 1992 and 82% of physician services, it covered only 72% of the cost of pharmaceuticals (Health Insurance Association of America 1994). Hence, data for 1992 shows that pharmaceuticals comprise over 30 percent of all out-of-pocket expenditures for health services (Health Insurance Association of America 1994). For the elderly this situation is even more pronounced, for they consume some 35% of all drugs, a disproportionately large share. The situation is exacerbated by greater health care needs of the elderly and the lack of insurance coverage for ambulatory drugs by their major source of health insurance, Medicare. Long (1994) estimates that 45% of the elderly have no insurance coverage for pharmaceuticals. Thus patients are more sensitive to prices charged for pharmaceuticals than for other services. They "demand" pharmaceuticals in the true economic sense, both consuming the product and paying for it out of pocket, to a greater extent than they do for most other health services.

Other aspects of the demand for pharmaceuticals are also investigated. Pharmaceutical demand is influenced by the fact that drugs are both a traditional product, in the sense of other manufactured goods, and also a service, because of the professional component in selection and dispensing. Another important consideration is the degree of market concentration or competition in the industry, and how consumers—and their physician agents—receive information about therapeutic alternatives.

Pharmaceutical Prices

Pricing of pharmaceuticals is perhaps the most controversial aspect of the industry. Consumers, and their elected legislative representatives, are highly attuned to drug prices. In fact, hearings into drug pricing have been held in Congress for over 30 years! It appears that consumers are more sensitive to the prices of pharmaceuticals than they are to other health services which are far more expensive. With the relatively low level of insurance coverage for pharmaceuticals, and their appearance as a "product" rather than a sophisticated "service," it is not surprising that consumers are more likely to complain about a $50 bottle of tablets than a $500 radiology procedure, or a $5000 hospital stay!

To understand how drug prices are set, one must return to the structure of the industry. Perhaps its most differentiating characteristic is that it is particularly intensive in fixed costs. Estimates of the cost of bringing a new drug to market are up to $259 million (DiMasi et al. 1991). Once those fixed costs are expended, the remaining costs of drug marketing, manufacturing, and distribution—while far from insignificant—are relatively small. The model of price-setting in a perfectly competitive market suggests that prices are based upon marginal costs. But this model obviously does not apply for pharmaceuticals, for if they were priced according to their marginal costs, they would be very inexpensive, but in the long run no expenditures on R&D would be made. A more applicable model allows either buyer or seller to act more as an oligopolist, with some control over price. Such oligopolistic markets allow prices to exceed marginal cost in the long run. There are many drug markets with only a few products within a drug class: calcium channel blockers, recombinant erythropoietin, and antifungals are examples of such classes. Indeed, there are relatively few markets within the pharmaceutical industry which come close to satisfying the conditions of perfect competition. This result is, in part, the objective of many institutional arrangements whose purpose is to reward innovation through protection of intellectual property.

On the other hand, many pharmaceutical markets are highly competitive. As we shall see, even new drugs, which enjoy full patent protection, often compete with other products in the same drug class and with older drugs that have a favorable reputation and product loyalty. Just how competitive is the pharmaceutical industry? Obviously the answer to this vexing question involves more than the total number of pharmaceuticals in the marketplace or the number of pharmaceutical manufacturers, either domestic or foreign.

Product differentiation among competing drugs highlights the role of consumer tastes and preferences in price determination for those competing drugs. Both product differentiation and consumer preferences underscore the importance of demand in pharmaceutical price determination. This appears counterintuitive at first because the cost of drug development, a supply-side variable, is so often blamed for high costs. This argument is heard not only from industry critics but from the industry itself. But let us consider three pieces of evidence to the contrary.

The first is that launch prices of new pharmaceuticals relative to prices of existing drugs in the same therapeutic class are substantially higher for drugs that are particularly innovative and offer major clinical advantages (Lu and Comanor 1996). In other words, better drugs command higher prices than less effective drugs do. But perception of drug quality is a demand factor, and not a supply variable.

Second, Lu and Comanor (1996) also observed that drugs introduced into a market where other brand products already exist are priced lower than they would be if there were no brand products already there. Not surprisingly, competition tends to moderate drug prices. Of course market competition is also a demand factor.

Third, price variation is extremely high in the industry, and some classes of buyers pay much more for the same drug than other classes do. The buyers who are best able to negotiate substantial discounts from list prices are health maintenance organizations (HMOs) and other managed-care plans because they are able to control prescribing decisions by their participating physicians. Retail pharmacies, which are passive in the product selection decision, are unable to obtain the same discounts. Economic theory describes this phenomenon as "price discrimination." We know that profit-maximizing sellers will attempt to charge different purchasers different prices, depending upon their demand elasticity. Purchasers whose demand is particularly price sensitive (e.g., HMOs) will receive a lower price than will those whose demand is less price sensitive (e.g., retail pharmacies). Price discrimination is not unique to pharmaceuticals, of course; the same behavior is observed among airlines, telephone companies, and even health services, where purchasers who can readily switch among sellers according to price pay less than buyers whose demand cannot be switched. Business purchasers with relatively inflexible schedules pay more for airfares and telephone charges than other consumers who can vary the timing of their purchase according to price. Thus, drug prices are substantially determined by purchaser demand elasticity, another demand factor.

Our conclusion is that price is largely determined by demand factors in this industry. The industry and its critics both argue that investment cost determines price and price determines demand. But the evidence suggests that demand determines price and price (and profit) determines subsequent investment.

Let us now turn to the evidence of actual trends in pharmaceutical prices and rates of return earned by pharmaceutical firms. Prior to 1980 price increases for pharmaceuticals were relatively modest. From 1960 to 1980 price increases were below the rate of increase for all medical care (Organization for Economic Cooperation and Development 1993), but a structural shift seems to have occurred around 1980, and since that time the rate of increase of pharmaceutical prices has exceeded that for all medical care and has remained higher. Why is this?

A better understanding is needed of the role that costs and risks of R&D play in pricing. Are regulatory factors influencing the costs and risks of drug development? If so, how do these affect rates of return on investment? There is considerable disagreement concerning the rate of return drug companies earn on their high fixed costs of R&D. In response to frequently voiced public concern regarding exorbitant drug industry profits, the Congressional Office of Technology Assessment (OTA) recently studied the revenues and costs of R&D for the pharmaceutical industry (US Congress, Office of Technology Assessment 1993). The study found that revenue for new products was greater than the development costs but that the amount by which the rate of return to investment in the pharmaceutical industry exceeded that in other industries was only modest (US Congress, Office of Technology

Assessment 1993). What is the significance of these "excess" profits? If they existed in an equilibrium situation, they would suggest that market competition is failing to moderate profits and that pharmaceutical firms have been able to generate abnormal profits—what economists term "economic rent." But industry R&D expenditures have been growing substantially in the past five years, suggesting that the excess profits observed by the OTA are only temporary and represent a state of disequilibrium which has stimulated increased R&D effort. If this is true, the increased investment will tend to lower yield, for investment decisions are "ordered," with the highest profit investments being made first, followed by those expected to yield lower profit, and so forth. The yield on the last investment will therefore be lower than that on the earlier investments. In the face of these increased expenditures, excess profits may not be sustained in the long run. In addition, each investment decision entails considerable risk, for most initial investments fail to produce a marketable drug, and of those drugs which do make it to market, few are commercially successful. A higher-than-average rate of return may represent the premium needed to attract each marginal investment into an industry with such high risk.

As noted previously, the study of pharmaceutical prices is made more complicated by the absence of a uniform price across buyers and geographic areas. The market for pharmaceuticals is highly segmented, both domestically and internationally, and price discrimination is common ("More Firms Give Medicaid Breaks on Drug Prices" 1990). Price discounting at the wholesale level is so widely practiced that it was the basis of a General Accounting Office (GAO) investigation into pricing practices of firms selling to the Veterans' Administration (VA) and Medicaid programs following passage of the 1990 Omnibus Budget Reconciliation Act (OBRA). OBRA required manufacturers to give state Medicaid programs at least the same discount they gave to any other purchaser (United States General Accounting Office 1991).* More recently, the National Association of Retail Druggists has successfully sued major drug manufacturers in order to obtain the same discounts (or rebates) that they give to chain pharmacies and managed-care providers (Genuardi et al. 1996).

Research studies do not even agree on the use of a common measure of wholesale price. Two commercial data sources are frequently used. Some researchers use the Average Wholesale Price (AWP), published by The Red Book, Inc. The GAO, on the other hand, used the Wholesale Acquisition Cost (WAC), published by Medi-Span in its recent studies of US, Canadian, and United Kingdom prices (United States General Accounting Office 1994). Unfortunately, neither of these measures captures actual transaction prices, including discounts and rebates.

---

*OBRA exempted the VA and other Department of Defense purchasers from "best price" comparisons (United States General Accounting Office 1991).

The Multinational Pharmaceutical Industry

Few industries are as multinational as pharmaceuticals. Although pharmaceuticals are ubiquitous and sold worldwide, the largest producers are based in relatively few countries, most notably the United States, Switzerland, the United Kingdom, Japan, France, Germany, and Sweden. However, each of the major firms has substantial operations in many countries, and it is often difficult to tell where a firm's R&D, manufacturing, or even strategic planning for a particular product occurred. Thus, describing the "nationality" of a firm or product in terms of the nation in which the corporate headquarters is located fails to identify such important concerns as employment generated or the relevant governmental regulatory jurisdiction.

An area of concern to multinational organization such as the World Health Organization (WHO) and the United Nations International Children's Emergency Fund (UNICEF) is how unevenly the pharmaceutical industry responds to health needs of developed and developing countries. The poorer countries of the world are dependent for many of their pharmaceuticals upon drug manufacturers which are primarily located in the wealthy countries—the United States, western Europe, and Japan. These firms seek markets primarily in the developed world because patients in poor countries have only a limited ability to pay for drugs. It is therefore not surprising that R&D is devoted to health problems of the developed world and not of poor countries. As firms export to developing countries there is often a gap between the importing country's health needs and the selection and price of products offered for sale. The problem is so serious that the WHO has recently suggested financing R&D into diseases prevalent in developing countries and then supporting the purchase of the drugs that result.

International Price Comparisons

The issue of drug pricing in an international context has recently been raised in the United States, since drugs appear to be more expensive in the United States than in other countries. For example, the GAO study referred to above compared the prices of the 200 top-selling drugs in the United States with the prices of those drugs in the United Kingdom and Canada. The finding was that Americans pay substantially more for drugs than patients pay in the other two countries (United States General Accounting Office 1992, 1994).

But price comparisons are more complex than they would appear to be on the surface. Should one merely compare prices of identical products, as the GAO did, or should one take into account differences in consumption patterns in different countries? If one country's price for a product is much higher than another's, but that product is only rarely used in the first country, does the price comparison have much meaning? Consumption patterns also become important when one considers the role of generic drugs. Countries differ in their reliance on generics. The market share for generics in the United States is relatively large. To compare the prices of a branded product in the United States and Canada, for example, is less interesting if that product is subject to more generic substitution in the United States than in Canada because of American reliance on cheaper generic versions. Another question, more technical, is whether international comparisons should be based upon official exchange rates or upon an adjusted rate of exchange that more accurately reflects the value of a nation's currency in purchasing similar products? Purchasing Power Parity is a technique that is often used to compare the purchasing power of different currencies. Danzon incorporated many of these complexities into her studies of international price variation and failed to find consistently higher US prices (Danzon 1993).

The Timing of Pharmaceutical Approvals

Another international aspect of the pharmaceutical industry is the varied timing of drug approvals. The speed of approval of new drug products by various nations' pharmaceutical review agencies is a major concern. Over 20 years ago Wardell first suggested that the US drug approval approval process was so slow as to create a harmful "drug lag" (Wardell 1973). The debate continues in the United States and elsewhere. It is common to hear physicians complain that a particular drug is available abroad but not yet approved in one's own country. But physicians are more likely to be aware of drugs which are not yet available in their own country but are available elsewhere than they are of drugs which *are* available domestically but are not yet available in other countries. Thus, the perception of most observers is that one's own drug approval system is too slow. In fact, this biased information would lead physicians in *every* country to conclude that their own system is slower than average!

The actual drug lag is difficult to measure, for it entails distinguishing between whether a country *never* approves a particular drug and merely does so *later* than other countries do. One must also decide which drugs will be included in the comparison. Should one consider all drugs, or only important ones? And how should one measure importance? One approach measures worldwide sales, on the grounds that the marketplace can identify which drugs are most "important." But if a major country fails to approve a new drug, its worldwide sales would be reduced, and so the apparent importance of that product would be lessened. A recent study by Schweitzer et al. (1996) attempted to address these issues by looking at the timing of drug approvals in eight developed countries. The speed of a country's drug approval should be dependent upon that country's general preferences concerning the benefits of new pharmaceuticals and the risks of those products. One might expect that one country would favor access so that patients would have the benefits of new products as quickly as possible, while accepting the risk of inadvertently approving a dangerous drug. Meanwhile, another country might be so concerned about the issue of safety that it would be willing to wait until more evidence is available before approving drugs. The authors found that *every* country lags behind others in approving many important products. While some countries, most notably Switzerland, are particularly quick in approving new drugs, even the Swiss frequently lag behind other countries. The United States is relatively fast in approving new drugs, together with the United Kingdom, Canada, and France. Other countries, such as Italy and Germany, are slower.

Government Intervention in the Pharmaceutical Sector

Few industries in industrialized countries are subject to as much direct regulatory control as the pharmaceutical industry: Every product produced for the prescription market is subject to intense scrutiny and government-mandated testing. The direct cost of these clinical trials is high, but more expensive is the indirect, time, cost. Premarketing approval in the US often takes as long a five to seven years, delaying the future revenue stream even for those drugs that successfully pass the trails and prove to be safe and effective. The United States' national drug approval agency is the Food and Drug Administration (FDA), part of the Department of Health and Human Services. Once a drug is approved by the FDA for a specific indication, the introducing firm is free to distribute and market the product for that use. The FDA continues to closely regulate marketing activities.

Research-oriented firms are both burdened and protected by the strictness with which the FDA approves new drugs. In 1962 Congress amended the Food and Drug Act, largely in response to a tragedy caused by a drug used widely in Europe but not yet approved in the United States, thalidomide (Silverman and Lee 1974). This drug was prescribed to alleviate nausea among pregnant women but produced severe birth defects among the infants who were subsequently born (Weekend Edition/Saturday 1995). The amendments required firms to demonstrate efficacy, as well as safety of new products, through extensive use of human clinical trials (Bezold 1981). These more rigorous requirements have lengthened the premarketing period for new products, thereby raising the barriers to new market entrants and shortening the effective marketing period of approved drugs. The effect was as if the patent period itself had been shortened! In 1984 Congress responded to public and industry criticism of the long regulatory delays by enacting the Drug Price Competition and Patent Term Restoration Act (the Waxman-Hatch Act), which simultaneously lengthened the period of patent protection for some new drugs while facilitating approval of generic products when the patent does expire.

Increasingly, drugs must also be approved for use by a multitude of third-party payers who agree to cover the cost of pharmaceuticals for their subscribers or beneficiaries. Until recently, for example, approximately one-third of the states used formularies in their Medicaid programs as the basis for authorizing reimbursement to pharmacies for drugs dispensed to indigent patients in the respective states (Schweitzer et al. 1985). Soumerai and Ross-Dengnan (1990) found that only four states had a completely "open formulary" for their Medicaid programs in 1988. Congress attempted to deal with the problems produced by restrictive formularies in passing OBRA, which guaranteed a state's Medicaid recipients access to all drugs manufactured by any company that agreed to grant to that state's Medicaid program the greatest price discount it offered to any other purchaser. For example, drug manufacturers had frequently granted especially large discounts to public hospitals and the Public Health Service.

Today managed care is growing rapidly, and many of these health plans cover drugs as part of their benefit package. One estimate of the importance of managed care to the entire pharmaceutical sector was made by Schondelmeyer, who found seven to ten percent of all retail prescriptions in 1986 were covered by managed-care plans (Schondelmeyer 1988). This proportion has been rising rapidly since then, and the influence of managed-care coverage decisions on the pharmaceutical industry has grown to become a critical factor determining industry strategy and marketing tactics. Formularies are frequently used by managed-care plans to reduce pharmaceutical costs by restricting drug utilization to those products which are viewed as cost-effective.

Another important government intervention in the pharmaceutical sector is the granting of patent protection. Both the approval process and patent protection are barriers to entry purposely established to protect the innovative process. But both are intensely debated because their effects on patients are frequently unfavorable as well as favorable. While many argue, for example, that patent protection is essential if the pharmaceutical industry is to recoup its enormous investment in R&D, others note that this protection comes at a price: It restricts access to markets by less expensive generic products, often depriving patients of cheaper, essentially identical products. Generic drugs are typically manufactured by firms that have not engaged in any of the original R&D work and therefore have only modest fixed costs.

While patents limit competition from generic products, competition also comes from similar (but not identical) products produced by other R&D firms, so it is easy to overstate the benefit that barriers to entry create for drug companies. The pharmaceutical industry is highly competitive in many markets. There is serious pressure on firms to diversify and maintain a large number of new drugs under development ("in the pipeline"). Not only does the diversity limit the loss from any one drug that fails during clinical trials (others will succeed—putting eggs in more than one basket), but it also protects a firm from substantial loss of revenue when one of its products loses market share due to competition.

But concern over the kinds of drugs under development by pharmaceutical companies is frequently raised because so many R&D and marketing resources are allocated to products which are similar to drugs already on the market (so-called "me-too" drugs) rather than to truly innovative entities. This was the view expressed in 1995 by Dr. David Kessler, director of the Food and Drug Administration, who asserted that there is little social benefit in developing imitative drugs (Kessler et al. 1995). Commissioner Kessler's concern, however, fails to note the downward pressure that additional drug entrants apply to prices of products already in the market. Thus, even patented "me-too" drugs help make drug markets more competetive.

Lastly in this book, we discuss various approaches used to evaluate the cost and effectiveness of new drugs. These assessments are increasingly used by health plans and national health insurance programs in other countries in deciding which drugs to include in their pharmaceutical benefit program. These assessments are made and interpreted in a variety of ways, and it is important to understand what their implications are, for such assessments are central to the process of diffusion of technology in any field.

This brief overview of pharmaceutical economics and policy highlights a number of health policy choices that face both the public and private sectors in the United States and other countries. In fact, these choices must be faced by countries with widely differing health systems, whether they are socialized, based on social insurance, or largely market oriented. The following questions are illustrative of issues discussed throughout the book.

- Can the rapid growth in technological development of drugs be maintained while assuring that the benefits are widely accessible to the population?
- Are physicians provided sufficient information at reasonable cost regarding drug therapy alternatives to enable them to make informed, cost-effective treatment decisions?
- Can a financing program for pharmaceuticals be developed that will provide access to new drugs, encourage drug compliance by patients, and lead to efficient allocation of resources among drug alternatives?
- Are US drug prices close enough to those in other countries to assure American patients that they do not bear a disproportionate burden of the worldwide costs of R&D for each product?
- Can the drug approval process be streamlined so that the burden it imposes on both pharmaceutical firms and potential patients is held to the minimum level necessary to assure both safety and access?
- Is market exclusivity protection sufficient to provide for an acceptable rate of return to R&D investment, while offering the consuming public the lowest possible price for their medication?
- Can wealthy countries, perhaps through multilateral arrangements, encourage the diffusion of pharmaceutical technology to developing countries, where the burden of disease is enormous, but the commercial market for drugs is small?

Each of these policy issues is best framed in terms of choices, which are made all the more difficult because society frequently makes inconsistent demands: consumer safety *and* access, or low prices *and* corporate incentives to invest. The discipline of economics—the science of resource allocation among alternative uses—is well suited for exploring these difficult choices pertaining to the pharmaceutical industry.

References

American Hospital Association, *ICD-9-CM Workbook*, Chicago: American Hospital Association, 1978.

Bezold C, *The Future of Pharmaceuticals*, New York: John Wiley, 1981.

Bowman MA, "Pharmaceutical company-physician interaction," *Archives of Family Medicine* 152(4):317–318, 1994.

Comanor WS, "The political economy of the pharmaceutical industry," *Journal of Economic Literature* 24:1178–1217, 1986.

Comanor WS and Schweitzer SO, "Pharmaceuticals," in Adams W and Brock JW (eds), *The Structure of American Industry*, 9th edition, Englewood Cliffs, NJ: Prentice Hall, 1994.

Danzon PM, "International drug price comparisons: uses and abuses," Unpublished Manuscript, The Wharton School, University of Pennsylvania, 1993.

DiMasi JA, Hansen RW, Grabowski HG, and Lasagna L. "The cost of innovation in the pharmaceutical industry," *Journal of Health Economics* 10:107–142, 1991.

Genuardi JS, Stiller JM, and Trapnell GR, "Changing prescription drug sector: new expenditure methodologies," *Health Care Financing Review* 17(3):191–204, 1996.

Health Insurance Association of America, *Source Book of Health Insurance Data, 1993*, Washington, DC: HIAA, 1994.

Kessler DA, Rose JL, Temple RJ, Schapiro R, and Griffin JP, "Therapeutic class wars—drug promotion in a competitive marketplace," *New England Journal of Medicine* 331:1350–1353, November 17, 1995.

Long S, "Prescription drugs and the elderly: issues and options," *Health Affairs* Spring (II), 1994:157–174, 1994

Lu JZ and Comanor WS, "Strategic pricing of new pharmaceuticals," UCLA Research Program in Pharmaceutical Economics and Policy, working Paper 95–1, February 15, 1996.

Martin BC and McMillan JA, "The impact of implementing a more restrictive prescription limit on Medicaid recipients: effects on cost, therapy, and out of pocket expenditures," *Medical Care* 34(7):686–701, 1996.

"More firms give Medicaid breaks on drug prices," *Los Angeles Times*, September 17, 1990.

Organization for Economic Cooperation and Development, *OECD Health Systems: Facts and Trends 1960–1991*, Paris: OECD, 1993.

Schondelmeyer SW, "Impact of third party and managed care programs on pharmacy practice," *Welcome Trends in Pharmacy* 10:2–10, November 1988.

Schweitzer S, Salehi H, and Boling N, "The social drug lag," *Social Science and Medicine* 21:10(1077–1082), 1985.

Schweitzer SO, Schweitzer ME, and Sourty-LeGuellec M-J, "Is there a United States drug lag? The timing of new pharmaceutical approvals in the G-7 countries and Switzerland," *Medical Care Research and Review* 53(2):162–178, 1996.

Silverman M and Lee PR, *Pills, Profits and Politics*, Berkeley: University of California Press, 1974.

Soumerai SB and Ross-Dengnan D, "Experience of state drug benefit programs," *Health Affairs* 9(3):36–54, 1990.

United States Congress, Office of Technology Assessment, *Pharmaceutical R&D: Costs, Risks and Rewards*, OTA-H-522, Washington, DC: US Government Printing Office, February 1993.

United States Department of Health and Human Services, *Health United States, 1994*, Washington, DC: US General Accounting Office, 1995.

United States General Accounting Office, *Medicaid: Changes in Drug Prices Paid by VA and DOD Since Enactment of Rebate Provisions*, GAO/HRD-91–139, September 1991.

United States General Accounting Office, *Prescription Drugs: Companies Typically Charge More in the United States Than in Canada*, GAO/HRD-92–110, September 1992; and ibid., *Prescription Drugs: Companies Typically Charge More in the United States than in the United Kingdom*, GAO/HEHS-94–29, January 1994.

Wardell WM, "Introduction of new therapeutic drugs in the United States and Great Britain: an international comparison," *Clinical Pharmacology Therapeutics* 14: 773–790, 1973.

Weekend Edition/Saturday, *Thalidomide Use by AIDS, Cancer Patients a Controversy*, Washington, DC: National Public Radio, September 30, 1995.

Wilkes MS, Doblin B, and Shapiro M, "Assessing prescription drug advertising," *Journal of the American Medical Association*, 1992.

THE INDUSTRY

1

Pharmaceutical Industry Research and Development

The US pharmaceutical industry invests 16% of its revenues into R&D. Only the office, computing, and accounting machine industry invests a larger percent. Although the rate of profit is higher than in similar industries, the risk is also higher, perhaps justifying company assurances of high return on the investor dollar. As a result, the US pharmaceutical industry has been the world's leading innovator in internationally accepted dugs for the last two decades. Domestically, US pharmaceutical firms hold patents on 92 of the 100 most commonly prescribed drugs, affirming that the US pharmaceutical industry is successful in investing its R&D resources in areas of high demand.

Pharmaceutical R&D is a lengthy and costly endeavor. On average, it is 10 years from the time a scientist first has a research idea until a product is marketed, at a cost of $259 million in 1990 dollars. Even more disheartening is the fact that only about one in 60,000 compounds synthesized by pharmaceutical laboratories could be regarded as "highly successful" (US Congress, OTA 1993).

The initial decision to proceed with R&D on a new drug begins early in the basic research phase. The decision to pursue a potential drug used belong to the chemists and biologists, but now it is a collective company decision: Clinicians, the marketing department, and the manufacturing team all contribute input. Key factors considered during the decision-making process include the project's likely costs and expected returns, the likelihood of FDA approval, the company's ability to carry out the project with existing resources, behavior of competitors, liability concerns, and possible future federal policy changes that may increase costs or reduce the likelihood of FDA approval. The decision to continue or drop a project may occur at any stage of R&D.

Once preclinical, basic research studies are completed and the new potential drug has been proven efficacious and safe on animals, the drug sponsor applies to the FDA for Investigational New Drug (IND) status. Upon authorization, the drug company will begin clinical phase I trials in which the drug will be tested on healthy human volunteers in order to document safety as well as the responses that it produces. During phase II clinical trials, the drug is administered to a larger number of human subjects, usually numbering several hundred. The groups selected consist of patients the drug is intended to benefit. The third, and final, premarketing phase involves large-scale controlled clinical trials of a drug's safety and efficacy in hospital and outpatient settings. Phase III studies gather a wider and more significant amount of information on a drug's efficacy and the best method of administering it to patients.

Upon successful completion of all three phases of clinical trials, the drug sponsor seeks FDA marketing approval by submitting a New Drug Application (NDA) to the appropriate subagency. If the application is approved, the drug can be marketed immediately. More often than not, the FDA requires at least one amendment by the company before granting NDA approval.

Concentration Among Pharmaceutical Manufacturers

Economists use market concentration, the market share controlled by the largest producers, to measure the degree of competition in a market. Usually, a market tends to be more competitive if there are many manufacturers producing the same product, while it tends to be more monopolistic if only one or a few suppliers provide the commodity. In the former case, the market concentration is smaller than that in the latter situation. There are a number of ways to calculate the market concentration, C. The most widely used measure is the concentration ratio, which measures the sum of the shares of the top n firms; that is,

$$C = \Sigma^n_{i=1} S_i$$

where S_i is the market share of firm i. All the firms included in the measure are treated equally. In other words, they are all given the same weight. The choice of the number of firms, n, is arbitrary and is dictated by information available in censuses of production. The concentration ratio obviously gives only very limited information on the number and size distribution of firms. For example, if the largest four pharmaceutical firms accounted for 15% of US drug sales, $C = 0.15$. The more competitive the market the lower C will be. In the case of an oligopoly, with very few firms, C will be close to 1.00, and it will be equal to 1.00 for a pure monopoly.

Another measure is the Herfindahl index, which takes account of *all* the firms in an industry. It is defined as:

$$H = \Sigma^n_{i=1} (S_i)^2$$

where n is the total number of firms in the industry and S_i is the share of the ith firm. The maximum value of the index equals 1 and occurs where there is only one firm. The index falls as the number of firms rises (as the market becomes more competitive). For example, when $n = 100$, the value of the index $= 0.01$ if all firms have an equal market share. The squaring of the shares means that smaller firms contribute proportionately less to the value of the index. The index rises as the inequality in shares among market participants increases (as a few firms tend to dominate the others).

In the pharmaceutical market the degree of market concentration changes as we look more and more narrowly at specific therapeutic products. When the industry is viewed as one market producing all drugs, there are hundreds of firms producing products. Such a market, with so many producers, appears competitive. But when one considers a specific therapeutic class, the number of firms producing such drugs will be much fewer.

Drugs with similar characteristics are often grouped together in families. The family name may denote chemical structure (e.g., barbiturate), mode of action (e.g., antacid), physiologic action (e.g., diuretic), or therapeutic effect (e.g., anticonvulsant, analgesic). Drugs are frequently classified into 12 major drug families and each family can be viewed as a market (see, for example, *Drug Facts and Comparisons 1992*). The families include the categories of anti-infectives, central nervous system (CNS) drugs, analgesics, cardiovascular drugs, gastrointestinal drugs, sex hormones, and antidiabetics. Each of these markets can be further divided into therapeutic areas or drug classes, such as calcium antagonists for treating hypertension, a condition within the cardiovascular disease category. Therefore the competitiveness of the pharmaceutical "market" depends upon the definition of market—which family and what therapeutic area. Market concentration indices will have different values for different drug families and in different therapeutic areas.

At the industrial level, the top-selling 100 products in the US account for a large percentage of all prescriptions, new and refill, but the percentage tends to be declining (Chang 1995). In 1980, the top 100 products represented 50.3% of all prescriptions dispensed in US drugstores. But the proportion declined to 47.7% percent in 1983 and to 42% in 1988. In 1992, the top 100 products accounted for only 40% of all prescriptions.

The 227 products that constituted the top-selling 100 drugs between 1980 and 1992, as reported by the *American Druggist*, an industry trade magazine, are manufactured by 53 pharmaceutical companies. These firms com-

Table 1.1 Twenty Leading Pharmaceutical
Firms Ranked by Number of Products Within
the Top 100 (US)

Rank	Manufacturer	Number of Products
1	Merck Sharp & Dohme	17
2	Wyeth-Ayerst Laboratories	13
3	Schering-Plough	12
4	Ciba-Geigy	11
5	Upjohn Co.	9
6	Parke Davis	9
7	Bristol-Myers Squibb	9
8	Burroughs Wellcome	8
9	Rugby Labs	8
10	SmithKline Beecham	7
11	Abbott Laboratories	7
12	Roche Laboratories	7
13	Sandoz Pharmaceuticals	7
14	Pfizer Laboratories	6
15	Ortho Pharmaceuticals	6
16	Eli Lilly	6
17	A.H. Robins	5
18	Boehringer Ingelheim	4
19	Glaxo	4
20	Searle & Company	4

Source: Chang (1995).

prise approximately one-tenth of all R&D-oriented drug manufacturers in
the country. Ten leading firms produce 103 of these products (45% of total).
The top 20 firms (including seven European firms) produce 159 of the products (70% of the total 227 products) (see Table 1.1).

In a single therapeutic area, both the number of products and number
of manufacturers are substantially reduced. For instance, angiotensin-
converting enzyme (ACE) inhibitors constitute a drug class used as an antihypertensive. There are 18 ACE inhibitors on the market. But four of these
products are produced by only five firms, and sales of these four made up
about 91% of the total US market share in 1992 (see Table 1.2).

Table 1.2. Market Concentration (US) of ACE Inhibitors, 1992

Product	Manufacturer	Market Share (%)
Vasotec	Merck Sharp & Dohme	40
Capoten	Bristol-Myers Squibb	24
Zestril	Stuart Pharmaceuticals	15
Prinivil	Merck Sharp & Dohme	1
Monopril	Mead Johnson Laboratories	2
Others		7

Source: Chang (1995).

Using the data in Table 1.2, the Herfindahl index for ACE inhibitors is approximately 0.26, indicating relatively high market concentration.

Pharmaceutical R&D and Prices

The pharmaceutical industry is unusually research intensive. According to National Science Foundation data on R&D expenditures as a percent of sales for 15 industries, shown in Table 1.3, the broad "Drugs and Medicines" sector ranks second only to the "Office, Computing, and accounting" heading in its R&D effort. And according to the Federal Trade Commission, the prescription drug component of the pharmaceutical industry spent over 10% of its revenue on R&D in 1977. Since then outlays on R&D expenditures have increased far more rapidly than sales, so that in 1991, the industry spent approximately $8.2 billion on R&D, 16% of its total global sales (Mossinghoff 1991; Comanor and Schweitzer 1994), and in 1992 outlays were 16.4% of domestic sales (including export sales; Pharmaceutical Manufacturers Association, 1993). Between 1966 and 1991, leading pharmaceutical companies nearly doubled the percentage of resources allocated to R&D from revenues, from 8.5 to over 16%, as indicated in Figure 1.1. In contrast, production costs fell during that same period. But the extent of these investments and their effect on prices and profits have raised criticism of the industry.

Some of the major complaints directed at the industry are that pharmaceutical companies are making too much profit and that drug companies are not investing enough on worthwhile research and development (see, for example, Kessler et al. 1994). In order to evaluate these concerns, the Congressional Office of Technological Assessment (OTA) undertook an extensive study of the costs, risks, and rewards of pharmaceutical R&D based on the industry's claim that the rising costs of R&D are the cause of rising drug prices (US Congress, OTA 1993). The OTA found that pharmaceutical manufacturers, on average, earned a net profit of $36 million from each new drug introduced between 1981 and 1983. On top of a normal rate of return of about 10%, the OTA found an excess 4.3 percent profit over a drug's life cycle. Further, profits by pharmaceutical manufacturers exceeded those of companies in industries with similar risks by 2 to 3% in each year from 1976 to 1987.

In response to these allegations, the Pharmaceutical Manufacturers Association (PMA), now called the Pharmaceutical Research and Manufacturers of America (PhRMA), asserted that such criticism reveals a lack of understanding about the drug-discovery process and the nature of research itself. It unfairly dismisses the value of incremental improvements in existing drug therapies, and it simply ignores the extent of pharmaceutical company investment in R&D compared to other industries and compared to the government's own investment in biomedical research (Mossinghoff 1991).

Although profits are higher in the pharmaceutical industry than in other similar industries, the risks are also higher in drug R&D. Only a small pro-

Table 1.3 Nonfederal R&D Funds as a Percent of Net Sales by Industry: 1980–1990

Industry	SIC Code	Percent		
		1980	1985	1990
Total		2.1%	3.0%	3.2%
Food, kindred, and tobacco products	20, 21	D	0.6	0.5
Textiles and apparel	22, 23	D	0.5	0.4
Lumber, wood products, furniture	24, 25	0.8	0.8	0.7
Paper and allied products	26	1.0	0.8	0.8
Chemicals and allied products	28	3.3	4.9	5.7
Industrial chemicals	281–82, 286	2.8	4.2	4.5
Drugs and medicines	283	6.1	8.0	9.8
Other chemicals	284–85, 287–89	1.9	3.1	3.9
Petroleum refining and extraction	13, 29	0.5	0.9	0.8
Rubber products	30	D	1.8	1.8
Stone, clay, and glass products	32	1.3	2.3	2.3
Primary metals	33	0.5	0.9	1.0
Ferrous metals, products	331–32, 3398–99	0.5	0.5	0.6
Nonferrous metals, products	333–36	0.6	1.4	1.5
Fabricated metal products	34	1.2	1.4	1.0
Machinery	35	4.5	6.7	8.4
Office, computing, and accounting	357	10.4	12.4	15.4
Other, except electrical	351–56, 358–59	2.2	2.6	3.0
Electrical equipment	36	3.9	4.8	4.9
Radio and TV receiving equipment	365	2.7	4.3	3.1
Communication equipment	366	5.4	5.4	4.9
Electronic components	367	5.9	8.2	8.6
Other electrical equipment	361–64, 369	2.5	2.0	2.2
Transportation equipment	37	—	3.4	3.7
Motor vehicles and equipment	371	4.2	3.1	3.9
Other transportation equipment	373–75, 379	0.3	2.3	1.9
Aircraft and missiles	372, 376	3.8	3.9	3.5
Professional and scientific equipment	38	6.1	8.3	7.6
Scientific and mechanical measuring	381–82	6.2	8.4	9.4
Optical, surgical, photographic, other	383–87	6.0	8.1	6.9
Other manufacturing industries	27, 31, 39	0.4	1.0	1.1

Source: National Science Foundation (1992).

*(D) Data have been withheld to avoid disclosing operations of individual companies

portion of the new compounds prepared in drug companies' laboratories ever reach the market, and of those drugs approved for use, few produce a financial return that covers the associated costs of R&D. Between 1961 and 1983, only about one in 60,000 compounds synthesized by pharmaceutical laboratories could be regarded as highly successful when success was measured in terms of a global sales performance in excess of $100 million annually

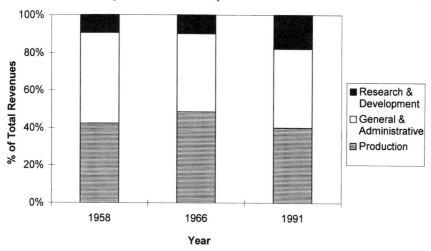

Figure 1.1 Revenue Allocation (%) for Leading Pharmaceutical Companies. Source: Comanor WS, Schweitzer SO. Pharmaceuticals. In: Adams W, Brock JW (eds.), *The Structure of American Industry*. New Jersey: Prentice Hall, 1994.

(Redwood 1993). According to Grabowski, only about three out of 10 drugs that are brought to market cover the development costs after taxes due to the many unsuccessful products that are developed (Beardsley 1993). In addition, Scherer (1993), estimates that about 55% of industry profits come from about ten percent of the drugs. Since the risk of failure is so high, drug companies must assure their investors that the return on their dollar will also be high; otherwise investors would be reluctant to take such risks. In short, increased expenditures on R&D and need to reward investors are two major motives for drug manufacturers to maintain high drug prices.

Congressional leaders such as Representative Henry A. Waxman (D–CA), former chairman of the House Energy and Commerce Committee's panel on health and the environment, and one of the congressmen who requested the OTA report, have advocated price controls for pharmaceuticals either through government controls or market forces (Blankenau 1993). While government price regulation for pharmaceuticals is not imminent, aggressive managed-care cost containment strategies are. Until quite recently, physicians were the primary target of pharmaceutical marketing efforts because the physician was the ultimate decision-maker concerning drug product selection. This situation has changed dramatically as health maintenance organizations (HMOs) have grown: In HMOs, physicians' decisions are influenced by regulations and financial incentives that restrict their choices of drug products. HMOs and pharmaceutical benefit management (PBM) programs rely on formularies, or lists of approved drugs, to control demand especially for costly drugs. Physicians who prescribe drugs that are

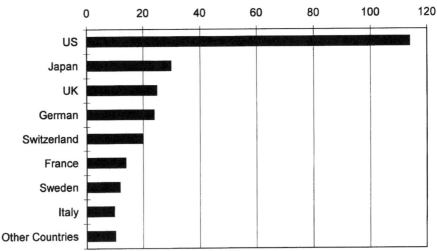

Figure 1.2 Development of Internationally Accepted Drugs. Note: Other countries include Denmark, Netherlands, Norway, Hungary, Belgium, Czechoslovakia, and Austria. Source: Redwood H. New drugs in the world market: incentives and impediments to innovation. *American Enterprise.* 1993, 4(4):72–80.

not on the formulary must either justify their choice of a nonapproved drug or be subjected to a variety of sanctions, ranging from counseling to financial penalties (Pollard 1993). The awareness that purchasers such as HMOs can leverage their buying power in the market for pharmaceutical products is adding new pressures on drug companies to lower their prices. In most drug classes today, there are several competing therapeutic alternatives, which enhances the buying power of hospital and managed-care systems. The major risk of price controls, whether governmentally imposed or market driven, is that lower profits will weaken the industry's ability to accept the risk inherent in efforts to discover and develop innovative drugs and to compete effectively on a global scale (Redwood 1993). The evidence suggests that price controls will also place obstacles in the way of genuine therapeutic progress by encouraging imitation instead of innovation (US Congress, OTA 1993).

Figure 1.2 shows the country of origin of 265 drugs that had spread to major pharmaceutical markets worldwide between 1970 and 1992. The United States has clearly dominated the development of internationally accepted drugs for the last two decades. Japan, the United Kingdom, Germany, and Switzerland follow the United States at a considerable distance. In fact, the combined number of such drugs produced by these four countries is still less than the number produced by the United States. Private industry, not academia or government, is the source of nearly all of the new drugs that

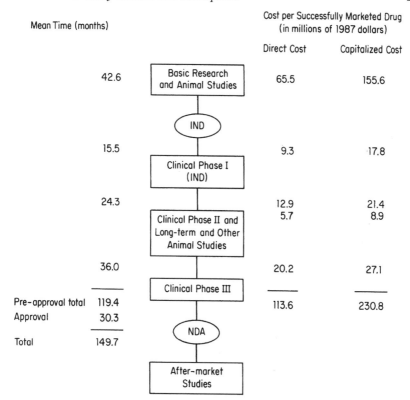

Figure 1.3 The Stages of Pharmaceutical R&D. Source: DiMasi JA, Hansen RW, Grabowski HG, Lasagna L. Cost of innovation in the pharmaceutical industry. *Journal of Health Economics*. 1991, 10(2):107–142.; US Congress, Office of Technological Assessment. *Pharmaceutical R&D: costs, risks and rewards*. Washington, DC: US Government Printing Office, 1993.; Wiggins SN. The pharmaceutical R&D decision process. In: RB Helms, ed. *Drugs and health: issues and policy objectives*. Washington, DC American Enterprise Institute; 1981:55–83.

reach the market. Of the 100 most prescribed patented drugs in the United States, 92 were patented by private industry (Mosinghoff 1991).

The discussion thus far gives the reader some perspective on US pharmaceutical industry R&D issues. A description of the pharmaceutical R&D process, from the time a scientist first has a research idea until a product is marketed, follows. A better understanding of the R&D process allows a better understanding of the important decisions every company faces throughout each phase of a drug's creation.

The stages of R&D are complex, time-consuming, and expensive. Figure 1.3 is a schematic, illustrating the R&D process from beginning to end. The left-hand column shows the average time for each of the stages, and the right-hand columns show the direct and capitalized costs of each stage of development for drugs successfully marketed, as estimated by DiMasi et al. (1991). Direct costs underestimate the true cost of drug development because they omit the cost of time. This cost is substantial because the entire development process from beginning to end is so long. DiMasi et al. (1991), Grabowski and Vernon (1990), and Hansen (1979) have all attempted to estimate the costs of R&D, including time costs. Additionally, the OTA included the effects of tax concessions, as well (US Congress OTA 1993). According to these estimates, the costs of developing a successful new drug were over $259 million in 1990, or $302 million in 1995 dollars.

Preclinical Pharmaceutical Development

Even before scientists set about to tackle a disease, an analysis of market potential is made to see if an investigation has economic potential. This "needs assessment" considers the incidence or prevalence of a condition and the likelihood that a drug, if successfully produced, could be marketed. This analysis may include the socioeconomic characteristics of the patients or a forecast of their health insurance coverage. Drugs for end-stage renal disease (ESRD) will, in all likelihood, be purchased by Medicare, the agency that assumed financial responsibility for ESRD treatment costs in 1974. On the other hand, insurance coverage for oral or mental health problems is more limited and will alter the market potential of a drug for these clinical areas. This analysis will be discussed in greater length in Chapter 5, where we discuss why drug companies, primarily located in developed countries, have been slow to address health needs of the developing world. Although the number of patients afflicted with diseases such as tuberculosis and parasitic diseases is huge, the economic demand is limited by low incomes.

Once a disease is thought to have economic potential, the scientists go to work. The first step in discovering a major new drug is understanding what causes a disease. In the past, many drugs were tested in the absence of a clear understanding of the etiology of a disease or symptom or the specific mechanism necessary to be employed to resolve the problem. Screening techniques developed by pharmaceutical companies were used to discover the pharmacological action of a particular class of drugs. The vast majority of chemical compounds screened would fail, but those proven successful would continue on to the next stage of biological testing—on animals (Wiggins 1981a). So many drugs were discovered by this clinically happenstance approach that it suffers from diminishing marginal returns, and yield has fallen considerably. Today, there is increased reliance on more focused, science-based biomedical research to help elucidate the disease process and act as a guide in discovering new drugs (US Congress, OTA 1993).

Basic Research

Basic research is the longest and most expensive of all R&D phases (see Figure 1.3). Once a new molecular entity (NME) is identified with the potential to produce a desired change in the biological system, preliminary studies are then performed to explore the pharmacological activity and therapeutic potential of the compound. Initially, these tests involve computer models, isolated cell cultures and tissues, enzymes, and cloned receptor sites. If the results of the tests suggest potential beneficial activity, related compounds—each a unique structural modification of the original—are tested to see which version of the molecule produces the highest level of pharmacological activity and exhibits the most therapeutic promise and has the smallest number of potentially harmful biological properties (US Congress, OTA 1993).

In 1990 the federal government and industry each funded approximately 45% ($9.9 billion) of health R&D undertaken in the United States (US Department of Health and Human Services 1990a). Federal support for biomedical research is as important as it is enormous. Sixty-two percent of National Institutes of Health (NIH) funding for R&D and 53% of all federal health R&D money went to colleges and universities, which rely almost solely on federal funds for research training (US Department of Health and Human Services 1990a). This federal investment in the R&D infrastructure develops the fundamental knowledge and techniques upon which current drug discovery depends. The advances in molecular biology, which is the core of biotechnology, include recombinant DNA processes, monoclonal antibodies, and gene synthesis and splicing (US Congress, OTA 1993). Biotechnology firms maintain in-house research teams, often doing research parallel to that performed in academic centers, and in many cases, there is a collaborative effort between pharmaceutical firms and academia (US Congress, OTA 1993).

The two most common collaborations are project-specific research support and consulting arrangements with pharmaceutical firms. In 1984, between 8 and 24% of all funds available for project-specific biomedical research in academia came from pharmaceutical firms (Blumenthal et al. 1987). Such projects tend largely to be endeavors in biology and pharmacology. In addition, life-science faculty receive support through consulting arrangements with private firms; 40% of such US faculty consulted for monetary compensation at least once in a recent 3-year period (Blumenthal et al. 1987).

The drug-discovery process is, more often than not, initiated by a member of a scientific department of a company who has an idea for a possible future research endeavor. Some companies assemble teams to focus on finding drugs to treat a disease or organ system. Some firms make research targeting decisions in committees, while others delegate authority to research directors (US Congress, OTA 1993; Wiggins 1981a).

After the idea is conceived and evaluated by the scientific unit, it is officially introduced as a potential project at an annual meeting explicitly organized for this purpose. According to Wiggins (1981a), the criteria used to assess the project include chemical and biological feasibility; clinical feasibility; rough estimates of the probable clinical cost of the project; estimates of the overall development cost; and prospects for (FDA) approval. Potential sales and marketability and a determination of whether the existing marketing system will be able to handle the product without extensive retraining or expansion are also considered. Whether the project can be carried out with existing research facilities and personnel and whether it will mesh synergistically with existing research and product lines of the company must also be decided (Wiggins 1981a).

The Management of Research

The three most important scientific decision-makers at this stage are the chemist, biologist, and clinician. The chief biologist estimates whether the proposed project has a reasonable chance of biological success. The chemist makes a similar prediction about the feasibility of making small amounts of the compound for research purposes, and later, larger amounts for general use. Finally, the clinician is expected to decide how possible it is to test whether the chemical compound is, indeed, efficacious. The reliability and validity of the testing process, the number of patients needed to achieve a successful and clinically significant outcome, the length of time required for the study, and the types of tests required all are estimated by the clinician. In short, the only factor that discourages a project with a high probability of chemical and biological success is a clinician's unfavorable opinion on the technical and statistical effect of the drug (Faust 1971).

During project selection, an economic report on expected annual and overall costs is produced. If the chances of success are projected to be low, if the costs dramatically exceed the norm, or if this testing stage is expected to continue past a reasonable time limit, there is little chance that the company will decide that the project is an acceptable economic investment.

The aging of the US population is a an important influence on industry R&D portfolios. Almost 70% of the R&D currently sponsored by the pharmaceutical industry is devoted to organ systems and diseases affecting the health of older Americans (PMA 1989). Most new drug therapies are maintenance medications aimed at reducing symptoms, such as pain, associated with disease processes of the older population. These drugs may yield significant financial gains to the manufacturers, for the patient must often continue therapy for the rest of his or her life in order to maintain the therapeutic effect (Pollard 1993). Prominent examples are drugs that arrest benign prostatic hyperplasia; or that control hyptertension, stomach ulcers, or gastric reflux; or that alleviate joint inflammation.

As noted before, a company's marketing department has a substantial input into the R&D decision process. Experts are given a description of the product and asked to estimate sales potential. These estimates are based on forecasts of what the health care market will look like in 5 to 10 years' time. Important product factors, such as specific disease applications, potential side effects, and alternative modes of administration (e.g., oral, injectable, patch, intravenous, or inhalent) may very well affect the chances for eventual market success (Wiggins 1981a).

R&D decision-makers must also consider whether existing facilities and personnel can handle the potential project. If the protocol requires time-consuming or expensive tests, specialized equipment, and/or personnel education on new equipment and techniques, the company may choose to drop the project, or contract out to another research firm (Pisano 1990). This is especially true in the case of biotechnology drugs.

Basic research in molecular biology during the 1970s yielded a number discoveries about how the genetic structure of cells might be manipulated to induce them to produce specific proteins. These discoveries created a methodology for synthesizing potential therapeutic drugs that were too complex to be synthesized through the chemical methods traditionally used in pharmaceutical research. The biotechnological method of synthesizing therapeutic compounds, required technical skills that were fundamentally different from those with which established pharmaceutical firms were familiar (US Congress, OTA 1984). These new methodologies and the scientific bases underlying them make biotechnology ventures unusually risky. Therefore, in today's cost-conscious health care industry, biotechnology firms are finding it difficult to acquire financial backing for drug projects which appear speculative. As a result, many of them are forming alliances with major pharmaceutical companies. These alliances help both parties. They give the small biotech companies needed cash to continue the extensive and time-consuming research and testing that will be needed. The biotech company may also benefit from management expertise available from the larger company, and the small firm also gains marketing expertise and opportunities that would otherwise be expensive to obtain. These alliances also offer major drug firms access to biotech R&D, which seems to be difficult for them to develop internally (Marsh 1995).

The final consideration that enters the basic research decision-making process is the likelihood of FDA approval of the product. Since the enactment of the 1962 amendments to the Federal Food, Drug, and Cosmetic (FD&C) Act (21 USC 301 et seq.), which order pharmaceutical companies to show drug effectiveness in addition to safety, researchers have studied the extent to which these regulations stifle, delay, or raise the cost of innovation in the pharmaceutical market. Evidence suggests that the 1962 law at least doubled the R&D costs of new drugs (Grabowski et al. 1978), decreased the introduction of new products by about 60% (Wiggins 1981b), and was associated with an additional 14-month delay in the introduction of new products with no evidence of greater safety or effectiveness (Eisman and Wardell

1981). These criticisms became particularly strident in 1987, when AIDS (acquired immune deficiency syndrome) activists protested the FDA's rigid adherence to safety standards in the context of investigational drugs that demonstrate efficacy for patients with catestrophic, or even terminal, illnesses (FDA 1988). In May 1987, the FDA issued new regulations allowing earlier access to investigational new drugs (INDs) for patients with life-threatening or serious illnesses (US Congress, OTA 1993). These regulations allow physicians to use certain INDs for treatment purposes when such drugs have demonstrated therapeutic effectiveness during early human clinical trials. There have also been recent attempts by the FDA to identify and expedite the review of new drugs deemed therapeutically important. These new measures may ease the burden on pharmaceutical companies by reducing the overall costs of the R&D process (US Congress, OTA 1993).

Animal Studies

Once a project is underway, and a potentially therapeutic compound is identified, the biological screening process begins. Laboratory tests are performed on animals to determine how the substance reacts physiologically with the target disease or affected organ system. Next, acute toxicological animal tests are performed to determine the highest doses that two species of animals (including one nonrodent) can receive without risking overt toxic reactions and death. Finally, chronic toxicological animal tests are performed to determine whether repeated exposure to the drug changes any toxic effects discovered in the acute tests (Gogerty 1987).

For toxicological tests requiring nonrodents, researchers choose species in which the organ systems of interest closely resemble those of humans. Table 1.4 lists the species of animals used in the most common toxicological tests. Animal testing is not performed solely during the preclinical phase; it may be continued or initiated concurrent with later clinical phases, as well. DiMasi et al. (1991) estimated that long-term animal testing begins, on average, 20.2 months after the commencement of phase I human testing. In addition, other animal testing sometimes takes place before long-term animal testing, sometimes after it, and at still other times both before and after it. These tests usually include chronic toxicity tests designed to identify the drug's impact on living tissue when administered repeatedly for anywhere from 6 months to the lifetime of the animal. They also test to determine whether the drug adversely affects the reproductive process or produces congenital deformities in offspring over two successive generations of animals, whether it causes cancer, and whether it produces genetic changes that form tumors or other illnesses. For some drugs, tests are conducted to determine whether the intended dose form or route of administration causes any toxic effects (US Congress, OTA 1993).

Table 1.4 Toxicological Tests Used in the US Regulatory Process

Type	Species	Number Used	Measured Outcomes
Acute toxicity	Rats	50 per sex	Death
	Dogs	10 per sex	Morbidity
Subacute toxicity	Rats	50 per sex	Morbidity, histopathology, blood chemistry, body weight, organ weights, hematology
Subchronic toxicity	Rats	100 per sex	Same as subacute
	Dogs	20 per sex	Same as rats
	Monkeys	12 per sex	Same as dogs
Reproductive toxicity			
Segment I	Rats	50 per sex	Fertility and reproductive
	Rabbits	50 per sex	Performance
Segment II (teratology)	Rats	50 per sex	Malformed offspring
	Rabbits	50 per sex	
Segment III	Rats	50 per sex	Growth of
	Rabbits	50 per sex	offspring
Cancer bioassay	Mice	250 per sex	Tumors
	Rats	250 per sex	Tumors
Mutagenicity			
Dominant lethal	Rats	40 males	Dead implants (embryos)

Source: US Congress, Office of Technological Assessment (1993).

Clinical Pharmaceutical Development

At the conclusion of animal tests the firm developing the new product must apply to the FDA for an designation. This approval to begin human tests to determine a drug's safety and efficacy does not specify the design of the studies, but usually the experimental drug is compared to a placebo because the likelihood that the drug's effectiveness will be statistically significant is maximized. These trials are usually designed as double-blind randomized clinical trials (RCTs) so as to remove bias in the findings that may result from either the patient or the physician knowing which patients are receiving the experimental drug and which are receiving placebo. The double-blind design presents many difficulties for investigators because the appearance of adverse events cannot be readily attributed to the study medication. The investigator cannot know whether the patient actually took the study drug unless the trial is "unblinded" a process undertaken only rarely. The RCT design also produces difficulties because patients must be enrolled in the study not knowing whether they will be receiving an experimental drug or no drug at all. Many potential subjects, excited by the opportunity of participating in medical research and eager to try an experimental therapy, are disappointed when they are told that there is a likelihood that they might *not* receive the drug.

A third difficulty arises when a drug previously approved for another condition becomes commonly used for a new purpose. Although this "off-label" use is not sanctioned by the FDA and cannot be promoted in any way by the drug manufacturer, the situation is not uncommon, and doctors are legally free to prescribe drugs in this fashion. If the manufacturer wants to expand FDA approval for the new use, clinical trials must be undertaken to demonstrate safety and efficacy, just as was done for the earlier indication. But the common use of the drug presents the investigator with a dilemma. If the placebo arm of the trial requires denying use of the drug, the patient is not offered "standard" care. This violates one of the ethical principles of an RCT, that patients should not be made worse off by agreeing to participate.

The sequence of the human trials is described more fully in Chapter 7.

Product Liability

An area of concern for the US health care system as a whole, and for the pharmaceutical industry in particular, is product liability. Of the 85,694 different federal product liability cases filed between 1974 and 1986, pharmaceuticals and health care products represented 13.5% of the total (Dungsworth 1988). Over the past 20 years, the courts have broadened the circumstances that determine when injured parties may collect from pharmaceutical manufacturers. Observers noted that the frequency of large jury awards has increased for cases proceeding to trial (Hensler et al. 1987). Some argue that these changes successfully protect the public from unsafe drugs. Others suggest that increased liability may affect R&D, in two ways: (1) Costs associated with bringing a new drug to market may increase due to additional research that firms conduct to ensure safety (Lasagna 1991) and (2) firms may decide not to pursue areas of research or product development where they fear that excessive liability costs will critically lower the potential return for a particular drug (Kuhlik and Kingham 1990).

The number of large, US-based pharmaceutical firms engaged in contraceptives R&D has dropped in recent years from nine to two (Connell 1987), and many companies are wary of pursuing drug research relevant to pregnant women because of two recent liability suits: the Dalkon Shield (Mastroianni et al. 1990) and Bendectin (Brody 1986).

The Dalkon Shield is a contraceptive device for women that was marketed by A. H. Robins in 1971. During the first 3 years of marketing, the firm received evidence that the product's use was associated with uterine infections and septic abortions, but it did not change the product or its labeling. In June 1974, the company withdrew the device from the market after the US Centers for Disease Control (CDC) had reported complications among 62% of women who became pregnant while wearing the Dalkon Shield (Mastroianni et al. 1990). All together, 320,000 suits were filed against the firm. Of the 4,400 claims resulting in litigation, Robins paid $250 million in out-of-court settlements and another $25 million in punitive awards imposed by 11 juries. As a result, the company went bankrupt.

Bendectin was first sold in the United States by Merrell Dow in 1956. It is a combination drug consisting of a vitamin, an antispasmodic, and a sedative. It is the only pharmaceutical ever approved in this country for the treatment of morning sickness associated with pregnancy (US Congress, OTA 1993). Beginning in 1969, the medical literature reported cases of congenital defects in babies born to women who had taken Bendectin during pregnancy. Although the FDA concluded in 1980 that there was not enough evidence to ban Bendectin from the marketplace, it required the company to change its package insert to reflect the possible risk associated with the drug. In the 1980s, the courts consolidated 1,100 claims into a single class-action suit that Merrell Dow offered to settle for $120 million. The plaintiffs rejected this offer, and the manufacturer successfully defended itself in a jury trial. According to Brody (1986), total costs to Merrell Dow of defending itself against Bendectin's liability suits exceeded the $13 million in annual revenues the company received from sales of the drug, prompting the firm to remove it voluntarily from the marketplace in 1985.

Recently, several initiatives have been proposed to change the FDA clinical testing guidelines to include women, pregnant women, and a surveillance on the development of their babies. This presents several concerns for drug firms, of course. First, drug companies will increase their risk of liability by including women of childbearing age in studies, for women who agree not to become pregnant during the testing phase may become pregnant, nonetheless, thereby inflicting possible injury upon them or their fetus. Second, firms will have difficulty finding female volunteers for trials when there is a potential risk to present or future pregnancies. Last, the inclusion of potentially pregnant women in study populations will increase the costs of R&D as well as lengthen the time until project completion. The inclusion of these groups will necessitate larger clinical trial samples, already thought to be one of the major causes of the increased cost of phase III trials (DiMasi et al. 1991).

US pharmaceutical R&D is motivated by market-driven consumer demand and not necessarily by consumers' or physicians' perceptions of need. To complement this private sector activity the federal government has targeted pharmaceutical R&D in specific areas which the private sector has not entered. Most of this research takes place at the NIH and specifically targets pharmaceutical research by funding 13 programs, accounting for $387 million in fiscal year 1989 (US Congress, OTA 1993).

In order to further stimulate private industry R&D in areas with modest project potential, Congress enacted the Orphan Drug Act of 1983 to encourage the development of treatments for rare diseases and conditions.

Table 1.5 Percent Distribution of Causes of Death for the Leading Noninjury Diseases in Developing Countries, 1990

Disease Type	Developing Countries	Developed Economies and Formally Socialist Nations of Europe
Cardiovascular disease[a]	25.28%	52.88%
Respiratory infections	11.17	3.28
Malignant neoplasms (cancers)[a]	10.36	24.13
Diarrheal diseases	8.04	0.07
Perinatal diseases	6.73	0.88
Respiratory conditions[a,c]	6.55	5.05
Tuberculosis	5.54	0.38
Childhood cluster[b]	5.21	0.00
Digestive disease[a,c,d]	3.97	4.24
Malaria	2.60	0.00
Total	85.50%	90.91%

Source: World Bank 1993.

[a]Noncommunicable disease

[b]Includes pertussis, polio, measles, and tetanus

[c]Includes chronic obstructive pulmonary disease and asthma

[d]Includes peptic ulcer disease and cirrhosis

There are four incentives in the legislation: (1) FDA assistance in protocol design for new drug approval (NDA) or product license approval (PLA) applications, (2) research grants for preclinical and clinical studies of orphan products, (3) grants of 7 years of exclusive US marketing rights to the first firm receiving an NDA for an orphan drug within a class, and (4) a tax credit for clinical research expenditures (US Congress, OTA 1993). The drug company making the request for an orphan drug IND must show that the disease or condition that the drug is intended to treat affects less than 200,000 persons in the United States or affects more than 200,000 persons in the United States but that there is no reasonable expectation that the cost of developing and manufacturing the drug will be recovered from sales in the United States (US Congress, OTA 1993).

Between January 1985 and the end of September 1992, the FDA granted orphan status to 494 drugs and biologicals, thus proving that governmental subsidies can induce the US pharmaceutical industry to pursue R&D for much-needed drugs, even though the demand for those drugs is meager. Unfortunately, these efforts by the US government do little to promote the development of drugs badly needed in developing countries, as discussed in Chapter 5. Table 1.5 compares the 10 leading causes of noninjury death in developing versus industrialized countries. The major difference in death rates resides in the frequency of communicable and perinatal disease in the developing countries. With the exception of respiratory infections, these causes of death have been nearly eliminated in industrialized countries, but they remain important killers in developing countries (Comanor 1995).

References

Beardsley T, "Blood money: critics question high pharmaceutical profits," *Scientific American* 269(2):115–118, 1993.

Blankenau R, "OTA takes a closer look at cost of drugs," *Hospitals* 67(7):48–50, 1993.

Blumenthal DB, Gluck ME, and Epstein S, *University-industry relationships in Biotechnology: Implications for Federal Policy*. Final report to the Assistant Secretary for Planning and Evaluation, US Department of Health and Human Services, US DHHS Grant #100A–83, 1987.

Brody M, "When products turn into liabilities," *Fortune* 113:20–24, 1986.

Chang RR, "The top 100 pharmaceutical products in the United States from 1980 to 1992," UCLA Department of Health Services unpublished paper, 1995.

Comanor WS, "Pharmaceutical research and the health needs of developing countries," UCLA Research Program in Pharmaceutical Economics and Policy, unpublished manuscript, 1995.

Comanor WS and Schweitzer SO, "Pharmaceuticals," in Adams W and Brock JW (eds), *The Structure of American Industry*, 9th edition England Cliffs, NJ: Prentice Hall, 1994.

Connell EB, "The crisis in contraception," *Technology Review* 90(5): 47–55, 1987.

DiMasi JA, Hansen RW, Grabowski HG, and Lasagna L, "Cost of innovation in the pharmaceutical industry," *Journal of Health Economics* 10(2):107–142, 1991.

Drug Facts and Comparisons, 1992 edition, St. Louis: Facts and Comparisons, 1992.

Dungsworth T, *Product Liability and the Business Sector: Litigation Trends in Federal Courts*, Santa Monica: The Rand Corporation, 1988.

Eisman MM and Wardell WM, "Incremental time study: an analysis of time spent in the development and approval of drugs for the US market," in *Economic costs of FDA regulation*, Washington, DC: Pharmaceutical Manufacturers Association, 1981.

Faust R, "Project selection in the pharmaceutical industry," *Research Management* 14: 46–55, 1971.

"FDA speeds drug approval," *World News Digest*, November 25; 875 F:2, 1988.

Gogerty J, "Preclinical research evaluation: pharmacology; toxicology; drug metabolism," in Guarino RA (ed), *New Drug Approval Process: Clinical and Regulatory management*, New York, NY: Marcel Dekker, 1987.

Grabowski HG and Vernon JM, "A new look at the returns and risks to pharmaceutical R&D," *Management Science* 36(7): 804–821, 1990.

Grabowski HG, Vernon JM, and Thomas LG, "Estimating the effects of regulation on innovation: an international comparative analysis of the pharmaceutical industry," *The Journal of Law and Economics* 21(1):133–163, 1978.

Hansen R, "The pharmaceutical development process: estimates of development costs and times and the effects of proposed regulatory changes," in Chien RA (ed), *issues in Pharmaceutical Economics*, Lexington, MA: D.C. Health, 1979.

Hensler DR, Vaiana ME, and Kakalik JS, *Special Report—trends in Tort Litigation: The Story Behind the Statistics*, Santa Monica, CA: The Rand Corporation, 1987.

Kessler DA, Rose JL, Temple RJ, Schapiro R, and Griffen JP, "Therapeutic class wars: drug promotion in a competitive marketplace," *New England Journal of Medicine* 331:1350–1353, 1994.

Kuhlik BN and Kingham RF, "The adverse effects of standardless punitive damage awards on pharmaceutical development and availability," *Food Drug Cosmetic Law Journal* 45: 693–708, 1990.

Lasagna L, "The chilling effect of product liability on new drug development," in Litan RE and Huber PW (eds), *The Liability Maze: The Impact of Liability Law on Safety and Innovation*, Washington, DC: The Brookings Institute, 1991.

Marsh B, "Biotech blues: firms go begging for money to test new drugs," *Los Angeles Times*, D:3, July 9, 1995.

Maugh TH, "Baboon use to fight man's AIDS is OK'd," *Los Angeles Times*, A:1, July 15, 1995.

Mosinghoff GJ, "Pharmaceutical research is expensive but well worth the cost," *Endocrinology* 128(1):3–4, 1991.

Mastroianni L, Donaldson PJ, and Kane TJ (eds), *Developing New Contraceptives: Obstacles and Opportunities*, National Research Council and Institute of Medicine, Washington, DC: National Academy Press, 1990.

National Science Foundation, *Selected Data on Research and Development in Industry: 1990*, Washington, DC: National Science Foundation, 1992.

Pharmaceutical Manufacturers Association, *Annual Survey Report, 1987–1989*, Washington, DC: PMA, 1989.

Pharmaceutical Manufacturers Association, *Trends in US Pharmaceutical Sales and R&D, 1990–1993*, Annual Survey Reports, Washington, DC: PMA, 1993.

Pisano GP, "The R&D boundaries of the firm: an empirical analysis," *Administrative Science Quarterly* 35:153–176, 1990.

Pollard MR, "Pharmaceutical innovation in the United States," *International Journal of Technological Assessment in Health Care* 9(2): 167–173, 1993.

Redwood H, "New drugs in the world market: incentives and impediments to innovation," *American Enterprise* 4(4):72–80, 1993.

Scherer FM, "Pricing, profits, and technological progress in the pharmaceutical industry," *Journal of Economic Perspectives* 7(3):97–115, 1993.

US Congress, Office of Technological Assessment, *Pharmaceutical R & D: Costs, Risks and Rewards*, Washington, DC: US Government Printing Office, 1993.

US Congress, Office of Technological Assessment, *Commercial Biotechnology: An International Analysis,* Washington, DC: U.S. Government Printing Office, 1984.

US Department of Health and Human Services, Public Health Service, National Institutes of Health, *Data Book 1990*, Washington, DC: US Government Printing Office, 1990a.

US Department of Health and Human Services, Public Health Service, Food and Drug Administration, *From Test Tube to Patient: New Drug Development in the US, an FDA Consumer Special Report* DHHS Pub. No. (FDA) 90–3168. Washington, DC: US Government Printing Office, 1990b.

Wiggins SN, "The pharmaceutical R & D decision process," in Helms RB (ed), *Drugs and Health: Issues and Policy Objectives*, Washington, DC: American Enterprise Institute, pp 55–83, 1981a.

Wiggins SN, "Product quality regulation and new drug introductions: some new evidence from the 1970s," *The Review of Economics and Statistics* 63(4):615–619, 1981b.

World Bank, *World Development Report 1993: Investing in Health*, Oxford: Oxford University Press, 1993.

2

Marketing Pharmaceuticals

The pharmaceutical industry produces so many new products each year that it is crucial that prescribers be informed about the innovations on a continuing basis. This activity is marketing. Few other pharmaceutical company activities have received as much public scrutiny as their marketing (US Senate, Committee on Labor and Human Resources 1990). According to a report by the Pharmaceutical Manufacturers Association (PMA) pharmaceutical companies in the United States employed nearly 160,000 people in the late 1980s. Twenty-eight percent of these employees were involved in marketing, 23% in R&D, and 36% in production (PMA 1989). The size of the marketing effort in terms of expenditures is seen in Figures 2.1, 2.2, and 2.3, which show the sales, R&D expenses, and marketing and administrative expenses in 1992, 1993, and 1994 for three of the largest US pharmaceutical manufacturers—Merck, Pfizer, and Eli Lilly. While the R&D expenses varied between 11 and 15% of annual sales for these firms, marketing and promotional expenses ranged from 21 to 40% of annual sales.

Marketing is critical to the success of any firm. The Tagamet–Zantac battles in the late 1980s underscore its importance. Tagamet, the first H_2-blocking antiulcer agent, was introduced in the United States in 1977. Glaxo's version of an H_2-blocking drug, Zantac, was released in 1981. While Zantac had fewer side effects than Tagamet, its real advance over Tagamet lay in Glaxo's marketing strategy. Rather than relying entirely on its own sales force, Glaxo contracted with salespeople from Hoffman–La Roche to promote Zantac worldwide. Despite a 4-year entry lag and a price that was 50% higher than Tagamet's Zantac sales increased dramatically, totaling $2.4 billion worldwide in 1990 compared to Tagamet's $1.2 billion ("Drugmakers under attack" 1991). Pharmaceutical marketing takes six major

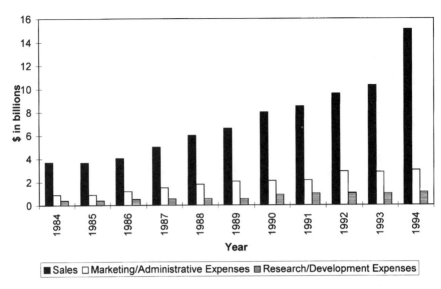

Figure 2.1 Sales, R&D and Marketing Expenditures: Merck

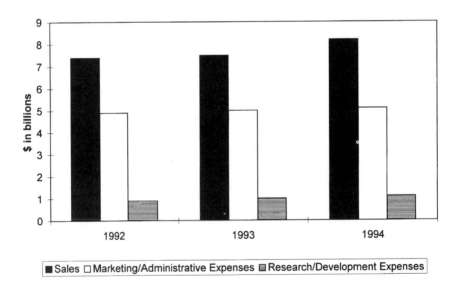

Figure 2.2 Sales, R&D and Marketing Expenditures: Pfizer

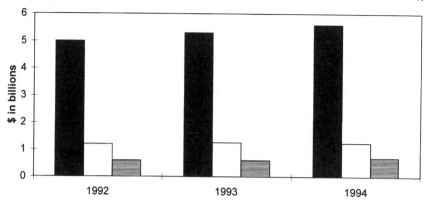

Figure 2.3 Sales, R&D and Marketing Expenditures: Eli Lilly

forms: sales representation ("detailing"), direct mail, samples provided to physicians ("sampling"), medical journal advertising, sponsorship of continuing medical education, and public media advertising.

In an era of cost constraints, marketing assumes an increasingly important role as companies seek to differentiate themselves from their competitors and to create brand names that can be exploited in the newly emerging markets of managed-care and over-the-counter (OTC) drugs. Traditionally, drug manufacturers have promoted their products with advertising aimed at physicians via direct mail, detail sales forces, and scientific symposia. Growing competition in the pharmaceutical industry and a shift in the locus of product selection from individual physicians to managed-care organizations has led to new forms of promotional activities aimed not only at physicians but also at consumers, hospitals, and increasingly, third-party payers, all of whom now influence drug purchases. The new promotional activities include press conferences, media tours, media coverage of scientific symposia, video news releases, sponsored single-issue publications, discussions with the investment community of drug development, along with advertising aimed directly at the consumer (Kessler and Pines 1990). In another new approach pharmaceutical manufacturers participate in developing disease management protocols for managed-care providers.

The FDA's oversight and regulatory authority covers every aspect of these pharmaceutical firm activities. The FDA has expanded its role beyond assuring the safety and efficacy of drugs and now sets standards for drug advertising and marketing. Many of the agency's regulations restrict physician access to information and have become intensely debated. This chapter therefore ends with a discussion of the FDA's activities and some of the controversies surrounding it.

The Size of the Marketing Effort

According to a recent study, nearly 1.7 billion prescriptions are dispensed annually in the United States which is almost seven for every man, woman, and child in the country (Schondelmeyer and Thomas 1990). The drugs prescribed are made by some 1300 manufacturers worldwide. They are prescribed by 773,000 physicians and dentists. But before they can be dispensed by 168,000 pharmacists working in 65,000 pharmacies, they pass through 100 drug wholesalers. And they are paid for either by patients or by 1900 third-party payers (National Wholesale Druggists Association 1992; US Department of Commerce 1990). *Marketing* is how manufacturers notify all of these intermediaries of their products.

It is estimated that the industry spends at least $5 billion annually on advertising and marketing—more than *$8000* for every physician in the United States (Rennie 1991). In fact, the drug industry spends approximately $1 billion more on marketing and advertising than on research (US Senate, Staff Report of the Special Committee on Aging, 1991).

Does it Work?

The purpose of advertising is to affect doctors' prescribing habits in ways favorable to the manufacturers. Nearly 30 years ago the strategy was put succinctly in an advertising manual, as follows:

> medical men are subject to the same kinds of stress, the same emotional influences that affect the laymen. Physicians have, as part of their self-image, a determined feeling that they are rational and logical, particularly in their choice of pharmaceuticals. The advertiser must appeal to this rational self-image, and at the same time make a deeper appeal to the emotional factors which really influence sales. (Smith 1968)

The role of marketing in providing information to physicians has been studied extensively for many years. An analysis of the Canadian pharmaceutical market, published in 1981, showed that the most significant determinant of a drug's sales was the amount of promotion it had (Pazderka and Rao 1981). And Lexchin (1994) notes how difficult it has been to control Canadian pharmaceutical marketing activities. Scott and Ferner (1994) document the strategy of pharmaceutical firms in influencing prescribing patterns of British physicians, and Zarate and Liosa (1995) describe the influence of marketing on Latin American physicians. A similar study in Finland found that 64% of physicians considered information provided by pharmaceutical representatives to be useful and only 14% considered it to be useless (Laitinen 1973). Jensen and Lunde (1972) reported that doctors selected their drugs for standard therapy most commonly from commercial drug catalogues, short review articles, and advice from other colleagues (Jensen and Lunde 1972). In a study by Dunnell and Cartwright (1972) 25% of general practitioners considered information from drug firms, and 25% considered information from medical journals, the most helpful source of information about new drugs (Dunnell and Cartwright 1972). Cleary (1992) describes the importance of pharmaceutical marketing efforts in prescribing patterns of antibiotics, and Girard (1992), Lichstein et al. (1992), and Bowman (1994) all note the importance of interactions between drug sales representatives and advertisements in informing physicians-in-training about new drugs.

Avorn and colleagues studied physician prescribing decisions by surveying primary care physicians about their perceptions of the efficacy of two highly promoted agents: propoxyphene-containing analgesics and cerebral vasodilators. The physicians were more supportive of these products than would have been expected, considering the negative scientific reports of the drugs' value. Although the physicians were not always able to recognize the products' commercial messages and although the vast majority of practitioners perceived themselves to pay more attention to scientific papers than to drug advertisements and detailers, their beliefs about the effectiveness of the index drugs revealed quite the opposite pattern of influence in large segments of the sample (Avorn et al. 1982). Another correlate of knowledge about drugs is the age of the physician. The longer one has been removed from one's academic training the greater the influence of commercial (as opposed to scholarly) sources of information. Glickman et al. (1994) related physicians' knowledge of the costliness of drugs and found that "younger physicians were more likely than older physicians to make correct [price] estimates."

The general agreement that advertising affects physicians' prescribing habits raises concern about its possible detrimental effects for medical decision-making. In Canada, multinational pharmaceutical companies spent an average of 17% of sales on promotion in the early 1980s; an estimated $1.40 out of the average prescription cost of $8.50 (Report of the Commission of Inquiry on the Pharmaceutical Industry 1985). According to Lexchin (1987), while advertising makes physicians more aware of the products, it also promotes poor prescribing. Aggressive promotion is thought to be the cause of inappropriate use of cefoxitin a second-generation cephalosporin antibiotic, in 43% of hospitalized patients for whom it was prescribed (Jewesson et al. 1983). A similar situation is blamed for the 60–86% inappropriate use of cimetidine (Kopala 1984). Drug promotion is thought to be responsible for a significant proportion of the estimated 135,000 life-threatening adverse drug reactions that occur each year in Canadian hospitals (Lexchin 1987).

Types of Promotion

Of the six means of drug promotion, five of them: detailing, sampling, direct mailing, journal advertising, and general media advertising, carry messages pertaining to particular products. Note that one of these, media advertising, is directed to the general public rather than to physicians. One other means of promotion, directed at physicians, is sponsorship of continuing medical education. Its purpose is to promote general corporate image rather than any specific product.

Detailing

Pharmaceutical sales representatives ("detailers") have traditionally been important in informing physicians about new products, answering questions, and maintaining goodwill. In the United States, more than 55% of drug company promotional budgets, or about $115 million, was spent on all aspects of detailing in 1983. This represented 15% of company revenue—the single largest expenditure, even greater than the cost of the raw materials used to manufacture the drugs. The number of detailers has increased rapidly in the last 20 years. While the ratio of physicians to detailers in the United States in the early 1970s was 76 to 1, it was approximately 31 to 1 by the mid-1980s (Lexchin 1987). The ratio is even closer in Canada, where there is a detailer for every 18 physicians. It is estimated that each call to a doctor's office costs about $80. Although the FDA regulates the content of printed drug promotional material, the content of face-to-face detailer–physician interactions cannot be monitored, leading Lexchin (1987) to conclude that detailing is an almost unregulated activity. In addition, many drugmakers have three or four sales teams so that detailers can rotate interacting with a single physician.

This interaction between the detailers and physicians often begins in medical school. The FDA has forbidden what had been one of the most visible signs of pharmaceutical largesse—pharmaceutical-firm gifts to medical students of the familiar black bag. Medical students are still provided with educational gifts such as pocket reference guides. To foster goodwill, companies donate money to sponsor student research and research forums, to aid students traveling to conferences, and to underwrite educational programs for students and faculty. Drug fairs allow companies to promote their products, providing product information together with an array of promotional gifts, many with company insignia (Mick 1991).

In a study of seven midwestern teaching hospitals, Lurie (1990) reported that medical faculty and house staff averaged 1.5 contacts per month with pharmaceutical representatives (PRs), and house staff (interns, residents, and fellows) averaged more than one meal per month at pharmaceutical company expense. Twenty-five percent of faculty and 32% of the residents reported changing their practices at least once as a result of PR contact. Faculty members who had received honoraria or research support were more likely to request addition of that company's drug to the hospital formulary. A similar conclusion was reached by Chren and Landefeld (1994), who found that requests by physicians for drugs to be added to a hospital's formulary were strongly associated with the physician's interactions with the manufacturers. The types of interactions were traditional detailing, acceptance of money from drug companies to support attendance at educational symposia, acceptance of money to speak at educational symposia, and acceptance of money for research.

Detailers are often knowledgeable, not only about the products they represent, but about competing products as well. Many, in fact, are licensed pharmacists. Nonetheless, dubious selling practices do sometimes occur. A survey of internal medicine residency directors in 1991 revealed that 14.3% had observed "unethical" marketing activities, and 37.5% reported that residents had participated in pharmaceutical-company-sponsored trips during the 3 years prior to the survey (Lichstein et al. 1992). One of the most famous of these activities was the Frequent Prescriber Plan of American Home Products (AHP). In 1987, AHP launched a program that allowed doctors to earn airline tickets by submitting patient profiles and prescribing Inderal, an antihypertensive medicine which was facing competitive pressure from cheaper generic drugs. Massachusetts Medicaid officials determined that this was illegal and forced AHP to cancel the program and refund $195,000 to the state (Drugmakers under attack 1991).

Direct Mail

Approximately 4 to 6% of total promotional expenditures is spent on direct mail promotions. This is usually in the form of free copies of controlled-circulation journals and direct advertising flyers from drug companies (Lexchin 1987). The content of the advertising is strictly regulated by the FDA. And firms are forbidden to distribute material suggesting use of a drug for an indication that has not been approved by the FDA. This prohibition even extends to scientific reports and journal articles.

Sampling

Providing free samples represents nearly 9% of total promotional expenditures. The drug industry's rationale for sampling is that a doctor must be personally acquainted with a drug before it will be prescribed with confidence. This notion is undoubtedly true, although one might question whether findings based on a small sample of patients selected as a "convenience sample" are as valid as those from a larger-scale clinical trial adhering to a rigorous protocol. A survey by Lichstein et al. found that pharmaceutical company representatives provided samples in 70% of the resident clinics and that 35% of the residents depended on these samples "moderately" or "a lot" (Lichstein et al. 1992). In many instances these samples are an important source of drug supply for clinics that serve the indigent; such patients are unable to purchase pharmaceuticals in the normal way.

Medical Journal Advertising

Advertising in medical journals is one of the main avenues for drug promotion. In 1991, approximately $352 million was spent on journal advertising alone (Klein and Secunda 1992). As a majority of doctors subscribe to medical journals, it is impossible for them to avoid being exposed to this form of advertising. Drug advertising makes up approximately 40–60% of the total content of Canadian medical journals (Lexchin 1987). The only limit to the number of advertising pages a journal can carry is set by the postal service. To continue mailing *JAMA* at a second-class rate, the ratio of advertising to editorial content must not exceed 0.75 in one-half of the journals mailed during the year.

Advertisements emphasize the positive aspects of a product but do not provide objective data that would be required for comparative analysis. The FDA requires full disclosure of a drug's indications, contraindications, side effects, and normal dosage in the format of the package insert. This information is usually on the back side of prominent advertisements. In a study of pharmaceutical advertisements in US medical journals, Wilkes et al. (1992) found that 92% of the advertisements did not comply with the FDA regulations. The advertisements were frequently misleading and had little or no educational value. A large proportion of advertisements (62%) were deemed to require major revisions before publication.

Surveys in Australia have found that 16 to 31% of advertisements are thought to be misleading. Exaggerated safety and efficacy claims, inadequate warnings of adverse effects, and promotion for inappropriate indications were the most egregious errors (Wade 1989). An official of the FDA has stated that "the vast majority" of promotional materials submitted to the FDA for consideration are misleading in some respect, but the agency takes regulatory action in only 5% of the cases, mainly because it lacks resources ("FDA's drug promotion problems" 1989).

In every developed country, regulations and regulatory bodies exist to govern the content of pharmaceutical advertising and promotion. In Canada, the Pharmaceutical Advertising Advisory Board (PAAB) screens drug advertisements prior to their publication in Canadian medical journals. Although this body is composed of representatives of the pharmaceutical industry, physicians, and pharmacists, its powers are limited, and sanctions for violations of the voluntary code are limited to withdrawal or modification of the offending advertisement.

The Medical Lobby for Appropriate Marketing (MaLAM) acts as a watchdog for advertisements appearing in medical journals circulated in the developing countries. This group attempts to use physicians' influence to encourage companies to provide accurate information so that prescribing and dispensing are better informed. The MaLAM sends letters to senior executives of pharmaceutical companies, requesting evidence in support of claims made in the company's advertisements in order to encourage honest advertising. Wade et al. (1989) found that many of the references used by drug companies in their advertisements to support their claims are from proceedings of unrefereed symposia, or journal supplements, or are unpublished.

In Britain, the Association of the British Pharmaceutical Industry (ABPI) has judged pharmaceutical advertisements on the basis of a voluntary code of practice. Section 93 of the Medicines Act forbids promotion that is likely to mislead as to the nature or quality of medicinal products . . . or as to their uses or effects. The Act also states that promotional material should not be inconsistent with particulars contained in the data sheet and that products should not be promoted for "purposes other than those specified in the license." Studies have shown that this voluntary code was breached nearly 300 times between 1983 and 1988, with the most frequent offenders being Organon (32 breaches), Smith Kline and French (23), Glaxo (21), A. H. Robins (18), Bayer (17), and Merck (17) (Herxheimer and Collier 1990).

In Australia, the code of conduct of the Australian Pharmaceutical Manufacturers Association (APMA) empowers its committee to examine advertisements and to ensure that an offending member issues a retraction statement which is subject to approval in detail by the committee before its release. The *Medical Journal of Australia* has recently begun to publish summaries of APMA decisions on violations of its code.

Leffler (1981) views pharmaceutical advertisements more as reminders to physicians to consider particular products and not as definitive sources of drug information. He suggests that continuing medical education is a better mechanism for diffusing knowledge about drugs and that advertisements should not be a major source of such information for physicians. Clearly there are two ways of viewing pharmaceutical advertising (and perhaps detailing activities, as well). One view expresses concern because these advertisements are self-serving, one-sided, and incomplete. On the other hand, this is exactly what advertising is—a way for manufacturers to tell potential consumers (or prescribers) of the merits of their product. Advertisements are paid for by the sponsoring organization, and so one would hardly expect them to provide comprehensive comparative data on all competing products.

The answers to two questions can largely determine whether advertising and promotion should be a policy concern:

1. Are there sources of comparative drug information in the marketplace that physicians can access in order to maintain high standards of prescribing quality?
2. Do physicians obtain most of their drug knowledge from unbiased and comprehensive sources of comparative information rather than from the narrowly focused advertising material?

If the answers to these questions are positive, whether advertising is complete and balanced or not becomes irrelevant. If the answers are negative, better physician education is called for, but advertising is surely not the best medium for this educational effort.

Evidence suggests that the answers to the questions are not entirely positive or negative. There are excellent sources of comparative drug information in the marketplace. Examples are *Drug Facts and Comparisons*, published by Facts and Comparisons, St. Louis (published annually) and *The Medical Letter on Drugs and Therapeutics*, published by The Medical Letter, Inc., New Rochelle, NY (published biweekly).

The studies cited previously, however, suggest that physicians rely too much on marketing material for their information, suggesting a greater need for wider distribution of the comparative information that is published. Leffler's suggestion that continuing education may be the best medium for disseminating this information may be appropriate.

Continuing Medical Education (CME) Programs

Expenditures by the top ten pharmaceutical manufacturers on symposia rose from $6.5 million in 1974 to $85.9 million in 1988 (Kessler 1991). According to the American College of Physicians, a substantial percentage of the estimated $200 million spent on medical education by pharmaceutical companies (as distinct from promotional activities) is used to subsidize programs given under the auspices of traditional CME programs (ACP 1990). Without industry support, many of the CME programs currently offered in North America either would not be offered or would be prohibitively expensive. One study of prescribing decisions by general practitioners found that seminars, conferences, and lectures organized by pharmaceutical companies had more influence than advertisements, promotional material (e.g., samples, calendars, or diaries), or direct mail. Moreover, many of the doctors surveyed did not interpret such "educational" activity as promotion (Pitt and Nel 1988).

Many physicians are uncomfortable in distinguishing between activities that primarily support the business of the company from those that are primarily educational. In response to these ethical concerns, the American Medical Association (AMA) issued a report entitled *Gifts to Physicians from Industry to Guide the Ethical Relationships of Individual Physicians* (AMA 1990) and in 1991 the Accreditation Council on Continuing Medical Education (ACCME) issued its *Guidelines for Commercial Support of Continuing Medical Education*. This document must be adhered to by providers of continuing medical education who have, and wish to retain, accreditation by the ACCME.

The Food and Drug Administration regulates pharmaceutical firm promotional activities, but only if they fall within the legal definitions of labeling or advertising. Criteria used by the FDA to distinguish educational from promotional activities include the independence of the program, the control of the agenda, selection of speakers, and what is said. Inducements such as free meals, travel refunds, and entertainment make the presentation more likely to be seen as promotional. Publications resulting from symposia are regarded as labeling by the FDA if they are distributed by the drug company (Kessler and Pines 1990).

Public Media

Since the late 1980s pharmaceutical companies have attempted to use the various media—including television and newspapers and magazines—to publicize new results from drug research. An example is the concerted action taken by a pharmaceutical company following the release of a study by Pollare et al. (1989) that compared the effect of hydrochlorothiazide and an angiotensin-converting enzyme (ACE) inhibitor, capotopril, on serum cholesterol levels and glucose metabolism. The results of the study were sent to many newspapers before it was published in the medical journals. The story appeared in more than 200 newspapers and appeared on the front page of the *New York Times*. Audio and video spots were sent to radio and television stations across the country, followed by a press conference called by the pharmaceutical company in New York. The *New York Times* story was titled "New Study Says Diuretics Raise Heart Attack Risks." The Associated Press urged its readers who were taking diuretics to contact their doctors "about a new study showing that drugs may increase the risk of heart attack." Although there were follow-up articles and a letter to the editor which attempted to put the study into proper perspective, these were not widely disseminated. New prescriptions for oral diuretic agents decreased from 2,155,000 in September 1989 (the publication date of the study) to 1,874,000 in January 1990, a decrease of 13% (Moser et al. 1991). Following the release of the results of this study, numerous symposia were held across the country to reiterate the relationship between hypertension and insulin resistance; these meetings were largely promotional and were hosted by the pharmaceutical company.

Moser et al. question the appropriateness of this form of marketing saying it is unethical because it does not take into consideration input from the physicians, who are in the best position to decide the relative merits of different medications for each individual patient. Moreover, in this particular case the results of the study were not new, and the medical community already knew about the effect of a short-term increase of serum cholesterol in patients taking diuretics such as hydrochlorothiazide (Moser et al. 1991). Marketing through the media illustrates the attempt by pharmaceutical companies to expand the markets for their products by increasing the information available to consumers; the attempt is to urge them to influence their physician's choice of drug.

Disguising Marketing as Research

In an increasingly competitive and crowded marketplace, drug firms are also adopting new strategies in the "me, too" drug market. While a company hopes that its product will be an improvement over the other current members of its class, even when a drug fails to offer a substantial advantage over existing products, the company is likely to market the product as long as the size of the market is large enough. Often, of course, a "me, too" drug will be different in some respects from existing products and some consumers or doctors will find it advantageous.

Some company-sponsored trials of approved drugs appear to serve little or no purpose other than to encourage physicians to try using the drug. Such a trial was associated with the launch of a new antihypertensive agent, a latecomer to its therapeutic class. The stated objectives of the study were to study the efficacy and tolerability of this agent in controlling mild-to-moderate hypertension. The company used its sales force to recruit 2500 office-based doctors as "investigators" who would be paid $85 for each patient they enrolled in the trial. The FDA determined that the study was incapable of meeting its stated objectives and informed the company that no data from this trial could be used to promote the drug (Kessler et al. 1994).

False and Misleading Claims

Claims of superiority over competing products from a safety, efficacy, or cost-effectiveness perspective have increased dramatically in response to competitive pressures. For example, in the antiulcer product market, manufacturers have sometimes seized upon unproved and relatively unimportant differences to distinguish their products from competing ones. The FDA has challenged these dubious claims of cost-effectiveness, as evidenced by its case against the manufacturer of an antiepileptic drug who attempted to justify the drug's higher cost by its superior clinical efficacy (Kessler et al. 1994).

Traditionally the role of the FDA has been limited to assuring safety and efficacy. It has done so first through the approval process, but it has extended its resonsibility to cover drug promotion, making sure, for example, that drugs are not promoted for uses for which safety and efficacy have not been demonstrated. Should the FDA also monitor claims by manufacturers concerning a product's relative efficacy compared to other products, or the validity of claims of cost-effectiveness? Some would argue that the FDA's responsibility should not extend beyond issues of safety and efficacy. This would implicitly put reliance back on the Federal Trade Commission to monitor the accuracy of advertising claims in areas where the FDA has far greater expertise.

A related issue is whether the FDA should restrict the diffusion of information concerning unapproved, "off-label," uses of drugs that have been approved for other uses. Under present guidelines, the FDA prohibits drug manufacturers from engaging in *any* promotion activities for off-label uses, including the distribution of scholarly and scientific journal articles describing such use. Inherent in this policy is the assumption that physicians will be mislead by this information. A compromise position that stimulates, rather than retards, diffusion of knowledge about drugs would allow dissemination of studies together with a warning that "FDA approval for the use of this drug described in the attached study has not been granted."

Some marketing campaigns attempt to induce patients to switch from their originally prescribed medications to the products marketed by other companies. Although switching can lower costs and improve quality in some circumstances, the FDA has proscribed the practice of using monetary payments to pharmacists who convince physicians to change prescribing patterns. In early 1994, several states reached a settlement with two major pharmaceutical firms with regard to their payments to pharmacists for this practice (Kessler et al. 1994).

Marketing in an Era of Managed Care

Dramatic changes in the marketplace have forced pharmaceutical companies to develop new product marketing strategies. Generic drugs, whose share of the market doubled from 15% to 30% between 1983 and 1989, are one reason for this shift. Another significant reason is the growth of managed care and its use of strategies to control costs. Of all HMOs, 49% use drug formularies, 70% mandate generic substitution, and 48% have mandatory drug utilization review. According to The Boston Consulting Group, (1993), managed care now influences approximately 50% of the drug market volume. Table 2.1 shows the growth of cost containment efforts in HMOs from 1988 to 1991.

The growth of managed-care organizations wishing to use cost-effectiveness information to influence drug choice has created the need for the industry not only to develop expertise in health economics but also to communicate the results of these analyses.

The need to evaluate drugs on economic as well as clinical grounds occurs because of the large numbers of drugs available to treat many common conditions, the wide variation in price of these competing products, and the highly competitive nature of the health insurance industry.

Frequently a new drug is introduced into a therapeutic class with existing

Table 2.1 Use of Cost-Containment Techniques

	Percent of HMOs using	
Containment Techniques	*1988*	*1991*
Formularies	40%	49%
(% of enrollees)	58%	61%
(% listing 1000 + drugs)	31%	24%
Mandatory Drug Utilization Review	37%	48%
(% applying to all drugs)	38%	69%
Required generic substitution	65%	70%

Source: *Marion Merrell Dow Managed Care Digest.*

drugs. When the cost of health care was not such a critical concern, physicians selected a drug on the basis of clinical effectiveness—either the drug most likely to work or the one with the least-dangerous side-effect profile. Occasionally convenience for the patient was also considered. Cost was rarely an important consideration. Now, third-party payers demand value for their reimbursement dollar because they compete aggressively with one another for beneficiaries, so-called "covered lives." Today a more effective drug is not necessarily the product chosen, especially if the gain is relatively small and the price premium for the new drug is large. This joint clinical and economic assessment is the heart of outcries raised by physicians (and, increasingly, by patients themselves). Patients and (typically) their employers demand lower-cost health care coverage but resent that with this often comes the denial of health care whose cost is thought by the insurer to be disproportionate to its benefit.

Pharmaceutical companies have responded to the changing environment by increasing the number of marketing employees with specific responsibility for managed care (Figure 2.4). The growth of managed care has entailed changes in the detailing staff, with more specialization and a higher level of training in health services and economics to strengthen both the representatives' technical product knowledge and their ability to communicate that knowledge effectively to the prescriber (The Boston Consulting Group 1993). Similarly, as the complexity of drug prescribing has increased, the marketing mix has shifted toward forums that allow communication of more complex information. For example, the number of symposia sponsored by the pharmaceutical industry increased fivefold, to 34,688, between 1974 and 1988 (The Boston Consulting Group 1993).

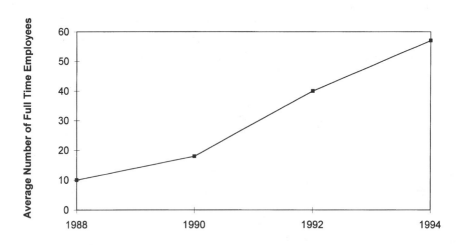

Figure 2.4 Number of Pharmaceutical Company Employees With Managed Care Responsibility

Direct-to-Consumer (DTC) Advertising

Direct prescription drug promotion first began in England when Syntex Laboratories promoted its antiarthritis drug Naprosyn (naproxen) on British talk shows, generating high sales volume in a few months. Drugmakers spent an estimated $200 million in 1992 on DTC advertising of prescription products.

Proponents of this form of promotion suggest that it has several beneficial effects. It makes the consumer more aware of the possible existence of a disease, and that a remedy is available for it. By treating the disease in its early stage, money may be saved in the long run. It also hastens the adoption and utilization of important medical advances and satisfies the consumer's desire to know more about prescription drugs and become more involved in medical decision-making.

Opponents, however, argue that this form of promotion could lead (1) to patients pressuring physicians to prescribe unnecessary drugs, (2) to confused patients believing that a minor difference represents a major therapeutic advance, (3) to use of brand-name products rather than cheaper generic versions, and (4) to increased drug taking in an already-overmedicated society (Morris et al. 1986).

In the United States, one of the earliest examples of DTC advertising was Pfizer's Partners in Healthcare series, which ran in the print and broadcast media to increase awareness about conditions such as arthritis, angina, and depression. Merck undertook a targeted marketing campaign in the late 1980s for its hepatitis B vaccine with advertisements in periodicals whose readers included many homosexuals—a group at special risk for contracting this disease. Merck also cosponsors a national prostate awareness program in association with the US Prostate Health Council and the National Council on Aging. This promotional effort ties in with advertisements Merck has placed in many seniors magazines for Proscar, its drug for treating benign prostatic hyperplasia (BPH). Physicians reported that 88% of patients asked for a drug by brand name in 1992, up from 45% in 1989 (Liebman 1993).

Consumers are generally receptive to DTC advertising. A survey by Morris et al. (1986) found that 66% of consumers believed that prescription drug advertisements provide useful information, and 50% felt that this information would benefit the consumer. Physicians, on the other hand, initially opposed this form of advertising. Of physicians surveyed by the AMA in 1984, 84% said that they were opposed to such advertisements in television. Reasons cited for this attitude were the public's inability to understand medications' complexities, therapeutic indications, and drug interactions. They also felt that advertising undermined the doctor–patient relationship by encouraging patients to make demands for drugs not medically indicated (Freshnock and Shubat 1984). The AMA House of Delegates passed a resolution disapproving of prescription drug advertising directly to consumers. However, physicians' attitudes are changing. The AMA modified its position in 1992 to allow direct consumer advertisng on a case-by-case basis when such advertisements are in the patient's best interest, conform to guidelines established by the AMA and FDA, and meet other criteria outlined by the AMA.

An example of this current trend is the national advertising campaign for diltiazem HCl (Cardizem CD) launched by Marion Merrell Dow. Cardiazem CD advertisements have appeared in magazines such as *Newsweek*, *Time*, *Woman's Day*, and *McCall's Silver Edition*. Upon calling a toll-free number listed in the advertisement, customers receive free brochures, a newsletter, and a discount coupon for the drug.

Over-the-Counter (OTC) Drugs

Many drugs are sold that do not requires a doctor's prescription, and the size of the OTC market has increased because many widely sold prescription drugs are now "switched" to OTC status when their patents expire. This $1.6 billion market saw more than 40 new product introductions in the early 1990s backed by more than $410 million in advertising.

The prescription and OTC pharmaceutical markets used to be separate entities. There was little movement of products from the former to the latter, and competition between the two only affected relatively few patients who consciously chose OTC drugs rather than prescribed drugs. As one might expect, however, this pattern was income sensitive; more lower-income than upper-income people decide to forgo prescribed drugs in favor of OTC products.

But recent patent expirations of prominent prescription drugs have created a strategic marketing opportunity for firms faced with patent loss. Drugs that lose patent status face loss of market share as generic drugs enter the market. In fact, the Waxman-Hatch Act of 1984 made it easier than before for generic manufacturers; only an abbreviated New Drug Application (ANDA) showing use of the same active ingredient and not requiring the full gamut of tests that new drugs must undergo, is now necessary. Grabowski and Vernon (1996) have shown that the market share of brand products 18 months after patent expiration fell from 53% for 1989–1990 expirations to only 28% for 1991–1992 expirations. What can firms do in the face of imminent generic competition?

One approach is to apply to the FDA to allow the product to be switched to OTC status so that the drug can continue to be marketed by its trade name. For the FDA to approve the switch the applicant must satisfy the agency that the drug would not be a safety hazard if it were available without a prescription. When a drug is a prescription drug, physicians will tend to write prescriptions in such a way so as to allow pharmacists to substitute generic for brand versions. And managed-care plans further encourage this substitution. The trade name has little value. But as an OTC product, the firm can keep marketing its trade name—directly to the patient rather than to the physician. All this comes with a cost, however. While drug insurance might have covered the prescription version of the product (probably the generic version), drug coverage is unlikely to extend to OTC drugs. Therefore the patient has to pay the full price for the OTC product rather than only the cost-sharing portion of the prescription version. The brand-name manufacturer's gain appears to be achieved partly at the expense of the patient.

The OTC market is segmented between brand and private label products, and name products now face increasing competition from private store labels. Sales of private label cough and cold medicines sold in food and drug stores were $106 million in 1992. In order to differentiate their products from the competition, manufacturers of brand OTC products are introducing new forms of drug administration, including liquid caps, gelcaps, enteric coating, alcohol-free hot liquids, and even skin patches. Large advertising budgets are allocated to these OTC products, which are often differentiated only by method of administration. Ciba-Giegy launched its Efidac 24-hour nasal decongestant with a $50 million advertising campaign, and Proctor & Gamble spent $22 million promoting its competitor, Nyquil (Riddle 1993).

The market for OTC antacids and heartburn medication has grown rapidly recently because of the strategic switch referred to above. This market was estimated to be about $770 million in 1992; the brand leaders are Maalox (Rhone-Poulenc Rorer), Mylanta, (Johnson & Johnson) and Metamucil (Proctor & Gamble). The prescription market for heartburn drugs was estimated to be $5 billion and was led by Glaxo-Wellcome's Zantac (prescribed for 240 million patients worldwide with $3.6 billion in sales), SmithKline Beecham's Tagamet (it earned the company a total of $14 billion in the 17 years it was under patent protection), Johnson & John/Merck's Pepcid, and Eli Lilly's Axid. When Tagamet came off patent on 1994 its sales dropped to $400 million, from $600 million in 1993. The company sought and received approval to market the product as an OTC drug; permission was also granted to Axid, Pepcid, and Zantac. The OTC antacid market is now estimated to have grown by $1 billion since the entry of these drugs. SmithKline Beecham and Johnson & Johnson/Merck are each spending over $100 million to promote their products ("Fire in the belly, money in the bank" (1995). Table 2.2 shows the changes in market share that have occurred since the introduction of Tagamet HB and Pepcid AC. Table 2 shows that as the two formerly prescription drugs, Tagamet and Pepsid, entered the market the share of the previously OTC products fell.

While marketing these products, companies have to be careful not to cannibalize sales of their older OTC products already established in this category. For example, SmithKline has to avoid comparisons with Tums, its antacid product, and Johnson & Johnson/Merck must prevent a direct comparison between Pepcid and Mylanta. The high cost of these products is

Table 2.2 Shift in Market Share of Major Antacids

	1994	1995
Tums (SmithKline)	25%	19%
Tagamet HB (SmithKline)	Not yet launched	19%
Pepcid AC (J&J/Merck)	Not yet launched	15%
Rolaids (Warner-Lambert)	18%	13%
Pepto-Bismol (P&G)	13%	9%
All others	18%	9%
Mylanta (J&J/Merck)	15%	8%
Maalox (Ciba)	9%	6%
Gaviscon (SmithKline)	2%	2%

Source: "Biotech companies abandon go-it-alone approach" (1995).

another concern. While Tums costs less than 3 cents per tablet, the cost for Pepcid AC and Tagamet HB is more than 40 cents per tablet ("Fire in the belly, money in the bank," 1995).

Another example of a successful switch from prescription to OTC is Proctor & Gamble's Aleve painkiller. This is the OTC version of its prescription analgesic Naprosyn, and it quickly achieved a 5.9% share of the $2.4 billion OTC analgesic market in a few months after its introduction, helped, no doubt, by the $100 million campaign to launch it (Weisz 1994).

Switching pharmaceuticals from prescription to OTC appears to be advantageous to third-party payers for drugs. Gurwitz et al. (1995) have noted the cost savings for managed-care plans as drugs are switched, but they note that the net effect is unclear, because pharmaceutical costs are not necessarily being reduced—they are being shifted from health plans to consumers.

Joint Marketing

As marketing becomes a critical element in a drug's financial success, small companies, which do not have national sales forces, are associating with those companies that have them, and are jointly marketing products. Figure 2.5 shows the increasing number of strategic alliances in the industry from 1986 to 1992. An example is the joint agreement between Astra, a Swedish drug firm, and Merck, the American firm, to form Astra Merck for the sole purpose of marketing Astra's drugs in the United States. The licensing agreement gives Merck the US rights to market new drugs of its choice developed by Astra in return for financing the FDA trials and all marketing expenses. In addition, Astra Merck has contracted with Marion Merrell Dow to increase its marketing power for the drug Prilosec. It is estimated that this venture will gross $1.3 billion in 1995 and will split over $500 million in pretax profits between the partners ("Ulcer busters" 1995).

Such arrangements can be crucial to the survival of small biotechnology firms which have strong R&D programs but almost no sales and marketing forces. Between July 1994 and June 1995, biotechnology companies signed

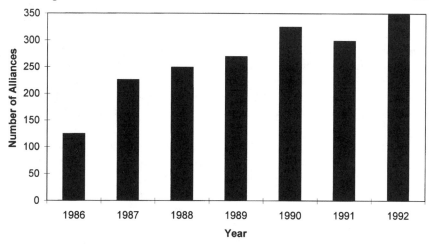

Figure 2.5 Strategic Alliances in the Pharmaceutical Industry

246 alliances with drug companies, up from 152 in the previous year ("Bio-tech companies abandon go-it alone approach" 1995). For example, Cen-tocor, a small biotechnology firm, has signed marketing agreements with Eli Lilly to market a new anticlotting drug, Reopro.

Pharmacy Benefit Managers (PBMs)

With the increasing shift toward managed care, prescribing power no longer remains exclusively in the hands of the physicians. Physicians now have to prescribe drugs that are available in the formulary of the managed-care or-ganization, so marketers are increasingly focusing their marketing efforts on pharmacy managers and others who decide whether a drug is to be placed on the formulary or not.

In addition, many organizations are hiring institutions known as phar-macy benefit managers (PBMs) to oversee prescription claims processing. Companies like Medco (now a unit of Merck) oversee pharmaceutical serv-ices for some of the largest companies in the country, including AT&T, Texaco, Bell Atlantic, and Continental Airlines. They also handle pharma-ceutical claims processing for insurance companies such as Blue Cross of Western Pennsylvania, Trigon Blue Cross Blue Shield, and the State of South Carolina. Cost savings in this $1.5 billion market for PBMs are achieved by guiding physicians toward cheaper alternatives. In the Medco Prescribing Program, Medco pharmacists telephone doctors and inform them that a cheaper alternative is available for the same indication and sug-gest that the physician switch to the lower-cost alternative. Pharmacists may also be sent to visit physicians and suggest ways to eliminate unnecessary prescriptions. One study found that approximately 35% of physicians called by Medco agree to switch their prescriptions ("Drugmakers under attack" 1991). As of 1993, 100 million people were in health plans served by at least 40 PBMs. Eighty percent of the PBM market is controlled by five big PBMs: Merck-Medco, Diversified Pharmaceutical Services, PCS Health Systems, Value Health's Value Rx, and Caremark International's Prescription Service unit (US Congress GAO, 1995a). The number of people who receive their prescription drugs through PBMs increased from 60 million in 1989 to 100 million in 1993.

The acquisition of PBMs by major pharmaceutical companies is another important development. Medco was bought by Merck, SmithKline Beecham bought Diversified Pharmaceutical Services, and Eli Lilly bought PCS Health Systems. Congressional concern over antitrust issues raised by these mergers resulted in a study by the General Accounting Office (GAO). The GAO found that a few months before it was acquired by Merck, Medco's formulary included only a few Merck drugs. Following the merger, the number of Merck drugs in its formulary increased while those of its competitors (such as Bristol Myers Squibb's cardiac drug Monopril) were dropped from its formulary. While the report did not find evidence of anticompetitive behavior, it did urge the need for continued scrutiny of the mergers between drug companies and PBMs (US Congress GAO 1995a). This report follows the recent consent agreement signed between Merck-Medco and 17 state attorneys general in which Medco pharmacists are now required to disclose their affiliation with Merck when they call doctors urging them to use Merck drugs.

The wealth of physician prescribing information now available to pharmaceutical manufacturers enables them to virtually "customize" new marketing approaches. Through its PCS subsidiary, Eli Lilly has compiled comprehensive information on the prescription transactions of more than 55 million patients. It will attempt to link this master database with physicians' offices and pharmacies so that Lilly will have access to a patient's patterns of drug use, including whether a prescription was actually filled. The goal is not only to enable physicians and pharmacists to make more accurate diagnoses and prescribe the most effective medications but also to enable Lilly to target consumers and physicians more selectively in their marketing (Eli Lilly 1994).

These databases can contribute to medical outcomes research. Such research will allow companies to demonstrate the effectiveness of different courses of treatment for a disease from both a therapeutic and cost perspective. This would permit doctors, patients, and payers to make both financially and clinically informed decisions regarding health care (US Congress, GAO 1995b).

But the ability of a claims processor, such as a PBM, to construct physician and provider profiles raises new legal and ethical challenges with regard to confidentially. Consumers typically sign releases with their insurers upon enrolling in a health plan to allow the use of claims data for administrative purposes. When this data is allowed to flow from the insurer (contracting with the PBM) to a manufacturer (merged with the PBM) the potential for abuse rises. These issues are only beginning to be raised and undoubtedly guidelines or boundaries will have to be drawn defining the extent to which patient and plhysician data can be transferred among corporate entities, and for what purposes.

In the managed-care market, medications are often selected based on cost benefit or cost-effectiveness analysis or medical outcomes research. This is discussed more fully in Chapter 10. Manufacturers are now incorporating these themes into their marketing efforts in addition to traditional safety and efficacy criteria. The aim is now to justify use of new products to pharmacy committees of managed-care organizations on the basis of potential cost savings. For example, when Genentech announced the availability of Pulmozyme, its new drug to treat cystic fibrosis, it went to great lengths to supply cost data to justify insurance coverage for the drug. The company calculated the mean reduction in hospital and antibiotic costs which could be expected from the drug's use, thereby permitting a comparison with the purchase price ("Finding a new marketing Rx for pharmaceuticals" 1994).

In its *Annual Report* for 1994, Eli Lilly declared that in a major case study of patients having lower respiratory tract infections, Ceclor produced estimated savings of $388 per patient, primarily, due to lowering hospital costs. Another study showed that adding Prozac to a state Medicaid program would save almost $2 million a year in treating patients not responding to tricyclic antidepressants (Eli Lilly 1994).

Studies of the economic effect of new drugs vary widely in design, methodology, and quality partly because there is so little agreement on many of the analytical aspects of the study design, and hence little standardization and little comparability in results. The situation is similar to that of medical outcomes literature: An astute reader is required to discern when observed differences between procedures are both statistically significant and meaningful and whether the study has policy, clinical, or managerial implications.

Pharmaceutical companies also have become more sensitive to other outcomes in their approach to institutional buyers. They now include multicultural promotions, disease-specific instructional videos, tie-ins with nonprofit or advocacy groups, and lifestyle-oriented compliance programs like Zeneca's Wellspring Service in their sales strategy. In part they do this to overcome cost considerations, creating incentives beyond price to encourage selection of a branded product over a generic. Generic manufacturers rarely have the funds to offer similar value-added programs ("Finding a new marketing Rx for pharmaceuticals" 1994).

Disease Management

"Disease management" is a systems approach to identifying and then promoting "best practice" for a condition. It is based on the realization that a piecemeal approach to improving quality or reducing costs, such as by limiting prescriptions, shortening hospital lengths of stay, or restricting use of emergency rooms, is likely to have unexpected consequences that may thwart the stated objectives. Drug firms have contracted with health services research consulting organizations to develop protocols for best practice. Some of these guidelines may promote a firm's own products (especially if the firm actually produces the most cost-effective product for a given condition). Producing these protocols may also promote the image of the firm through the goodwill that can be generated. And of course firms will benefit if they can demonstrate that more restrictive regulation of pharmaceutical use (common in managed-care organizations) is not an optimal cost-containment or quality-enhancing strategy.

This approach addresses the entire spectrum of pharmaceutical-related needs—diagnosis, treatment, compliance, and patient follow-up—in an attempt to treat disease in an integrated fashion. Hypertension, a major killer, can be easily treated with drugs. However, only 33% of Americans with hypertension are treated being treated this way. And for hypercholesterolemia, another serious chronic condition, only 15% of patients are treated with cholesterol-lowering agents such as Merck's Mevacor or Bristol-Myers Squibb's Pravachol. And only a minority of noninsulin-dependent diabetics are adequately treated for their condition.

Warner-Lambert has adopted a unique marketing approach for hospitals and HMOs for patients with epilepsy: The firm will help identify epilepsy patients, provide them with educational materials, and help monitor their treatment compliance, thus decreasing unnecessary hospitalizations and long-term system-wide costs ("A dry period" 1995). Warner-Lambert claims that seizures may require hospitalization with bills of $12,000 to $18,000 per episode, which is more than enough to provide a lifetime supply of seizure-preventing medicine such as Dilantin. This is a strong message to health insurers.

In 1994 Pfizer reorganized its US marketing along disease management lines. Its Diabetes Control Network coordinates treatment protocols and product supplies, monitors diet and exercise, and provides educational and psychosocial services for diabetics being treated in managed-care organizations. The firm has also developed a diagnostic tool, PRIME-MD, which helps primary care physicians identify the existence of common mental ailments.

Similarly, Merck is promoting Fosamax, its treatment for osteoporosis in postmenopausal women, through disease awareness programs and coalitions with women's groups. Zeneca's Wellspring Program is aimed at improving compliance among hypertensive patients. Patients participating in Wellspring receive a free newsletter, telephone reminders to fill their prescriptions, and pharmacy coupons and discounts. Zeneca estimates that enrolled patients average $94 less a year in medical expenses than those not in the program. These programs and protocol development activities illustrate how pharmaceutical firms shift from the traditional product manufacturer role into a health service professional role, making diagnostic and treatment decisions as well as the drug products themselves.

The Role of the FDA in Marketing

The federal Food, Drug, and Cosmetic Act of 1938 granted the FDA jurisdiction over the labeling of all drugs. In 1962, Congress further expanded the FDA's mandate by transferring jurisdiction over advertising of prescription drugs from the Federal Trade Commission to the FDA, while leaving jurisdiction of over-the-counter (OTC) drugs with the Federal Trade Commission. The definition of labeling used by the FDA is "any written, printed, or graphic matter upon or accompanying the drug." Brochures, calendars, mailing pieces, sound and film recordings, letters to formularies, exhibits, detailing pieces, references in published works like the *Physicians' Desk Reference*, and even books used to promote the sale of a product are considered labeling by the agency and regulated as such. The Act does not define what constitutes advertising, but the FDA views anything, other than labeling, that promotes a drug product and that is sponsored by the manufacturer as advertising. The definitions of labeling and advertising taken together cover virtually all information-disseminating activities that can be carried out by the drug manufacturer (Kessler and Pines 1990).

A particular area of controversy is the FDA's prohibition against advertising a drug for uses other than those specifically approved. Off-label use is widespread in medical practice, and in many cases FDA approval is eventually sought for new uses. Lidocaine, for example, was first approved as a local anesthetic but now has FDA approval for treatment of cardiac arrhythmias. The philosophy behind the FDA's concern, of course, is that it is wary of allowing any form of drug marketing for uses which have not been validated by clinical trials. As an exception, the FDA allows drug firms to help sponsor continuing education programs at which off-label drug use is discussed as long as the firm's sponsorship and relationship with speakers (if any) are fully disclosed. A related issue is advertising for drugs whose NDA approval is expected shortly. The FDA allows firms to distribute announcements of products whose approval appears imminent (so-called "coming soon announcements"), but without claims of efficacy.

In 1981 the FDA established the requirement that advertisements for drugs must "present true statements relating to side effects, contraindications, and effectiveness." Advertisements not meeting these requirements henceforth would be labeled false and misleading. They must also present a fair balance between the information relating to side effects and contraindications and information relating to effectiveness of the drug. Specifically, the regulations state that advertisements "are false, lacking in fair balance, or otherwise misleading" if they

1. Make claims about relative safety and efficacy or about the populations in which the drug is useful that are not supported by the current literature
2. Use literature or references inappropriately to support claims in the advertisement
3. Use statistics erroneously, or
4. Use headlines, subheadings, or pictorials or other graphic material in a way that is misleading

The guidelines also specify that advertisements "may be false, lacking in fair balance, or otherwise misleading" if they

1. Use statistical significance to support a claim lacking known clinical significance
2. Cite studies inadequate in design to support claims
3. Use tables or graphs in a way that is misleading
4. Contain claims about the mechanisms or sites of actions that are not supported by scientific evidence
5. Fail to provide sufficient emphasis on side effects and contraindications
6. Fail to present information relating to side effects and contraindications with a prominence and readability comparable with the presentation of information relating to efficacy, or
7. Promote use in a particular class of patients without emphasizing significant side effects and contraindications or dosage considerations applicable to the class of patients

Similar regulations apply to the package insert. The agency's assessment of an advertisement includes a comparison of the content of the advertisement with the package insert. Usually, the agency does not review or approve advertising and promotional materials before their dissemination by the drug company. All advertising and promotional materials are considered a representation of the package insert and are thus intimately linked to the scientific basis for statements contained in the package insert. The FDA commits substantial resources to the development of a package insert that will fully inform the practicing physician about the risks, limitations, and benefits related to a product's use.

If the drug's labeling or advertisements are found to violate these provisions, the drug is subject to seizure, and its manufacturer and certain employees are subject to prosecution. Usually, however, the agency merely requires that the advertisement be canceled or that the distribution of the detail piece be halted. If there are concerns about patient safety, the agency requires the offending manufacturer to send "Dear Doctor" warning letters to physicians.

The FDA's most common enforcement action is to write to a pharmaceutical company, identifying a violation of the law and proposing a remedy. A more serious transgression generates a "regulatory letter" which contains stronger language and is released publicly. If the company does not take suitable remedial actions, then the FDA can pursue criminal prosecution (Kessler and Pines 1990).

In recent years, the FDA has asserted its jurisdiction over emerging promotional methods also. The agency views its mandate as preventing physicians and consumers from being misled by spurious claims made not only on labels and advertisements, but via any promotional mechanism.

At present, the FDA has adopted the position that direct-to-consumer (DTC) advertising is permissible if it meets the regulation for fair balance and includes the brief summary information. The most controversial DTC advertisements are those that promote a specific drug. The FDA regulations in effect proscribe product-specific advertisements on network television, for it is difficult to include the brief summary information in a 30-second commercial. The FDA also requires that the advertisement refer to the prescribing information in the *Physicians' Desk Reference*, that it display a toll-free number that can be called for prescribing information, and that it meet the fair balance test.

Disease-specific advertisements, which do not promote a specific product but advise a viewer to "See your doctor," are acceptable to the FDA as long as there is no implication that drugs are the only suitable treatment for the condition and as long as there is no reference to a specific product (Kessler and Pines 1990). These ads are widely used for common conditions such as arthritis, hypertension, and hypercholesterolemia.

For drug company funding of continuing medical education, the FDA requires that emphasis be placed on the content of the information conveyed and not on how it is being delivered or by whom. It has developed various tests to assure the independence of such educational activities.

The FDA's role in regulating marketing implies that it has a substantial responsibility for controlling the flow of information between drug manufacturers and those who prescribe and consume drugs. Control over information is every bit as important to the public as control over the products themselves. In overseeing the content of advertising and other promotional activities the FDA is in effect deciding what information medical decision-makers have access to. While many see this role as appropriate for a regulatory agency and necessary for the protection of the public, others feel that the flow of information should be expanded, with physicians and others free to weigh and consider all possible evidence concerning therapeutic alternatives.

Rather than attempt to limit advertising beyond present constraints, it may be wiser public policy to supplement current advertising with wider diffusion to physicians of unbiased comparative drug information that is already in the marketplace. Given the complexity of new drugs and the rapid pace of innovation, it may be reasonable to require that physicians participate in continuing education programs to a greater degree than now required in order to improve their drug competency.

References

"A dry period," *Forbes*, 88, April 24, 1995.

American College of Physicians, "Physicians and the Pharmaceutical Industry," *Annals of Internal Medicine* 112(8):624–626, 1990.

American Medical Association, *Opinion of the Council on Ethical and Judicial Affairs— Gifts to Physicians from Industry*, Chicago: AMA, December 1990.

Avorn J, Chen M, and Hartley R, "Scientific versus commercial sources of influence on the prescribing behavior of physicians," *American Journal of Medicine* 73: 4–8, 1982.

"Biotech companies abandon go-it-alone approach," *Wall Street Journal*, November 16, 1995.

Bowman MA, "Pharmaceutical company–physician interactions," *Archives of Family Medicine* 152(5):317–318, 1994.

Chren MM and Landefeld S, "Physicians' behavior and their interactions with drug companies: a controlled study of physicians who requested additions to a hospital formulary," *JAMA* 271:684–689, 1994.

Cleary JD, "Impact of pharmaceutical sales representatives on physician antibiotic prescribing," *Journal of Pharmacy Technology* 8(1):27–29, 1992.

"Drugmakers under attack," *Fortune*, 48, July 29, 1991.

Dunnell K and Cartwright A, *Medicine Takers, Prescribers and Hoarders*, London: Routledge & Kegan Paul, 1972.

Eli Lilly, *Annual Report*, 1994.

"FDA's drug promotion problems," *Scrip*, 14, February 24, 1989.

"Finding a new marketing Rx for pharmaceuticals," *Public Relations Journal*, 24, March 1994.

"Fire in the belly, money in the bank," *Time*, November 6, 1995.

Freshnock L and Shubat S, *Physician Opinion on Health Care Issues*, Chicago, IL: American Medical Association, 1984.

Girard DE, "The relationship between physicians in training and pharmaceutical companies: A time for guidelines," *Archives of Internal Medicine* 152(5):920–921, 1992.

Glickman L, Bruce EA, Caro FG, and Avorn J, "Physicians' knowledge of drug costs for the elderly," *Journal of the American Geriatrics Society* 42(9): 992–996, 1994.

Grabowski H and Vernon J, "Longer patents for increased generic competition in the US: the Waxman-Hatch Act after one decade," *PharmacoEconomics* 10(suppl 2): 110–123, 1996.

Gurwitz JH, McLaughlin TJ, and Fish LS, "The effect of an Rx-to-OTC switch on medication prescribing patterns and utilization of physician services: the case of vaginal antifungal products," *Health Services Research* 30(5): 672–685, 1995.

Herxheimer A and Collier J, "Promotion by the British pharmaceutical industry, 1983–1988: a critical analysis of self regulation," *British Medical Journal* 300: 307–311, 1990.

Jensen PG and Lunde PKM, "Legens Anvendelse og Vurduring av Legemiddelinformasjonen I Norge. Resultatet av en Generell Rundsporring Hosten 1970 og en Tilleggsundersokelse Hosten 1971," *T Norske Laegeforen* 92:407, 1972.

Jewesson PJ, HOR, Jang Q, Watts G, and Chow AW, "Auditing antibiotic use in a teaching hospital: focus on Cefoxitin," *Canadian Medical Association Journal* 128: 1075–78, 1983.

Kessler DA, "Drug promotion and scientific exchange," *New England Journal of Medicine* 325:201–203, 1991.

Kessler DA and Pines WL, "The federal regulation of prescription drug advertising and promotion," *JAMA* 264:2409–2415, 1990.

Kessler DA, Rose JL, Temple RJ, Shapiro R, and Griffin JP, "Therapeutic class wars–drug promotion in a competitive marketplace," *New England Journal of Medicine* 20:1350–1353, 1994.

Klein T and Secunda E, "Rx for pharmaceutical ads: self regulate before government steps in," *Advertising Age* 20, August 17, 1992.

Kopala L, "The use of Cimetidine in hospitalized patients," *Canadian Family Physician* 30:69–71, 1984.

Laitinen A, "Laakareiden Asenteet Ammattikuntaansa Kohdistuvaan Laakemainontaan," *Suom LaakL* 28:1907, 1973.

Leffler KB, "Persuasion or information? The economics of prescription drug Advertising," *Journal of Law and Economics* 24:45–74, April 1981.

Lexchin J, "Canadian marketing codes: how well are they controlling pharmaceutical promotion?" *International Journal of Health Services* 24(1):92–104, 1994.

Lexchin J, "Pharmaceutical promotion in Canada: convince them or confuse them," *International Journal of Health Services* 17:77, 1987.

Lichstein PR, Turner RC, and O'Brien K, "Impact of pharmaceutical company representatives on internal medicine residency programs: a survey of residency program directors," *Archives of International Medicine* 152:1009–1011, 1992.

Liebman H, "Consumer, heal thyself: ads for prescription drugs are popping up more frequently in consumer media," *Mediaweek* 12: July 5, 1993.

Lurie N, Rich EC, Simpson DE, Meyer J, Schiedermayer DL, Goodman JL, and McKinney WP, "Pharmaceutical representatives in academic medical centers: interaction with faculty and house staff," *Journal of General Internal Medicine* 5:240–243, 1990.

Mick T, "Pharmaceutical funding and medical students," *JAMA* 265:659–664, 1991.

Morris LA, Brinberg D, Klimberg R, Rivera C, and Millstein L, "The attitudes of consumers toward direct advertising of prescription drugs," *Public Health Reports* 101:83–89, 1986.

Moser M, Blaufox MD, Fries E, Gifford RW, and Kirkendall W, "Who really determines your patients' prescriptions," *JAMA* 265:498–500, 1991.

National Wholesale Druggists Association, *1991 NWDA Directory*, Alexandria, VA: National Wholesale Druggists Association, 1992.

Pazderka B and Rao RC, *Market Share Competition in the Canadian Prescription Drug Industry: A Comparison of Several Therapeutic Markets*, Working Paper 81–8, School of Business, Queens University, Kingston, Ontario, September, 1981.

Pharmaceutical Manufacturers Association, *Annual Survey Report*, Washington DC: Pharmaceutical Manufacturers Association, 1989.

Pitt L and Nel D, "Pharmaceutical promotional tools—their relative importance," *European Journal of Marketing*, 22(5):7–14, 1988.

Pollare T, Lithell H, and Erne C, "A comparison of the effects of hydrochlorothiazide and captopril on glucose and lipid metabolism in patients with hypertension," *New England Journal of Medicine* 321: 868–873, 1989.

Rennie D, "Editors and advertisements: what responsibility do editors have for the advertisements in their journals?" *JAMA* 265:2394–2396, 1991.

Report of the Commission of Inquiry on the Pharmaceutical Industry, Ottawa: Supply and Services Canada, 1985.

Riddle JR, "There just ain't no cure for the store brand blues," *Brandweek* 19:16, July 19, 1993.

Schondelmeyer SW and Thomas J III, "Trends in retail prescription expenditures," *Health Affairs* 9:131–145, 1990.

Scott DK and Ferner RE, " 'Strategy and desire' and rational prescribing," *British Journal of Clinical Pharmacology* 37(3): 217–219, 1994.

Smith MC, *Principles of Pharmaceutical Marketing*, Philadelphia: Lea Febiger, 1968.

The Boston Consulting Group, *The Changing Environment for U.S. Pharmaceuticals*, Boston: The Boston Consulting Group, April 1993.

"Ulcer busters," *Forbes*, 94, May 8, 1995.

US Congress General Accounting Office, *Pharmacy Benefit Managers: Early Results on Ventures with Drug Manufacturers*, GAO/HEHS-96-45, Washington DC: GAO, November 1995a.

US Congress General Accounting Office, *Prescription Drugs and the Elderly*, GAO/HEHS-95-152, Washington, DC: GAO, July 1995b.

US Department of Commerce, *110th Edition of Statistical Abstracts of the United States*, Bureau of the Census, Washington, DC: US Government Printing Office, 1990.

US Senate, *Staff Report of the Special Committee on Aging*, Serial No. 102-F, Washington, DC: US Government Printing Office, 1991.

US Senate, Committee on Labor and Human Resources, *Advertising, Marketing, and Promotional Practices of the Pharmaceutical Industry: Hearing before the Committee on Labor and Human Resources*, 101st Congress, 2nd session, Washington, DC: US Government Printing Office, December 11–12, 1990.

Wade VA, Mansfield PR, and McDonald PJ, "Drug companies evidence to justify advertising," *Lancet*:1261–1264, 1989.

Weisz P, "Rx for profitable switch to OTC: brand before others join the fray," *Brandweek*, 30, September 12, 1994.

Wilkes MS, Doblin B, and Shapiro MF, "Pharmaceuticals advertisements in Leading medical journals: experts' assessments," *Annals of Internal Medicine* 116:912–919, 1992.

Zarate CE and Liosa IL, "Describing habits of Peruvian physicians and factors influencing them," *Bulletin of the Pan American Health Organization* 29(4):328–337, 1995.

II

THE CONSUMER

3

The Demand for Pharmaceuticals

Demand for pharmaceuticals, like the demand for other health care, is derived from the demand for health itself. Market demand, as distinct from the professionally determined idea of "need," entails a desire and willingness to pay for a product or service. In the United States, demand for pharmaceuticals is unusual because it is determined by four parties—the consumer; the physician, often serving as the consumer's agent; insurers, who actually pay for the drug that is purchased; and the pharmacist, who often decides which version of a drug to dispense, fills the prescription, and often provides the patient with health counseling and additional information on the drug's action, administration, and side effects.

Demand for pharmaceuticals is uneven across the population; demand is higher among the elderly, women, and African Americans. The quantity of drugs demanded varies with drug prices and also with prices of complements and substitutes, such as the price of physician office visits and over-the-counter (OTC) medications.

Pharmaceutical demand also varies by physician specialty: Some physician groups are nearly three times as likely to prescribe medication as others. This difference is no doubt related to a greater availability of useful products for some medical conditions than for others. Some physicians have begun dispensing drugs directly to patients, rather than referring them to a pharmacy.

Increasingly, third-party payers are interposing themselves between patients and their physicians and deciding which drugs will be covered. This reduction in physician autonomy is part of a new health care structure and is changing the way pharmaceuticals are demanded. Insurers use several cost containment strategies, including cost sharing, drug formularies, and utilization review.

Pharmacists have played an important role in product selection historically, but their professional autonomy is also threatened by managed care. Other efforts are being made to defend and enhance the phamacist's role as a primary care provider—as one who gives advice on health promotion and appropriate taking of pharmaceuticals. Managed care has been rapidly shifting from small drugstore pharmacies to chain and even health-plan-owned pharmacies. But a recent court decision prohibiting substantial discounts to drugstore chains brings into question the future ability of managed care to contain health care costs through negotiated price reductions.

How is Demand Determined?

Economic theory suggests that demand for a commodity is determined by a number of factors: consumer tastes and preferences, purchasing power, and the price of complementary and substitutional goods and services. Consumer demand exists only if the consumer has a desire to buy the product and the willingness and ability to pay for it. The quantity demanded is therefore directly related to one's income. Need, a term often used in health care, refers to professionally determined requirements unrelated to the factors deriving demand. Need is often quite different from a consumer's preferences and willingness to pay for a good or service. The difference between demand and need is more than semantic. It is important in differentiating between what "is," or what "will be," on the one hand, and what "ought to be," on the other. Need is an important measure of professionally determined objectives but it is often a poor predictor of consumer behavior, either in the health sector or more generally. It is also less useful than one might wish in making forecasts or simulations of policy decisions. Consumption is more determined by demand factors than need; this chapter deals primarily with the concept of demand and its effect on consumption.

Demand for pharmaceuticals is derived from people's demand for health. They are rarely purchased separately from other health services, but consumed jointly with other medical services—typically, physician office visits or hospital stays. Under some circumstances drugs are complements to these other services, and in some circumstances they are substitutes for them.

Physicians have primary authority to decide which medicine should be used, including the method of administration, dosage, and duration of usage. They act as the patient's agent, as discussed previously in the Introduction. But third-party payers, both public and private, pay for patients' health care expenses in the United States. Because the market for health insurance is competitive, insurers attempt to reduce premiums by reducing the cost of the underlying health services they cover. They try to contain pharmaceutical costs by offering health plans with cost-sharing arrangements, either deductibles or coinsurance or copayments, and by bargaining with drug manufacturers for price discounts. Even more important today is the rapid adoption of drug formularies and other disease management protocols by managed-care organizations, which limits physicians' prescribing options. Finally, pharmacists who provide drugs and counseling services to patients can influence the demand, as well.

Market concentration (or competitiveness) changes as we look more and more narrowly at specific products. The pharmaceutical industry as a whole is comprised of hundreds of firms within the United States, and several times that number if we look worldwide. But within particular classes of drugs there are far fewer producers. And if we look at a specific drug, there may be only a few producers if the drug is not patented, or there may be only one if it is. When one asks how competitive the pharmaceutical industry is, the answer obviously depends on how the question is asked.

The Changing Structure of the Pharmaceutical Market

As seen in Chapter 2, the demand for pharmaceuticals is affected by the unique structure of the market. Traditionally, in this market, those who make decisions concerning drug use neither pay for them, nor do they consume them. Prescribers make decisions on behalf of patients (the agency relationship) but are not involved in the financial consequences of their decisions. Consumers, on the other hand, are not decision-makers, and frequently they, too, are insulated from the economic burden of the product's costs by health insurance. The payers are frequently insurers who in the past have not been involved in making therapeutic decisions. Pharmacists, who actually sell the products to the patient, are responsible for assuring that the patient is informed about the drug's use—its method of administration, indications, contraindications, and side effects—and are obligated to verify that the prescription and dose are appropriate.

In recent years insurers have adopted managed-care systems that attempt to observe and change the behaviors of patients, physicians, and pharmacists in order to control rising pharmaceutical expenditures. The model of conventional drug prescription and dispensing practice has, in some settings, evolved toward one in which pharmacists take a more active role in counseling patients and conferring with physicians on medications. Although controversial, this evolution has some positive effects on the pharmaceutical market. It tends to reduce the cost of prescriptions and other health services. Counseling services offered by pharmacists are less expensive than physician counseling, may be more effective in improving patient compliance, and ultimately may reduce use of other health care services and improve health outcomes. This gives the pharmaceutical market new incentives to create more competition among drug retailers. Under managed care the interactions among the players in the pharmaceutical market tend to intensify both cooperation and competition. In the following section, we discuss both the traditional roles and their evolution for the four parties in the pharmaceutical market. We begin with consumers.

Consumers

An overview of the sociodemographic characteristics of those who are receiving medical services should give us a picture of who the consumers of pharmaceuticals are. Many sociodemographic factors have been found to be related to health care demand, including age, gender, and race.

Age: The elderly (aged 65 or above) are major consumers of both hospital and physician services. As shown in Table 3.1, the elderly accounted for a substantial proportion of hospital utilization, 62.6% of admissions and 52% of inpatient days, although they only represented 15% of the whole population in 1993. Their length of stay (7.9 days) were also much longer than those of younger cohorts (5.1 days).

The same pattern can be found in use of physician services. As shown in Table 3.2, the elderly accounted for 22% of physician office visits, far beyond their population percentage.

The elderly also consume a disproportionate share of drugs. Schondelmeyer and Thomas (1990) found that the elderly represented only 12.4% of the US population in 1988 yet accounted for 34.3% of retail prescription expenditures. Nelson (1993) analyzed the "drug intensity" of office visits by patient age. His data is presented in Table 3.2. The percentage of physician office visits which were "drug visits" (a visit in which medication was prescribed or provided by the physician) was approximately 65% for the elderly, compared with 60% for younger patients, although the elderly had only a relatively small share of office visits (12.27% for the 65–74 cohort and 9.49% for those 75 and over). Older patients were more likely to receive multiple-drug therapy while younger patients were more likely to receive single medication. For instance, a higher percent of visits by patients 75 years and over resulted in prescription or provision of three or more medications (22.51% than occurred for their younger counterparts (less than 20%). By contrast, patients under 15 years of age were administered more single-drug therapies (41%) than the elderly (29%) (Nelson 1993). The drug utilization rate (the average number of medications per visit) for those 65 or older was 1.4, significantly higher than that for the younger cohorts, which was under 1.2.

Table 3.1 Hospital Utilization by Age Groups, 1993

Age Groups	Admissions (1000s)	Inpatient Days (1000s)	Length of Stay (Days)
All ages	32,652	202,078	6.2
≥65	12,209	97,042	7.9
<65	20,433	105,036	5.1

Source: American Hospital Association: Data from the National Hospital Panel Survey.

Table 3.2 Office Visits Resulting in Prescriptions by Age and Gender of Patient, 1990

	Office Visits			Distribution of Patients by Number of Drugs Used (%)			Drug Utilization Rate
	Number (1000)	Percent (%)	Drug Visits	One	Two	Three	
All patients	704,604	100.00	60.26	32.74	15.73	11.78	1.80
Male and Female Combined							
<15 years	138,427	19.65	61.95	40.56	16.05	5.35	0.90
15–24 years	68,918	9.78	57.46	35.45	14.59	7.42	0.90
25–44 years	194,786	27.56	54.72	31.99	14.44	8.29	0.90
45–64 years	149,786	21.26	62.08	30.31	16.75	15.01	1.21
65–74 years	86,422	12.27	64.71	28.56	16.66	19.49	1.38
≥75 years	66,856	9.49	65.88	26.82	16.54	22.51	1.47
All Ages Combined							
Female	427,151	60.62	60.78	32.93	15.87	11.97	1.09
Male	244,452	39.38	59.46	32.46	15.52	11.48	1.06
Female, by Age							
<15 years	65,229	9.26	62.86	41.76	16.04	5.05	0.91
15–24 years	45,165	6.41	57.09	36.01	14.45	6.64	0.87
25–44 years	132,183	18.76	54.47	32.53	13.69	8.25	0.89
45–64 years	89,697	12.73	63.24	30.79	17.37	15.08	1.23
65–74 years	51,529	7.31	66.79	28.76	18.17	19.87	1.42
≥75 years	43,349	6.15	68.45	27.05	17.91	23.48	1.53
Male, by Age							
<15 years	73,198	10.39	61.15	39.48	16.07	5.62	0.90
15–24 years	23,753	3.37	58.15	34.38	14.86	8.19	0.96
25–44 years	62,012	8.80	55.25	30.85	16.02	8.38	0.92
45–64 years	60,089	8.53	60.34	29.59	15.84	14.91	1.18
65–74 years	34,893	4.95	61.63	28.28	14.43	18.93	1.31
≥75 years	23,507	3.34	61.14	26.40	14.02	20.73	1.34

Source: Nelson (1993).

Gender: Studies have also shown that drug utilization differs between men and women. For example, Leibowitz et al. (1985) found that annual drug expenditures were significantly higher for women than for men, based on their analysis of data from the Rand Health Insurance Experiment (HIE). For people below age 65, adult women spent twice as much as men. Children, although somewhat more likely than men to have had at least one prescription filled, averaged only half of men's annual expense for drugs. This finding is supported by Nelson's data in Table 3.2, showing that women had a higher likelihood than men of getting prescriptions in connection with physician visits. Women's drug utilization rate was 1.09 drugs per visit, while for men it was only 1.06.

For the elderly the gender difference in office visit drug intensity was

Table 3.3 Office Visits Resulting in Prescriptions by Race of Patient, 1990

Race or Ethnicity	Office Visits			Number of Drugs Used			Drug Utilization Rate
	Number (1000)	Percent (%)	Drug Visits	One	Two	Three	
All patients	704,604	100.00	60.26	32.74	15.73	11.78	1.80
Race							
White	597,306	84.77	59.88	32.86	15.47	11.56	1.07
Black	62,317	8.84	67.91	33.18	18.83	15.90	1.29
Other	23,694	3.36	60.46	32.89	16.55	11.03	1.04
Unspecified	21,287	3.02	48.21	28.04	13.33	6.84	0.79
Ethnicity							
Hispanic	35,456	5.03	62.31	36.21	16.13	9.97	1.04
Non-Hispanic	619,747	87.96	60.71	32.69	15.79	12.23	1.10
Unspecified	49,401	7.01	53.07	30.91	14.75	7.41	0.87

Source: Nelson (1993).

substantial. The percentage of women who received multiple prescriptions was much larger than that of men. For the age groups 65–74 and 74 and above, the drug utilization rates for women were 1.42 and 1.53 drugs per visit, respectively, compared with 1.31 and 1.34 for men.

Race: The drug intensity of physician visits also varied by ethnicity, as shown in Table 3.3. Black patients had a higher proportion of visits that yielded by at least one prescription (68% than did white patients (60%). The proportion for Hispanic patients (62%) is also higher than for white patients. The overall intensity was higher for black patients (1.3) than that for any of the other racial group, whose rates ranged from 0.79 to 1.07.

In addition to demographic factors, the intensity of prescribing varies by diagnostic group. The demand for pharmaceuticals is far from evenly spread across diagnostic categories. For example, office visits for respiratory and circulatory system diseases are more likely to involve prescriptions than are visits for surgically treated or gynecological conditions. Table 3.4 portrays the frequency of physician office visits and the intensity of their use drugs, by diagnosis, based on the International Classification of Disease, 9th Revision (ICD-9) (American Hospital Association 1978).

Thirty-three percent of physician visits were associated with diseases of the circulatory system (ICD 290–459), diseases of respiratory system (ICD 460–519), or diseases of the nervous system and sense organs (ICD 320–389). And these diagnostic categories were associated with particularly high intensity of drug use. For example, over 100 million visits to doctors' offices were in response to diseases of the respiratory system and 86% of these visits were classified as drug visits. Drugs were prescribed in 79% of the visits for circulatory system problems. The number of multiple drug visits was so high that the average drug utilization rate for diseases of the respiratory system was 1.65. It was even higher, 1.85, for diseases of the circulatory system.

Table 3.4 Office Visits Resulting in Prescriptions by Diagnosis, 1990

Diagnosis	ICD Code	Office Visits			Distribution of Patients by Number of Drugs Used (%)			Drug Utilization Rate
		Number (1000s)	Percent (%)	Drug Visits	One	Two	Three	
All diagnoses		704,604	100.00	60.26	32.74	15.73	11.78	1.80
Infectious & parasitic	001–139	27,075	3.84	66.83	46.32	14.32	6.19	0.97
Neoplasms	140–239	21,941	3.11	37.72	17.13	9.25	11.35	0.79
Endocrine, nutritional, & metabolic diseases, & immunity disorders	240–289	29,456	4.18	70.28	32.92	17.61	19.74	1.48
Diseases of the endocrine glands	240–259	19,289	2.74	74.22	30.89	18.33	25.00	1.69
Obesity	278	3,840	0.55	60.87	51.98	5.77	3.13	0.76
Diseases of blood and blood-forming organs	280–289	3,552	0.50	73.96	40.87	20.56	12.52	1.29
Mental disorders	290–319	29,929	4.25	58.79	33.12	16.02	9.65	1.01
Nonpsychotic disorders	300–316	22,612	3.21	51.31	30.48	12.98	7.85	0.87
Diseases of nervous system & sense organs	320–389	80,128	11.37	61.68	38.03	15.84	7.81	0.97
Diseases of central nervous system	320–349	4,799	0.68	77.43	35.18	23.68	18.56	1.52
Eye disorders	360–379	38,603	5.48	48.28	29.04	11.77	7.47	0.79
Oritis media	382	21,043	2.99	86.48	59.92	20.82	5.74	1.20
Diseases of circulatory system	390–459	55,989	7.95	79.21	29.96	19.71	29.54	1.85
Essential hypertension	401	27,310	3.88	83.96	36.46	23.36	24.14	1.73
Ischemic heart disease	410–414	9,210	1.31	80.11	16.94	18.17	45.00	2.34
Diseases of respiratory system	460–519	100,294	14.23	86.35	40.01	26.58	19.77	1.65
Acute upper respiratory infection	464	18,676	2.65	85.80	43.45	31.31	11.04	1.45
Asthma	493	7,137	1.01	91.41	20.42	22.20	48.79	2.53
Diseases of digestive system	520–579	26,154	3.71	61.49	33.40	17.14	10.95	1.09
Diseases of genitourinary system	580–629	41,067	5.83	56.34	37.39	13.05	5.90	0.84
Male genitourinary system	600–608	4,479	0.64	50.38	33.68	11.06	5.64	0.75
Female genitourinary system	614–629	20,377	2.89	57.48	37.66	14.87	4.94	0.83
Diseases of skin and subcutaneous tissue	680–709	36,836	5.23	69.73	35.90	20.32	13.56	1.24
Disease of musculoskeletal system	710–739	47,101	6.68	64.68	36.53	15.48	12.68	1.13
Symptoms, signs, & ill-defined conditions	780–799	27,221	3.86	52.86	29.59	13.54	9.74	0.94
Injury & poisoning	800–999	51,134	7.26	43.38	28.65	9.54	5.20	0.66
Normal pregnancy	v022	23,561	3.34	32.86	24.73	6.87	1.26	0.42
Health supervision of infant or child	v020	15,676	2.22	48.22	25.04	16.95	6.22	0.79
Other or undetermined		87,454	12.41	33.91	21.72	7.33	4.84	0.54

Source: Nelson (1993).

But the use of prescription drugs is only a part of the medication picture. It has been estimated that only about one-third of American adults suffering from illness or injury seek professional help. The rest either self-diagnose or use nonprescription medicines or do nothing at all (Industry Surveys 1993a). Health problems among older Americans, including arthritis, rheumatism, sleeping problems, muscle aches and pains, fatigue, eye problems, and other conditions, are widely treated with nonprescription products. According to Kline & Co., a market research firm in Fairfield, New Jersey, the total OTC pharmaceutical market is expected to expand from $11.5 billion in 1992 to $28 billion by the year 2010 (Industry Surveys 1993b).

As mentioned earlier, consumers recently have been encouraged to self-medicate with (OTC) medicines instead of going to the doctor and obtaining prescription drugs. According to the Nonprescription Drug Manufacturers Association, more than 70 applications for converting from prescription to OTC status are expected to be filed with the FDA over the next 5 years (Industry Surveys 1993b). As a result the number of important drugs once dispensed only with a doctor's prescription will continue to become available on shelves at groceries and convenience stores.

Physicians

In the health services market, possession of information is highly asymmetrical between physicians and patients, in part because of barriers placed by the medical profession. By training, the physicians has specialized knowledge in diagnosing and treating diseases. The patient, on the other hand, is usually poorly informed about the diagnosis, available treatment alternatives, expected outcomes, and prices charged by various service providers (Folland et al. 1993). As a result, the agency relationship, mentioned previously, has developed, in which the physician is trusted to act on behalf of the patient. The demand for drugs, therefore, is based upon physicians' behavior, which is determined in part by training and experience and in part by prevailing patterns of drug prescribing. Table 3.5 shows the drug-prescribing behavior of physician by specialty.

Physicians who specialize in cardiovascular disease, internal medicine, general and family practice, pediatrics, and neurology account for approximately 57% of all office visits. These physicians were also most likely to prescribe medications. Nearly 79% of visits to cardiovascular disease specialists resulted in prescriptions, and 42% of the visits resulted in three or more prescriptions; cardiovascular disease specialists have the highest drug utilization rate (2.24) of all the speciality groups. General and family practice visits accounted for nearly 30% of all visits and over two-thirds of the visits resulted in a prescription.

In the late 1980s, some physicians began dispensing drugs at their own offices. Although their counterparts in many other countries such as China and Japan customarily do this, it is a new aspect of physician practice in the

Table 3.5 Office Visits Resulting in Prescriptions by Physician Specialty, 1990

Physician Specialty	Office visits			Distribution of Patients by number of Drugs Used (%)			Drug Utilization Rate
	Number (1000)	Percent (%)	Drug visits	One	Two	Three	
All physicians	704,603	100.00	60.26	32.74	15.73	11.78	1.80
General & family practice	209,788	29.77	68.67	36.42	20.16	12.08	1.20
Internal medicine	96,622	13.71	74.48	33.70	29.82	20.97	1.55
Pediatrics	81,148	11.52	66.85	45.90	15.82	5.13	0.94
Obstetrics and gynecology	61,243	8.69	43.78	32.30	8.89	2.59	0.58
Ophthalmology	43,842	6.22	43.78	26.56	10.83	6.40	0.70
Orthopedic surgery	32,917	4.67	26.08	20.37	4.19	1.52	0.34
General surgery	22,402	3.18	31.07	18.38	5.40	7.30	0.56
Dermatology	24,009	3.41	63.99	29.48	17.96	16.55	1.23
Psychiatry	20,963	2.98	51.31	26.88	16.22	8.21	0.88
Otolaryngology	17,959	2.55	44.64	27.95	11.23	5.46	0.69
Urological surgery	9,546	1.35	40.37	30.23	7.70	2.44	0.54
Cardiovascular disease	11,240	1.60	78.53	19.47	17.45	41.60	2.24
Neurology	6,228	0.88	66.27	33.16	18.49	14.62	1.22
All other specialties	66,696	9.47	62.70	26.05	15.33	21.33	1.40

Source: Nelson (1993).

United States, and its effects on the pharmaceutical market are mixed. The separation in ownership between a medical practice and a pharmacy removes potential conflict of interest, of course.

The positive side of physician dispensing includes increased competition in the drug-dispensing market and more convenient services for patients. The following news report underscores this latter point:

> To Dr. Arnold D. Panzer, dispensing prescriptions simply makes good business sense. "I have a seven-day-a-week, walk-in, primary care practice, so dispensing medicine is in line with the focus of my practice—convenience," he said. . . . "Sure I make a profit from it," Dr. Panzer said. "We mark it up a certain amount, but it's often still cheaper than the local pharmacies." (Garret 1989)

There are two negative aspects to this development. The first is that dispensing physicians are no longer under the surveillance of pharmacists in terms of providing drugs appropriately. Of particular concern are those drugs that have addictive potential, important side-effect profiles, or inter-actions with other drugs prescribed by different physicians. This surveillance is an important function of pharmacists. A second problem is the potential conflict of interest for the physician because drug dispensing has become a source of additional income. This conflict is inherent in the fee-for-service system of paying physicians, of course, but it has been viewed as serious enough to invoke legislative controls in limited areas. Physicians are forbidden to hold ownership in pharmacies, for example. They are also now re-quired to disclose ownership interest in diagnostic laboratories to their patients, who might use this information to decide where to have their di-agnostic tests or whether to have them at all.

Alternatives to fee-for-service physician reimbursement alter the financial incentives of drug prescribing and dispensing. Managed-care plans fre-quently pay physicians by "capitation," a flat amount per month for every patient who has designated that physician as their primary care provider. Not only is the physician's income set independently of the quantity of services performed, but the physician may be financially responsible for serv-ices that are prescribed—referrals to specialists, or diagnostic procedures, or even prescriptions. Under these arrangements there is an economic *disincen-tive* to use these other services.

Even if the capitation arrangement does not explicitly put the physician at risk for ancillary services, the risk can take an implicit form if the man-aged-care organization actively seeks to restrict plan participation to physi-cians with especially conservative or inexpensive treatment patterns. Managed-care organizations, of course, receive their income in a capitated way, through subscriber premiums. They therefore have an incentive to re-duce their expenditures, and one approach is to use physicians who are frugal in their use of outside consultants, services, or drugs. A physician who rou-tinely refers patients to expensive specialists, diagnostic radiologic tests, or the latest and most costly prescription drugs may be asked to justify those patterns of care, and if acceptable explanations are not offered, may be dropped from the list of plan member physicians. The practice of following utilization patterns of either physicians or patients is termed "profiling," and it is another threat to physician autonomy and the integrity of the agency relationship between patient and doctor. Profiling is certainly expected to alter physician prescribing patterns.

Insurers

Health insurers influence demand for pharmaceuticals in two ways. Health plans have different cost-sharing provisions that will affect patients' demand for health services as well as medications. In addition, insurers frequently constrain the ability of physicians to prescribe by imposing formularies that restrict reimbursement to a select list of approved drugs. Furthermore, some insurers utilize "managed care" as a cost control strategy for pharmaceuti-cals, enabling them to bargain from a position of strength with pharmaceu-tical manufacturers for price discounts.

In the health insurance market, a variety of programs are offered, with different cost-sharing options in terms of deductibles, coinsurance, and co-payment. Table 3.6 describes the major insurance program types prevailing in the United States in 1991, together with their cost-sharing provisions as reported in a Health Insurance Association of America (HIAA) survey (HIAA

Table 3.6   Health Insurance Premiums and Cost Sharing, 1991

	Conventional Insurance	HMO		PPO		Medicare	
		IPA	*Staff/ Group*	*Preferred*	*Nonpreferred*	*Part A*	*Part B*
Monthly Premium							
Individual	$149	$130	$130	$147	$147	0	$29.9
Family	351	358	348	353	353	—	—
Deductible							
Individual	$205	—	—	$158	$283	$628	$100
Family	475	—	—	455	465	—	—
Coinsurance	20%	—	—	10–20%	20–30%	0	20%

Source: HIAA (1992).

1992). Health care organizations are divided into fee-for-service plans and two managed-care groups: Health Maintenance Organizations (HMOs) and Preferred Provider Organizations (PPOs). The table further distinguishes between Staff/Group-model HMOs, in which physicians are either employed by the HMO or are employed through an intermediary medical group, and Independent Practice Associations (IPAs) in which the HMO contracts with existing freestanding physician groups to provide service, often on a capitation basis. Preferred Provider Organizations (PPOs) are even-less-structured organizations in which insurers identify specific physicians who are authorized to provide covered services to plan members. These fee-for-service physicians have agreed to charge the insurer discounted fees and to accept utilization monitoring. PPO plans set different premium and cost-sharing requirements depending upon whether beneficiaries use the designated (preferred) providers or other, nonpreferred providers. The cost-sharing provisions of these private insurance options are contrasted with Medicare in the table, for both Part A (hospital and other institutional coverage) and Part B (professional services).

The relationship between the net price of health inputs, such as drugs, and the quantity demanded is described in Grossman's health demand model (1972). This model is especially useful for analyzing the demand for health care services because it acknowledges that consumers do not demand services directly. Their demand is derived from the demand for health itself. According to the Grossman model, consumers' utility is a function of market goods and healthy days. Because of disease, a person's health may fall below his or her desired level, which itself is a function of income and price of health as well as the price of other goods and services. The person will want to increase his or her stock of health by combining health inputs such as prescription drugs, physician services, and other inputs including time.

How does the patient select a combination of inputs that, taken together, will raise health status? Grossman sees this as a production decision, the same as faced by all firms engaged in combining inputs, or factors of pro-

Table 3.7 Actual and Predicated Drug Utilization by Plan

Plan Coinsurance Rate	Mean per Capita Expenditure	Cost per Prescription (1983 dollars)
Free	$54.41	9.06
25% plan	$49.91	9.43
50% plan	$36.12	8.18
95% plan	$33.95	8.73

Source: Leibowitz et al. (1985).

duction, to produce an output, in this case, "health." The patient, acting as a producer, will seek the cost-minimizing combination of inputs. When this combination is selected, the quantity chosen of each input will be such that the contribution to health of the last dollar's worth of each factor employed will be the same for all inputs. In other words, the producer will use each input up to the point that the marginal product per dollar is the same. This model predicts the (not surprising) behavior that as the price of an input falls, more of it will be consumed. The lower the price of a factor, or the higher its marginal productivity, the more of it will be used. Thus, assuming productivity is unchanged, the demand for drugs rises as their price falls and declines as price increases.

This theoretical construct has been supported by empirical studies, such as the study of Leibowitz et al. (1985) based on the RAND Health Insurance Experiment. Their results, presented in Table 3.7, show that mean per capita drug expenditure in an ambulatory setting rises steadily as cost sharing falls. The authors found that individuals with more generous insurance bought more prescription drugs than those with higher cost-sharing plans. The sample's mean annual drug expenditure ranges from a high of $54 (in 1983 dollars) for the free plan to a low of $34 for members of families with the highest coinsurance rate.

A later study by Foxman et al. (1987) found similar results. This study, using insurance claims for antibiotics from 5765 nonelderly people, found that people with free medical care are prescribed 85% more antibiotics than those who were required to pay some portion of their medical bills. The Foxman et al. study differs from the RAND experiment in that the former looks at *prescriptions*, while the latter looks at patient *expenditures*. The two measures can differ, of course, if patients choose not to have their prescriptions filled. While the RAND experiment is a direct test of the Grossman model, the Foxman study is not, for it asks whether patient cost influences prescribing behavior. It suggests another possible dimension of the agency relationship at work, with physicians looking out for the patient's *financial* as well as *clinical* health.

Another explanation is that drugs are usually consumed together, or jointly, with other medical care services, especially physician office visits. The two services are thus complements. Higher cost sharing would reduce an individual's likelihood of using physician service, so the chance of receiving medication prescriptions as a part of the service would consequently be reduced.

Third-party payers have played an increasing role in health care cost containment, during the last decade or so, using various managed-care approaches, including Diagnosis Related Group (DRG) and Resource Based Relative Value Scale (RBRVS) prospective payment systems first adopted by Medicare. The growth of managed care is expected to affect the US pharmaceutical sector, as well. Whereas in the past the decision as to what drug and brand to prescribe was almost entirely left up to the individual physician, it is now increasingly being determined by large payers. Managed-care providers use their collective purchasing power to secure discounts on purchases of pharmaceuticals and medical products, as well as on purchases of physician and hospital services. They then encourage use of those products purchased at a particularly advantageous price. These insurers also require substitution of less expensive generic products for brand products sold by leading drugmakers (Industry Surveys 1993a).

The most frequently used measure that insurers use to control drug utilization is the so-called "formulary." Formularies were discussed earlier, in the Introduction. A formulary limits the range of drugs that physicians are allowed to prescribe to one or two selections within a given therapeutic class. The managed-care industry has adopted Formularies as a powerful tool in holding down drug costs and eliminating use of the "me, too" drugs (Industry Surveys 1993a). More than half of the HMOs and PPOs in this country are believed to presently use formularies (Industry Surveys 1993a).

The evidence on the success of formularies is mixed, however. Sloan et al. (1993) Ross-Degnan and Soumerai (1996) have observed that health care costs actually rise when formularies are especially restrictive. This is consistent with evidence from Medicaid formularies noted by Schweitzer and Shiota (1992) and Martin and McMillan (1996). The problem is that pharmaceuticals, even within the same class, are not perfect substitutes for one another, and they are both complements to and substitutes for other health services. Therefore, if a suboptimal drug replaces a drug better matched to a patient's particular needs, the cost of the drug may be reduced, but the cost of other services may well rise. And overall treatment costs are highly sensitive to even slight changes in use of hospital and physician services because their cost is so high.

Another tool used by managed-care organizations to lower drug costs is the drug utilization review (DUR), a process of using screens based on clinically relevant criteria to identify potential prescribing problems. The DUR may be retrospective (RDUR) or prospective (PDUR). Under RDUR, a centrally administered system uses profiles to characterize past performance of prescribers, drug classes, or classes of patients against predetermined criteria. Under PDUR, information is supplied to the pharmacist at the time a patient presents a prescription (USDHHS 1994). The 1990 Omnibus Budget Reconciliation Act (OBRA 1990) required that all state Medicaid programs implement both RDUR and PDUR. In addition, approximately three-quarters of HMOs presently employ DUR programs (US Department of Health and Human Services 1994).

Using mail order pharmacies to dispense drugs at reduced cost is also an important development adopted by more and more managed-care insurers. The volume of prescription drugs sold via mail order has more than doubled over the past 5 years and should continue to expand significantly in the near future. A paper in the Industry Survey (1993a) notes:

> Fueled by increasing demand, the mail order drug market is projected to grow from an estimated $4 billion in 1992 to more than $7 billion within the next few years. Utilizing sophisticated computer technology and economies of scale in the handling of large volumes of shipments, mail order firms can usually supply drugs at lower prices than those charged by retail pharmacists. By making use of automated pharmacy techniques and offering prescription drugs at reduced cost, Medco Containment Corp. has become the largest factor in the mail order prescription drug field, with its sales increasing from $66 million in 1985 to an indicated $2.5 billion in the 12 months through June 1993. In August 1993, Merck & Co., the nation's leading ethical drug manufacturer, agreed to purchase Medco in a $6 billion cash and stock transaction.

Pharmacists

Traditionally, pharmacists act as both the seller of drugs and the counselor for those using the drugs. They provide OTC and prescription drugs and information about them, such as their indications, side effects, and expiration date. Meanwhile, physicians expect the pharmacists to provide additional services such as "monitoring drug interactions," "clarifying dosage directions," and "serving as a source of drug information" (Hirsch et al. 1990).

From the early 1970s, under cost containment pressure, pharmacists were required to participate in the campaign to lower drug costs. State antisubstitution laws have been repealed or amended so that pharmacists have the right to substitute a a less expensive generic product for a brand-name drug. Although studies found that substitution did not grow as quickly as might have been anticipated, it was the first step in modifying pharmacists' practice behavior (Salehi and Schweitzer 1985).

More recently, It has become normal practice for health insurers to contract exclusively with pharmacies, mostly large chains, that have negotiated substantial discounts, or rebates, with manufacturers. The following report from the *Washington Post* notes,

> HealthPlus [a local HMO in Washington, DC], which has 221,000 members, now contracts with Peoples Drug Stores Inc., Safeway Inc., Revco D.S. Inc., Rite Aid Corp., Kmart Corp. and nine independents located in areas not served by these chains. "We believe an important part of our managed care program is to market a restrictive provider network of physicians, hospitals and phar-

macies both to manage cost and to ensure the highest possible quality," said Jeff D. Emerson, chief executive for HealthPlus. (Singletary 1993)

Additionally, pharmacists could help reduce drug and health care demand by offering such services as drug counseling, education, and health promotion. A typical example is the control of hypertension. There are numerous reports of pharmacists entrusted with the management of therapy for hypertension through stepped-care protocols: If a first-line medication fails to achieve the desired result, the pharmacist might be authorized, through a protocol preapproved by a physician, to add to it or replace it with another drug (Talley 1994). This model reduces costs because the services provided by pharmacists cost less than those provided by physicians. It is also effective since pharmacists are more knowledgeable than other health care professionals about medication costs, adverse effects, and problems with patient compliance with therapy. Pharmacist counseling might also help patients alter their lifestyle with regard to such things as smoking, alcohol abuse, exercise, and diet.

The potential for reducing overall health care utilization through pharmaceutical counseling is substantial, for the following reasons:

- As much as 70% of the illness treated in our health care system is preventable.
- Poor health habits contribute substantially to the cost of treatment.
- Modest interventions, in which health care providers give consumers adequate information and guidance, reduce the overall medical services needed (Talley 1994).

Modern pharmacies, however, are under increasing financial pressure. One threat is competition from competing drug delivery systems such as mail order pharmacies and physicians who dispense pharmaceuticals directly. Strong growth in these outlets in recent years has cut into traditional retail drugstore volume. Market share of retail pharmacies shrank from 80% in 1985 to 65% in 1988 (Garrett 1989). Mail order prescription plans have captured about 6% of the outpatient prescription market and are expected to continue growing. Physician dispensing has also increased rapidly, capturing up to 3% of the outpatient prescription market in some areas (Schondelmeyer and Thomas 1990). The following report in the *New York Times* summarizes some of the challenges facing retail pharmacies:

> There is a drug war in America today that has nothing to do with crack dens and money laundering. Pharmacies are fighting to keep what was once their exclusive domain: the retail market for prescription drugs. Since 1985, health maintenance organizations, doctors and mail-order houses have cornered a growing share of that business and last year sold 15 percent of the nation's $28 billion in prescription drugs. (Garrett 1989)

The second pressure results from Pharmacy Benefit Management (PBM) organizations, which tend to exclude small, independent pharmacies from the contract pharmacy programs offered by HMOs and other health care providers. According to the National Association of Retail Druggists, many such stores may not survive as a result (Singletary 1993).

Retail druggists, both independent and chain, are also seriously worried about the effects of tiered pricing arrangements in which pharmaceutical retailers (including mail order pharmacies and those pharmacies closely linked to managed-care organizations) receive substantial wholesale discounts from the prices paid by nonaffiliated pharmacies and distributors. This form of price discrimination follows closely predictions of economic theory which suggest that a profit-maximizing firm will attempt to set prices to groups of buyers such that each group's price is inversely related to its demand elasticity. Retail pharmacies and wholesalers that are affiliated with managed-care plans will typically negotiate significant price discounts with the manufacturer because the plan has the ability to determine which drug will be used within each drug class. In other words, discounts will be sought from several competing drugs within a particular therapeutic drug class, and the drug with the most favorable efficacy, side-effect profile, and price will be selected. With this high elasticity of demand, substantial price discounts are not surprising. On the other hand, unaffiliated pharmacies and wholesalers cannot influence the choice of drug, so their role is strictly passive, furnishing the products local physicians prescribe. Demand elasticity is therefore low for these unaffiliated pharmacies and wholesale prices will consequently be higher. The ability of manufacturers to price discriminate is being challenged in the courts. "Unitary pricing" would protect unaffiliated pharmacies but would limit the ability of managed-care plans to reduce pharmaceutical costs to their subscribers.

Tiered pricing arrangements were challenged in federal court in a suit brought by the National Association of Retail Druggists which claimed that discounts and rebates between drug manufacturers and their PBMs, on the one hand, and large retailers and drugstore chains, on the other, were a restraint of trade because these discounts prohibited nonaffiliated drugstores from sharing in the prescription drug business of HMOs and other managed-care plans. The case concerning the ability of managed-care plans to negotiate discounted prices with participating providers has not yet been settled. If any providers seeking to participate (termed "any willing provider") are allowed to do so, one of the basic principles of managed-care cost containment would be made inoperative, bringing into question the ability of managed competition to constrain health care costs.

Conclusion

The demand for pharmaceuticals is unique. First of all, the structure of the market is unusual, with four players—patients, physicians, insurers, and pharmacists—all determining demand. Second, the role of each player is rapidly evolving. Pharmacists not only act as drug-dispensers but also as health counselors, educators and health promotors, substituting in part for physicians. Physicians, on the other hand, have started to dispense drugs in their own offices, usurping part of the pharmacist's professional responsibility. And health insurers not only pay medical bills but are increasingly engaged in managing the care they pay for, and they attempt to modify the behaviors of the other three players. Consumers have become more cost-conscious as their cost sharing is increased. In addition, more drugs can now be purchased without a prescription; consumers use more over-the-counter drugs, which requires them to be better informed about medications.

As society seeks more effective health care together with a slowed pace of expenditure increases, we expect to see even more changes in the pharmaceutical market. One can anticipate still further evolution and diffusion of organizational structures designed to achieve the two goals of effectiveness and economy.

References

American Hospital Association, *ICD-9-CM Workbook*, Chicago: American Hospital Association, 1978.

Folland S, Goodman AC, and Stano M, *The Economics of Health and Health Care*, New York: Macmillan, 1993.

Foxman B, Valdez RB, Lohr KN, Goldberg GA, Newhouse JP, and Brook RH, "The effect of cost sharing on the use of antibiotics in ambulatory care: results from a population-based randomized controlled trial," *Journal of Chronic Disease* 40(5):429–437, 1987.

Garrett EM, "What's new in prescription drugs," *The New York Times*, November 5, 1989.

Grossman M, "On the concept of health capital and the demand for health," *Journal of Political Economy* 80:223–255, 1972.

Health Insurance Association of America, *Source book of health insurance Data*, Washington DC: HIAA, 1992.

Hirsch JD, Gagnon JP, and Camp R, "Value of pharmacy services: perceptions of consumers, physicians, and third party prescription plan administrators," *American Pharmacy* NS30(3):20–25, 1990.

Industry Surveys, "Rx needed for ailing pharmaceutical industry," *Health Care*, September 9, 1993a.

Industry Surveys, "Rx-to-OTC conversions to boost market," *Health Care*, September 9, 1993b.

Leibowitz A, Manning WG, and Newhouse JP, "The demand for prescription drugs as a function of cost-sharing," *Social Science and Medicine* 21(10):1063–1069, 1985.

Levit KR, Sensenig AL, Cowan CA, Lazenby HC, McDonnell PA, Won DK, Sivarajan L, Stiller JM, Donham CS, and Stewart MS, "National health expenditures, 1993," *Health Care Financing Review* 16(1):247–294, Fall 1994.

Martin BC and McMillan JA, "The impact of implementing a more restrictive prescription limit on Medicaid recipients: effects on cost, therapy, and out of pocket expenditures," *Medical Care* 34(7):686–701, 1996

Nelson CR, "Drug utilization in office practice—national ambulatory medical care survey: 1990," *Advance Data*, Centers for Disease Control and Prevention, March 25, 1993.

Ross-Degnan D and Soumerai SD, "HMO formularies," *The Lancet* 347:1264, 1996.

Salehi H and Schweitzer SO, "Economic aspects of drug substitution," *Health Care Financing Review* 5(3):59–68, Spring, 1985.

Schondelmeyer SW and Thomas III J, "Trends in retail prescription expenditures," *Health Affairs*, pp 131–145, Fall, 1990.

Schweitzer SO and Shiota SR, "Access and cost implications of state limitations on Medicaid reimbursement for pharmaceuticals," *Annual Review of Public Health* 13:399–410, 1992.

Schweitzer SO and Comanor WS, "The cost of pharmaceuticals, Chapter 6," in Andersen RA, Rice TH, and Kominski GF (eds), *Beyond Health Reform*, San Francisco, CA: Jossey-Bass, 1996.

Singletary M, "Drugstores seeking Rx for survival," *The Washington Post*, February 15, 1993.

Sloan FA, Gordon GS, and Cocks DL, "Hospital drug formularies and use of hospital services," *Medical Care* 31(10):851–867, 1993.

Talley RC, "Reducing demand through preventive care," *American Journal of Hospital Pharmacy* 51:55, January 1, 1994.

US Department of Health and Human Services, *Medicaid Drug Use Review Demonstration Projects*, Report to Congress, Washington, DC: US Government Printing Office, 1994.

III

THE MARKET

4

Pharmaceutical Prices

Whether the drug industry is making above-average profits because of its alleged monopolistic structure has been a matter of policy debate for over 30 years. In this chapter we investigate some of the claims and counterclaims concerning drug prices. First we ask whether pharmaceutical prices are really high and increasing. And if they are, is this the result of the monopolistic structure of the pharmaceutical industry? Or are drug prices determined more by product quality, and do pharmaceutical profits function as a signal to the market to encourage increased investment in research and development?

First, we look at the changes in pharmaceutical prices over time and discuss the difficulties inherent in measuring drug prices. We note evidence that drug prices have not risen faster than prices in other health care sectors and that our measures of drug price changes tend to bias reported rates of increase upward.

Next, we analyze how drug prices are determined and what factors influence them. We consider evidence on the competitiveness of the pharmaceutical industry. We see that parts of market fit virtually *all* of the standard models of competition: monopoly, oligopoly, monopolistic competition, and even pure competition. In the debate over drug prices, a recurring theme is the question of whether or not prices are justified on the basis of high costs of R&D. We criticize the notion that these supply—side costs determine prices because these costs have already been spent and ought not to enter into any firm's pricing decisions. Especially important is evidence that price is determined substantially by product characteristics—a demand-side variable.

Lastly, we look at a new approach for studying drug prices, hedonic analysis, in which prices are related to product attributes. With hedonic analysis one can measure the value consumers place on drug characteristics such as convenience or absence of side effects. One can also assess whether particular products are priced at, below, or above the predicted price based upon the drug's characteristics and the values consumers tend to place on those characteristics for other products.

The Problem of Pharmaceutical Prices

It was the price of drugs that led to the 9-month-long hearing held by the Senate Subcommittee on Antitrust and Monopoly, which began in December 1959. The major concern of the hearings was that pharmaceutical products were overpriced, thereby justifying regulations. As Senator Estes Kefauver, who presided over the hearings, said in his opening statement,

> It is our purpose to inquire into the question of whether the drug manufacturers are setting their prices at excessive levels. It is also our purpose, this being a legislative subcommittee, to determine whether the antitrust laws as applied to this industry are adequate and, if not, to devise specific remedial legislation. (United States Senate 1960)

More harsh statements were made by another member of the subcommittee, Senator George Smathers from Florida.

> It is readily apparent that the American people, who are fortunate in having the most advanced medicines and drugs in the world, share alike the distinction of paying the world's highest premium for these basic human necessities. . . . This is a shameful condition in our present-day society which spends tremendous sums on research to promote health and increase lifespan, and yet the products are placed well out of reach of the average and low-income families. (United States Senate 1960)

Many of the same concerns are raised today by members of Congress and others. For example, in the 1993 hearings before the Senate's Special Sub-Committee on Aging, the chairman, Senator David Pryor, stated that "millions of older Americans go to bed at night wondering if they will be able to afford their medications." As in the first hearings 30 years ago, the major issue was price inflation of pharmaceuticals, because "from 1980 to 1993, drug inflation at the manufacturers' level increased four and a half times the rate of overall inflation" (US Senate Special Committee on Aging 1994). The committee concluded that significant manufacturer increases in the price of prescription medications commonly taken by older Americans, combined with the lack of prescription drug insurance, made it difficult for older Americans to take the prescription drugs that they needed.

But the pharmaceutical industry replied, to the contrary, that prices were low relative to the value afforded consumers and that high returns on successful products were required to balance the losses from the large number of unsuccessful ones. They argued that if drug prices were to be judged against marginal costs, as price determination under perfect competition would suggest, marginal cost must be defined to include the costs of developing and marketing new products. If marginal costs were defined this way, they went on, prices would not be seen as excessive at all. Although it admitted earning substantial profits, the industry argued that without these returns, research outlays would be limited and the number of new drugs reduced (Comanor 1986). According to Scherer the pharmaceutical industry was either the first or second most profitable industry for 24 out of 32 years between 1960 and 1991, as measured by the median after-tax profit return on stockholders' equity for the 500 largest US industrial firms (Scherer 1993).

But as Grabowski and Vernon noted, "without the real price increases which have occurred since 1980 . . . the drug industry would not have recovered total allocated costs from their 1970s drug introductions. The rapid rate of growth in industry research and development expenditures undoubtedly would also have been adversely affected if real prices had remained constant" (Grabowski and Vernon 1990).

Pharmaceutical Prices Over Time

Compared with other health care sectors in the United States, the share of expenditures devoted to pharmaceutical products declined from 1960 to 1990, as shown in Figure 4.1. And by 1994 the share was still lower, at 5.5% (Genuardi et al. 1996). Of total health care expenditures, the share of phar-

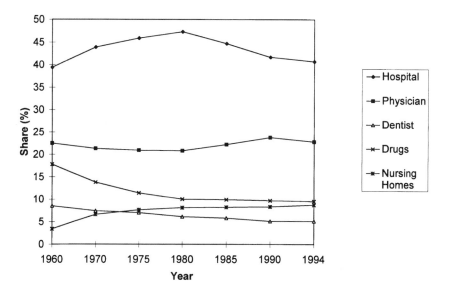

Figure 4.1   Share of Personal Health Expenditures: 1960–1990

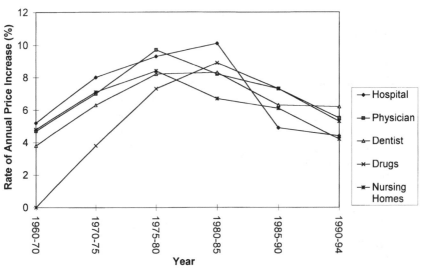

Figure 4.2 Annual Rate of Price Increase by Sector: 1960–1990

maceuticals in 1990 was 8.2%, down nearly 50% from its share in 1960. During this period, expenditures on pharmaceuticals grew, but at a far less rapid rate than expenditures for other health services.

The rate of increase in prices for the hospital, physician, dentist, and drug components during this period is shown in Figure 4.2. The figure shows that the rate of increase in pharmaceutical prices from 1960 to 1980 was substantially below that of the other sectors. Thus, pharmaceutical price increases actually moderated the overall rate of increase of health care prices rather than stimulated it during this period. However, pharmaceutical prices rose more rapidly after 1980. By 1980, the rate of increase in drug prices was as rapid as that for hospital services and higher than the rates of increase for either physician or dental services. But even after 1980 the rate of pharmaceutical price increases never exceeded those of the other components. However, the Bureau of Labor Statistics Product Price Index (PPI) for pharmaceuticals doubled between 1982 and 1993, while the PPI for all finished goods rose by only one-quarter. In other words, the average annual increase in pharmaceutical prices during this period (6.5%) was more than triple that for all finished goods (2%).

If pharmaceuticals constitute such a small portion of health care, and if price increases have often moderated, rather than led, overall health care price increases, why the public and Congressional criticism?

Part of the answer lies in the distinction between patient cost and total price in a market with substantial third-party market intervention. Table 4.1 shows the extent of third-party coverage and out-of-pocket expense for three health care sectors: hospital care, physician services, and pharmaceuticals.

Table 4.1   Third-Party and Out-of-Pocket Payment for
Health Care, 1992

Sector	Third-Party Payers	Out of Pocket
All Health Care	81%	19%
Hospitals	95%	5%
Physicians	82%	18%
Pharmaceuticals	72%	28%

Sources: Health Insurance Association of America, *Source Book of Health Insurance Data* (1993).

Over 8% of health care was paid for by third-party payers in 1992, with less than 20% paid directly by consumers as "out-of-pocket" expenses. But the percentage of care which is purchased directly is different across components of the health sector, and pharmaceuticals have relatively little third-party insurance coverage. Only 72% of pharmaceutical costs (defined as drugs and other medical durables) were covered, leaving consumers with the burden of paying for 28% directly. Thus, while consumers are sheltered from the burden of paying directly for most health care, this is not true for pharmaceuticals. The price of pharmaceuticals is therefore more visible to consumers than are prices of other components of health care. Because of the discrepancy in coverage levels, patients are more likely to complain about the cost of a $50 prescription than a $500 radiologic procedure or a $5000 hospital stay!

Aggravating the problem of the cost of pharmaceuticals is the large burden that drug costs have become for more and more people. There is a greater likelihood today than ever before of incurring truly catastrophic pharmaceutical costs. For example, drugs for patients with drug-resistant viral or bacterial infections may cost $5000 for a standard course of treatment, measured at the published wholesale level, while common drugs for cardiac patients cost as much as $400 per month and are taken chronically (*The Medical Letter*, selected issues). Transplant patients incur costs of $10,000 for immunosuppressive medications during their first year of treatment and $3000 each year afterward (UCLA Kidney Transplant Program, personal communication).

Measuring Drug Prices

How do we measure pharmaceutical price changes? And how accurate are our observations? Published statistics may seriously overstate actual price increases. The Bureau of Labor Statistics (BLS) measures the Consumer Price Index (CPI), together with its constituent parts, using a measure called a Laspeyre Index which relates the cost of a given bundle of goods and services (often referred to as the "market basket") purchased at current prices to the cost of that same market basket purchased at prior prices. The formula for the Laspeyre price index for the period t relative to t_o is the following:

$$P_t = (\Sigma_i p_{it} q_{it_0})/(\Sigma_i p_{it_0} q_{it_0})$$

where P_t is the price index at period t relative to period t_0. p_i and q_i are prices and quantity weights, respectively, for commodity i. The formula requires that we sum the product of p_i and q_i for all commodities for both the base time period, t_0, and the final period, t. The formula can be interpreted as computing the relative price of purchasing last period's market basket of goods and services at today's prices.

As a "base-weighted" index, this method for measuring price changes is designed to track prices of an *existing* market basket over time. But as the composition of the market basket changes, new weights must be incorporated into the index. This is especially important in health care, where new treatments for old problems, such as coronary artery disease and renal failure, have totally replaced techniques in use only a few years ago. In many cases improved techniques or drugs replace older products, but at a higher price. When this occurs, the price index should account for the quality improvement along with the price increase. If the technique fails to account adequately for technical change and quality improvement, measures of price changes are likely to be biased upward.

When items in the market basket change through substitution the BLS uses a "linking" technique. For example, when a new drug replaces an old one, price indices with the old and the new product are calculated and the new index is scaled upward or downward to equal (or "link" with) the old one. If the new good is more expensive than the old, the new index must be scaled downward, and vice versa. The index using the new item or service then replaces the old index for future calculations. No attempt is made to assess whether the improved product is more or less expensive than would be justified by the improvement in quality represented by the introduction of the technological change. The price index merely tracks the prices of all items comprising the former market basket and then recalculates the price index with the substitution.

In the case of pharmaceuticals, this failure to capture quality change is a serious deficiency, for the turnover of products is rapid, and many new products represent improved versions of old products, with greater efficacy, fewer side effects, or a more convenient regimen. The question of whether increases in drug prices exceed, fall behind, or accurately track changes in quality is left unanswered by the methodology used by the BLS in calculating the CPI (see Cleeton et al., 1992).

An analogous problem occurs because the BLS fails to recognize generic drugs as lower-price versions of the products they replace. Generic drugs are treated by the BLS as different commodities and their introduction is merely linked into the former CPI, as described earlier. The CPI therefore fails to reflect the price decrease, and is therefore biased upward. Grilliches and Cockburn (1994) have estimated that failure by the BLS to properly account for the introduction of generic drugs in one case led to a CPI *increase* measuring 14% over a 45-month period, while the correct figure was a *decrease* of 48%.

A third difficulty in the CPI is caused by the delay in new drugs making their way into the index. The lag is frequently 4 months or longer. The significance of this lag lies in the price changes associated with the introduction of new drugs. There is evidence that firms introducing new drugs frequently use a "penetration" strategy in which a drug is initially priced below existing products in order to penetrate the market and achieve market share, and only after several months is the price raised. If the new product is introduced into the CPI after a lag, the effect of the initially low price is missed, and only the subsequent *rise* in price is captured.

The inability of the CPI to account for quality improvement of new drugs, its failure to acknowledge price reductions associated with generic equivalents, and the lag in incorporating new products all tend to overstate changes in the drug component of the CPI. These difficulties in measuring changes in the producer price index (PPI) for pharmaceuticals were recently noted by the General Accounting Office (GAO) in its report on prescription drug prices. The report noted, "the evidence is strong that PPI-Drugs substantially overstated actual drug price increases for many years" (GAO 1995).

A number of (competing) models have been developed to better understand pricing behavior in less-than-perfectly-competitive markets. Many capture elements of corporate and consumer behavior well. Models of oligopoly, for example, deal with behavior of firms producing nearly the same product when there are so few of them that pricing decisions of one firm will cause a reaction by the others. Firms must therefore consider responses by competitors before acting themselves. Airlines and automobiles are examples of industries exhibiting this behavior. And we see examples in pharmaceuticals as well, especially when generic producers enter a market, inducing a price response from the firm whose patent has just expired.

While the theory of oligopoly deals with few firms engaging in rivalrous behavior, the theory of imperfect competition was developed to address markets in which there may be more producers where there is product differentiation among the products. Imperfect, or monopolistic, competition and oligopoly are not necessarily mutually exclusive from one another. Telephone services, airlines (again), paint, and pharmaceuticals are all examples of markets with products that may be virtually identical to one another, but firms realize that they can raise price above their marginal cost if they can convince consumers that their brand is different (and better) than other brands.

Another model addresses the inability of a company to measure accurately the position of consumer's demand schedules. How do you set a price when you don't know exactly what consumers will pay in order to purchase the quantity of output that will maximize the firm's profit? A simplification of the theory predicts that businesses will price by marking up their marginal cost. Of course, prices can be adjusted in order to obtain just the right sales level either by formally resetting price or by holding sales.

How Are Drug Prices Determined?

Underlying the debate over drug prices is the question of whether they are set primarily by supply-side factors such as costs or by demand factors such as drug attributes. The former would suggest monopoly power of the industry. In a competitive market, price is determined jointly by demand and marginal, not total, costs. We do not expect to hear industry representatives concur with their critics that costs—especially those of R&D—determine prices, as could occur only in a monopolistic or imperfectly competitive market. We will show that demand, and especially product characteristics, have a far greater role in pharmaceutical price determination than has been acknowledged, even by the industry itself.

Economic theory suggests that in a perfectly competitive market a consumer's demand curve for a particular good or service is perfectly elastic, with even small price increases leading the consumer to shift purchases completely to a competing product. Pefectly competitive markets are exceedingly rare today but do occur among commodities such as agricultural products, natural resources, and computer memory (RAM) chips. In such a market, prices will be bid down by producers to the point that $P=MC$, where P is the product's price and MC is the marginal cost for producing the product by the most efficient firm. P will be so low that any successive price reduction will cause all the producers to shut down. The price does include, however, normal profit for the producer, equal to the rate of return on their investment and their own labor that they would earn in the next-most-profitable industry.

Is this perfectly competitive market characteristic of pharmaceuticals? It may be argued that it is for some products, such as generic penicillin, where many firms produce the product and brand loyalty is slight. But product differentiation exists for most pharmaceuticals, even when the they compete with one another. Product differentiation and brand loyalty suggest that consumer demand is not perfectly elastic but is downward sloping. Now, when a firm produces at the level of output where MC equals marginal revenue (MR), price (P) will be above the intersection of the MR and MC curves because the demand curve the firm is facing is downward sloping (see Figure 4.3). Hence price is determined jointly by the shape and positions of the (marginal) cost curve as well as the shape and position of the demand curve. Prices cannot be set by either supply or demand factors alone. Because of the central role played by marginal costs, we look now at the cost structure of the industry.

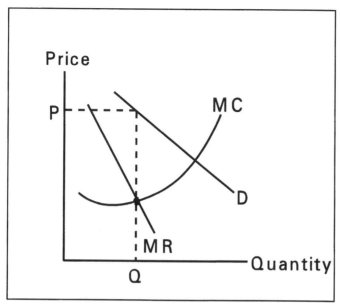

Figure 4.3 Price-setting under imperfect competition.

The Cost Structure of Pharmaceutical Firms

Data indicates that expenditures on pharmaceutical research and development have risen sharply. In 1991 the leading research-based firms spent 12% of their revenue on R&D, up from 10.2% in 1965 (Comanor and Schweitzer 1995). In 1992 the share rose to 16.1%. One reason for this growth is the high cost of drug development. The latest estimate of the cost of developing a successful new drug is $231 million (Grabowski and Vernon 1990).

Manufacturing costs are low in this industry, however. In fact, the pharmaceutical industry is less like other manufacturing industries and more like the computer software or film industry in this regard. It even resembles infrastructure investments such as roads and bridges, with high fixed costs and low marginal costs. The additional cost associated with producing an additional unit of output is very small in all of these industries. On the other hand, both research and marketing costs in the pharmaceutical industry are usually incurred before the final products are manufactured, so they do not change with the volume of production. Hence they are termed fixed or "sunk" costs. This is an important distinction because, as we have seen, marginal costs determine price in a competitive market, but fixed costs do not. Nonetheless, the industry's position has consistently been that these costs must be covered by the price of the final products. If these fixed costs

Table 4.2   Prices for New Pharmaceuticals Relative to
Those of Existing Drugs

FDA Designation of Therapeutic Advance	Ratio of Launch Prices of New Drugs to Prices of Existing Drugs	
	Acute	Chronic
Important advance	2.97	2.29
Modest advance	1.72	1.19
Little/no advance	1.22	0.94

Source: Lu and Comanor (1996).

are not covered, firms will lose incentive to develop and promote more innovative drugs. How does one resolve the question of whether these costs should be covered by the price of the product? The question of whether sunk costs determine price is so central to the controversy over drug prices that it is important to discuss the issue specifically.

Let us consider two models of price determination in the pharmaceutical industry. In the first, argued by both the pharmaceutical industry and its critics, R&D investment is predetermined. The costs of this investment determine total costs, which, together with profit goals, determine prices. Thus, prices determine demand and ultimately, profit. Prices are set according to cost. This model is shown in Figure 4.4.

This model assumes that investment is predetermined and that costs determine prices. An alternative model, shown in Figure 4.5, introduces product attributes as a demand variable determining price.

In this model price is determined by the drug's attributes, not cost. And profit determines future investment.

Are prices set by the costs of investment (Figure 4.3) or by demand-side variables such as product attributes (Figure 4.5)? Fortunately, evidence is now available to help us answer this question.

First, we observe that prices of new pharmaceuticals vary according to their degree of innovativeness (Lu and Comanor 1996). Table 4.2 shows the mean "launch" prices of pharmaceuticals introduced between 1978 and 1987 relative to the weighted mean prices of competing drugs already on the market. The drugs are divided into those used primarily for acute and primarily for chronic conditions. The degree of innovativeness of each of the products was determined by the FDA as part of its review process. We see that innovative drugs, whose offering a major therapeutic advance, are able to command a substantially higher price differential than are drugs offering

Investment------>Costs------>Price------>Demand------>Profit
Profit goal------------------

Figure 4.4   A Cost-Driven Model of Pharmaceutical Prices

Product attributes------>Price------>Demand------>Profit----->Investment
Costs---!

Figure 4.5   A Quality-Driven Model of Pharmaceutical Prices

only a modest therpeutic advance. Drugs embodying only modest improvement still allow firms to charge somewhat more than existing drugs. But
drugs offering little or no therapeutic advance are unable to charge much
more than existing drugs. Drugs offering substantial therapeutic improvement over existing drugs, in terms of efficacy, more favorable side-effect
profile, reduced likelihood of side effects, or convenience, do not have to
offer a price discount to gain market share. Purchaser willingness-to-pay for
a drug's performance allows a higher price to begin with.

Next we consider price changes after launch. We observe that firms follow either of two pricing strategies consistent with the Lu and Comanor
findings noted above. One is termed a "penetration" strategy, in which a
drug is initially priced at a low price in order to gain market share, and then
the price is raised over time. In contrast, other drugs are launched at a high
price, and price increases are small over time. This is referred to as the
"skimming" strategy. Reekie (1976) first observed these patterns in a study
of drugs introduced between 1958 and 1975. He noted that the skimming
strategy was followed by innovative drugs, while drugs with limited therapeutic gain followed the penetration strategy, undercutting competitors in
order to take away market share and then raising prices once brand loyalty
was established. The penetration strategy would help explain the rise in price
of "me, too" products during the 1980s, especially after their launch. The
Reekie evidence is also important because it shows that competition from
"me, too" drugs tends to lower prices of products within a drug class.

Another explanation for the rise in price of "me, too" drugs in the 1980s
is the spatial model developed by Perloff (1995). Perloff argues that even
though "me, too" drugs may not be superior to existing products, the fact
that they are *different* in such dimensions as side-effect profiles, convenience,
or efficacy makes them more attractive, and hence worth more, to some
consumers. The particularily interesting implication of the Perlman model
is that when patients switch from the innovative product to the better-suited
"me, too" product, the average "fit" between drug attributes and consumer
preferences rises for *both* drugs. This spatial model suggests that "me, too"
drugs might have the opposite effect of the competition model, allowing
prices of both innovative *and* "me, too" drugs to rise.

These results suggest a direct relationship between therapeutic improvement of new products and their launch and subsequent prices. Prices of
innovative drugs are different from those products which are less innovative
both at launch and later. In other words, price is related to the quality of a
drug.

The third observation supporting the importance of consumer demand in setting price is the widespread existence of price discrimination in the pharmaceutical market. Price discrimination occurs when the same commodity is sold at different prices to different consumers. There is considerable evidence that this pattern has occurred in the pharmaceutical industry, as it has for other consumer goods—telephone charges and airline fares, for instance. Firms want to price discriminate among classes of consumers because profits rise when price is set according to each consumer group's willingness to pay, as measured by the respective demand schedule. We expect to find different prices charged to different buyers where prices depend on demand conditions, and also where there are clear distinctions among types of buyers. The theory of price discrimination suggests that prices will depend primarily on the relevant price elasticities of demand of the various consumers. Whenever these elasticities differ among classes of consumers, prices are likely to be different. In the past, wholesale prices paid by an HMO were typically lower than those paid by a retail pharmacy. Consumers with high demand elasticity, especially managed-care programs, paid lower prices than did purchasers who are less price sensitive, such as retail pharmacies.

Although price discrimination is widespread across many markets, a suit was brought against major pharmaceutical manufacturers by alliances of retail pharmacies. The plaintiffs contended that contracts between insurers, primarily managed-care organizations and selected pharmacy chains, led to price discounts and rebates that were so large that nonaffiliated pharmacies could not compete for the managed-care enrollees. The implication for the retail pharmacy sector is unclear, for it is not certain whether discounts based upon volume will be permitted. Nor is it clear whether managed-care providers will be able to negotiate price discounts with pharmacies in return for large numbers of patient referrals. A decision will affect contracts that managed-care organizations have negotiated with other providers such as hospitals, physician groups, and diagnostic centers. If these discount arrangements are threatened, one of the bases of the entire concept of managed competition is jeopardized.

While pharmaceutical companies have established a list price for each drug, many sales have been made by discounting that price, and these discounts have been substantial. Why is this? Demand by hospitals and other major purchasers for specific products is likely to be elastic because they can decide a *priori* which products their physicians will use. Individual pharmacies, on the other hand, must stock a large number of products to fill individual prescriptions. Their role is much more passive in terms of product selection. Differences in demand elasticities (high for major purchasers, low for independent pharmacies) are reflected in differences in actual transaction prices at the wholesale level (low for major purchasers, high for independent pharmacies).

These discounts may also have differed between individual and chain-store pharmacies and between hospitals and HMOs. A critical fact about the pharmaceutical industry is that there was no single price for an individual product, even at a specific point in time; prices depend on the demand conditions presented by particular buyers.

When generic products enter the marketplace, they typically appeal more to some buyers than to others. For example, HMOs and hospitals pharmacies are more likely to use generic products because they have the knowledge and expertise required to evaluate them, in contrast to individual physicians. One therefore expects that generic rivals will make greater sales inroads to some buyers than to others. That being so, producers of innovative products will respond to generic competition more strongly in some market segments than in others. By setting much lower prices where generic competition exists, and keeping prices at their original levels or even higher where generic competition is less important, the original sellers of many products have been able to maintain a large proportion of their original sales revenue even after patent expiration.

There is evidence that major pharmaceutical firms have pursued this type of strategy and that they have been surprisingly successful in maintaining market share and revenue following patent expiration and generic entry. By the sixth year after patent expiration, average market shares for 35 products between 1984 and 1987 were fully 62% in physical units and 85% in dollar sales as compared to their previous levels (US Congress, OTA 1993). The strategy of charging lower prices where firms face strenuous competition and setting higher prices where they do not is the key to success. Managed care, however, is increasing pressure to substitute generic for brand products, and the proportion of patients who remain loyal to the original brand product is shrinking. Evidence of this comes from Grabowski and Vernon (1996), cited earlier.

In summary, "skimming" and "penetration" pricing behaviors together with price discrimination are characteristic behaviors of pharmaceutical firms and reflect the relationship between demand conditions and price in drug markets. Why does the market behave this way? One reason is competition, as we have discussed earlier in this chapter.

Is the Pharmaceutical Industry Monopolistic?

Both the Kefauver Committee and later critics of the industry have viewed drug companies as having substantial monopoly power which enables them to manipulate price. This market power allegedly comes mainly from two sources. One is barriers to entry, including legal barriers such as patents, regulatory barriers such as the 7–8-year process of getting a drug approved by the FDA, and economic barriers, including the large research infrastructure necessary to produce new and sophisticated drugs that can compete successfully in the marketplace. The small number of similar products within a drug class creates a market structure defined as a "differentiated oligopoly."

Other evidence of the degree of monopoly power includes the observed difference between price and direct manufacturing costs observed for a number of pharmaceutical products. A frequently used measure of the divergence is the Lerner Index, L, which is defined as $L = (P-MC)/P$, where P and MC are a product's price and marginal cost. The greater the divergence between price and marginal cost, the greater the monopoly power, and the closer L will be to 1. Over 30 years ago Steele estimated L to be between 0.05 and 0.15 for the pharmaceutical industry, suggesting little monopolistic power on the part of manufacturers (Steele 1962, 1964). More recent data, on the other hand, suggests that L might be considerably larger, indicating a greater degree of monopoly power. Comanor and Schweitzer (1995) cite evidence that in 1991 the share of revenue spent on manufacturing in the pharmaceutical industry was 28%. Of course, MC is much lower than total costs, especially for pharmaceuticals, so MC's share of revenue is undoubtedly less than 28%. But even if the entire amount were MC, L would equal 0.72, much higher than Steele's earlier estimates.

A monopoly cannot exist unless it is fully protected from competition by barriers to entry (Browning 1993). But some barriers may be no more than a minor hindrance to entry, in which case an industry could remain reasonably competitive in spite of noncompetitive elements. This is true for pharmaceuticals, a market with some monopolistic segments, some competitive segments, and many components that fall in between.

In general, a single-source drug becomes a multiple-source drug when a patent expires, although sometimes entry of competitors takes place well before that time either because the patent is contested or because the original patent holder licenses other manufacturers. When a product's patent expires, entry is not difficult, because the chemical composition of the drug's active ingredient is publicly known, and many manufacturing processes are not difficult or complicated. After passage of the 1984 Drug Price Competition and Patent Term Restoration Act (the Waxman-Hatch Act) achieving FDA approval for generic drugs became significantly easier. The FDA was empowered to grant an Abbreviated New Drug Application (ANDA). Before 1984, generic manufacturers had to prove safety and efficacy independent of the pioneer product. The bill accelerated the approval process for generic drugs by allowing use of the research undertaken on behalf of the pioneer product to gain generic approval. Now the prospective generic manufacturer only needs to show that the generic product contains the same active ingredient as the pioneer product. The result in the pharmaceutical market has been dramatic. In 1980, the generic share of prescriptions was 23.3 percent. (Masson and Steiner 1985). But by 1991 the share had risen to nearly 40 percent (Morrison, 1993). Grabowski and Vernon (1996) have shown the continuation of this trend, noting that generic market share rose after patent expiration for drugs with expirations between 1989 and 1992. According to Caves et al. (1991), some 70% of prescriptions were written for multisource drugs, both brand name and generic. Caves et al. also predicted that by 1995, over 50% of all new prescriptions in the United States would be dispensed using a generic substitute (Boston Consulting Group 1993).

As generic products do not have to go through the process of research, clinical trials, and marketing, their costs are much lower than those of the incumbent. And they are offered at substantially lower prices. According to Grabowski and Vernon (1996), for example, the mean price for the generic version of 15 drugs, 1 year after the patent on the brand product expired, was only 65% of the average price of the brand version. Whatever the price strategies the incumbent firm may use in an effort to maintain its market share, severe competition is unavoidable.

Even when a drug is made by only one company, this does not mean that it has no competitors. Often several different drugs appear on the market to treat the same medical condition (Congressional Budget Office 1994). Drugs developed for the purpose of taking market share from innovative drugs are frequently called "me, too" drugs, as discussed previously. Some of these imitative drugs can serve as important competitors for a single-source drug because they use the same biological mechanism as innovative drugs. Although similar to the innovative drug, the imitative products are distinct chemical entities. They can therefore introduce competition into the market well before patents expire, thus limiting the ability of the innovative drug manufacturers to sustain high prices. This story of the antidepressant market, told by the Congressional Budget Office (1994), is a typical example.

> When Prozac was introduced into the antidepressant market in 1988 it offered a new treatment with fewer side effects than many of the older antidepressants. The result was that Prozac became one of the five most widely prescribed drugs in the United States, enjoying worldwide sales of $1 billion in 1992. Such a market was a tempting target for other companies. Within five years, three lower-priced drugs, all using some variant of the same treatment, were on the market in the United States. Four other drugs are being sold in Europe and await FDA approval for U.S. sale. Because there are several close rivals, manufacturers of antidepressant drugs are being forced to offer discounts, even though their patents last until after the year 2000, when generic versions will be permitted to enter the market. (p. 7)

The above-normal profitability of drug firms is often cited as evidence that the pharmaceutical industry is monopolistic. These profit rates were cited in the Congressional hearings mentioned in the Introduction. But these profits are calculated using conventional accounting practices pertaining to measuring assets and return on sales that overstate profitability, and they may be inappropriate for this industry. Clarkson (1993) analyzed the effects of conventional accounting rules on the stated profit rates of 113 firms in 14 industries, including the pharmaceutical industry. He found that the conventional accounting measures distorted the profitability in many industries in different directions and to different degrees. Using more sophisticated measures that took intangible assets (especially goodwill, important to the pharmaceutical industry) into account, he found that the rate of return on equity of the pharmaceutical industry (which spent the greatest proportion of net sales on marketing and R&D) fell from 21% to 13%. This recalculation brought the drug industry's rate of return much closer to the mean (only two percentage points above, rather than the seven percentage points indicated by conventional measures) (CBO 1994). And another recent study of rates of return to investment by the pharmaceutical industry found that profits are only three percentage points above the average for companies in all industries (US Congress, OTA 1993).

Also supporting the monopoly model argument is the alleged indifference of doctors to pharmaceutical prices, so-called "physician loyalty" to brand names. But many authors, including Schwartzman (1979), Morrison (1993), and Grabowski and Vernon (1996), have observed that there is considerable generic prescribing once a drug is produced by several well-known manufacturers. Brand loyalty is not such a strong determinant of prescribing patterns. As far back as 1973, 50% of all ampicillin prescriptions were written generically. Advertising and promotion efforts by pharmaceutical firms have made information on therapeutic options available to all physicians. And studies have found that information provided directly to consumers by advertising tends to decrease consumer loyalty to particular brands, which implies that advertising increases the price elasticity of demand for any individual firm's products (Hyman 1988). The leading drug companies now spend about one-quarter of their total revenues on advertising and promotion (Comanor and Schweitzer 1995). Nearly 30% of the 185,900 people employed by the Pharmaceutical Manufacturers Association (PMA) member firms in 1989 were involved in marketing (Comanor and Schweitzer 1995). Physicians have access to information about all competitive products in a therapeutical area, so brand loyalty, resulting in part from imperfect information, can no longer support the thesis of monopolistic structure of the pharmaceutical industry.

How Drug Quality Influences Price

Additional evidence on the role drug quality plays in determining prices comes from the substantial degree of price variation observed in the pharmaceutical market. Price variation takes two forms. The first, discussed earlier, occurs with different purchasers paying different prices for the same product. In addition, relative prices for drugs within the same drug class—potentially substituting products—also vary across buyers, suggesting that different buyers are willing to pay different amounts for attributes of competing products. How is this to be explained?

We assume that a consumer obtains utility by consuming a commodity and will be willing to pay for the commodity as long as its marginal utility is at least as great its marginal cost. For example, a more thirsty person would place a higher value, and hence pay a higher price, for a glass of water than would a less thirsty one, for the thirsty person's marginal utility of the water exceeds that of the less thirsty one. But price is also related to the quality attributes of the commodity. Suppose there are two different types of water in the market, a mineral water containing nutritive elements and water without any such nutrients: Sellers of the mineral water could charge a higher price than for the plain drinking water, because consumers would obtain some value from the mineral water above and beyond its ability to quench thirst. The question is, How much higher will the mineral water be priced than the ordinary drinking water?

The price difference between these two types of water should be based on the difference in their perceived value or qualities, which is known as the hedonic, or quality-adjusted, price. If we can measure the hedonic values of the two products, we will be able to predict the price differential between the two types of water. Furthermore, we will be able to validate the appropriateness of the existing price differential, or that of any new similar products for which there are claims of higher quality. The theory of hedonic prices and the methodology for measuring them provide an important approach to the study of the relationship between price and quality of goods and services.

In the late 1970s, the US Department of Housing and Urban Development funded the RAND Corporation to study the behavior of housing prices in a Wisconsin county (Barnett 1979). The agency wanted to understand the reasons behind the differences in rental rates within an area. In other words, why do homes or apartments in the same neighborhood command different prices?

The study adopted a hedonic pricing model to analyze the question. The assumptions of the model were that tenants were willing to pay a higher price for a dwelling with higher hedonic value to them. Also, it was assumed that consumers value the attributes of dwellings rather than dwellings *per se*. The quality of a dwelling was described along 17 attributes or dimensions, such as number of rooms, ceiling height, plumbing facilities, and location. Each attribute was rated according to a set of criteria. Then these attributes were used as independent variables predicting the gross rent by using a multiple regression model. The results showed how important each of these attributes was to the price. With such a model, policy-makers could analyze whether the price of a specific dwelling was high or low compared to the predicted rent, based on the general ratings of housing attributes.

Pharmaceutical products can also be described as embodying a number of attributes as well, such as the duration of effect, the severity of side effects, and convenience. This suggests using hedonic values to analyze the price of pharmaceuticals, especially new innovative products that may have added hedonic value. To date, the number of studies that have analyzed pharmaceutical prices with the hedonic approach has been small (see, for example, Suslow 1991; and Jensen and Morrisey 1990). If future research can measure the hedonic values for pharmaceutical products in a way analogous to the way the RAND study analyzed the housing market, one will then be able to assess the cost-effectiveness of a drug more accurately. Then we will know whether pharmaceutical prices are "too high."

References

Barnett CL, *Using Hedonic Indexes to Measure Housing Quantity*, Santa Monica, CA: The RAND Corporation, October 1979.

Boston Consulting Group, *The Changing Environment for U.S. Pharmaceuticals*, Boston: The Boston Consulting Group, April 1993.

Browning E and Browning J, *Microeconomic Theory and Applications*, 4th edition New York: Harper Collins, 1993.

Caves R, Whinston M, and Hurwitz M, "Patent expiration, entry, and competition in the U.S. pharmaceutical industry," *Brookings Papers on Economics Activity: Microeconomics*, 1991.

Clarkson K, "Intangible capital and profitability measures: effects of research and promotion on rates of return," paper presented at the American Enterprise Institute Conference on Competitive Strategies in the Pharmaceutical Industry, Washington, DC, October 1993.

Cleeton DL, Goepfrich V, and Weisbrod B., "What does the Consumer Price Index for prescription drugs really measure?," *Health Care Financing Review* 13 (3): 45–51, 1992

Comanor WS, "The political economy of the pharmaceutical industry," *Journal of Economic Literature* 24:1178–1217, 1986.

Comanor WS and Schweitzer SO, "The pharmaceutical industry," in Adams W and Brock J (eds), *The Structure of American Industry*, 9th edition, 1995.

Congressional Budget Office, *How Health Care Reform Affects Pharmaceutical Research and Development*, Washington, DC: US Congress, Congressional Budget Office, 1994.

General Accounting Office, *Prescription Drug Prices—Official Index Overstates Producer Price Inflation, A Report to the Chairman of the Senate's Special Committee on Aging*, Washington, DC: General Accounting Office, 1995.

Genuardi JS, Stiller JM, and Trapnell GR, "Changing Prescription Drug Sector: New Expenditure Methodologies," *Health Care Financing Review* 17(3):191–204, 1996.

Grabowski H and Vernon J, "A new look at the risks and returns to pharmaceutical R&D," *Management Science* 36(7) p 816, 1990.

Grabowski H and Vernon J, "Longer patents for increased generic competition in the US: the Waxman-Hatch act after one decade," *PharmacoEconomics* 10(suppl 2):110–123, 1996.

Griliches Z and Cockburn I, "Generics and new goods in pharmaceutical price indexes," *NBER Working Paper* No. 4272, February 1994.

Health Insurance Association of America, *Source Book of Health Insurance Data*, Washington DC: Health Insurance Association of America, 1993.

Hyman DN, *Modern Microeconomics: Analysis and Applications*, 2nd edition, Homewood, IL: Richard D. Irwin, 1988.

Jensen G. A. and Morrisey MA, "Group health insurance: a hedonic price approach," *Review of Economics and Statistics* 72:38–44, 1990.

Lu JZ and Comanor WS, "Strategic pricing of new pharmaceuticals," UCLA Program in Pharmaceutical Economics and Policy Working Paper, 1996.

Mansfield E, *Microeconomics Theory and Applications* 6th edition, New York: WW Norton, 1988.

Masson A and Steiner R, *Generic Substitution and Prescription Drug Prices: Economic Effects of* State Drug Product Selection Laws, Washington DC: U.S. Federal Trade Commission, 1985.

Morrison S, *Prescription drug prices: The effect of generics, formularies, and other market changes*, Washington DC: Congressional Research Service, August 17, 1993.

Perloff J, "A spatial model of pharmaceutical pricing: a case study of H2 antagonists," Working Paper of the UCLA Seminar in Pharmaceutical Economics and Policy, Los Angeles, 1995.

Scherer FM, "Pricing, profits, and technological progress in the pharmaceutical industry," *Journal of Economic Perspectives* 7:98, summer 1993.

Schwartzman D, "Pricing of multiple-source drugs" in Chien RI (ed)., *Issues in Pharmaceutical Economics*, Toronto: Lexington Books, 1979.

Steele H, "Monopoly and competition in the ethical drugs market," *Journal of Law Economics* 5:131–163, 1962.

Steele H, "Patent restrictions and price competition in the ethical drugs industry," *Journal of Industrial Economics*, 12:198–223, 1964.

Suslow VY, "Competition and product differentiation in the ulcer drug market," working paper, School of Business, University of Michigan, October 1991.

The Medical Letter, New Rochelle, NY: The Medical Letter, Various volumes, 1994–1996.

US Congress, Office of Technology Assessment, *Pharmaceutical R&D: Costs, Risks and Rewards*, OTA-H-522, Washington, DC: US Government Printing Office, February 1993.

US Senate, *Administered Prices, Hearings before the Subcommittee on Antitrust and Monopoly of the Senate Committee on the Judiciary*, Washington, DC: US Government Printing Office, 1960.

US Senate Special Committee on Aging, *A report on 1993 Pharmaceutical Price Inflation: Drug Prices for Older Americans Still Increasing Much Faster than Inflation*," Staff Report, Washington, DC: US Government Printing Office, 1994.

5

The Worldwide Market for Pharmaceuticals

Both production and sales of pharmaceuticals vary greatly by region of the world. Problems of access to needed drugs by the populations of developing countries are severe and present serious dilemmas not only to those countries but also to developed countries and to international organizations such as the World Health Organization (WHO) and UNICEF (of the United Nations). And, of course, the policy responses by these countries and organizations affect the major drug manufacturers, which are located primarily in the United States, Europe, and Japan. A discussion of these access issues is therefore essential to understanding one of the major policy debates confronting the industry: How can the fruits of pharmaceutical R&D benefit populations in poor, developing countries?

While consumption and production are largely in balance in the wealthy regions of North America, Europe, and Japan, countries in Latin America, Africa, and Southeast Asia import a substantial share of their pharmaceuticals. There are several consequences of this imbalance, and several reasons for it. The most important result is that access to needed drugs is limited in poor countries, either because the prices charged for the products are beyond the means of their populations or because the major drug producers have not invested the R&D resources necessary to be able to produce some of these needed drugs. Underlying this situation is the fact that poor countries have large numbers of patients *in need* of effective drugs, but their low incomes do not permit them to create economic *demand* for them. As a consequence, all too often drugs that are inappropriate for efficient clinical practice are exported to developing countries. Here we look at case studies of several developing countries to see how they are attempting to cope with these problems.

To remedy this situation, strategies both for developing countries themselves and for multinational organizations are needed. Developing countries could combine their efforts, either as manufacturers or as purchasers of drugs. Collective action will improve their bargaining power when it is most efficient to import drugs from the major manufacturers in developed countries. And when manufacturing is the most efficient strategy, collaboration will allow firms in developing countries to attain economies of scale in R&D and manufacturing. In addition, these have been commendable efforts by developed countries to establish a fund that would create demand for essential drugs, that would promote their distribution when they are available, and that would promote needed R&D when the drugs do not yet exist.

Geographic Patterns of Pharmaceutical Production and Sales

Worldwide sales of pharmaceuticals were more than $200 billion in 1994 (Ballance et al. 1992). The three largest market areas are the countries of the European Union (approximately $37 billion), the United States (approximately $35 billion), and Japan (approximately $35 billion) (Ballance et al. 1992). The largest firms are also from these regions.

The developed countries of North America, western Europe, and Japan produce and consume a far greater quantity of drugs than do countries in eastern Europe or the developing world, as shown in Table 5.1. The table also shows that developed countries are nearly self-sufficient in their drugs, with production nearly equal to consumption for all three areas. Developing countries, on the other hand, import nearly 20% of the pharmaceuticals they consume. For African countries, the proportion is approximately 60%. Of the developing countries listed, only China is virtually self-sufficient.

The pharmaceutical industry has three components: research and development (R&D), marketing, and manufacturing and distribution (Comanor 1994). R&D is generally carried out in the large market areas and is thus concentrated in a relatively small number of countries. Manufacturing, on the other hand, is far more dispersed throughout the world. But neither R&D nor manufacturing is carried out in every country, so the variance in the distribution of supply and demand throughout the world is an important issue. Also important is the distinction between the directions taken by R&D programs in the wealthy countries and the disease patterns seen in countries of the developing world. Some of these asymmetries can be understood within the context of the definition of market demand. Table 5.2 shows that only ten firms accounted for a third of the world market; Glaxo Wellcome has the largest market share, at 5.5% (*The Economist* 1995a). Of these, six firms are American, two British, one German, and one Swiss. The industry

Table 5.1   Production and Consumption of Pharmaceutical Preparations, 1990 (in Billions of 1980 Dollars)

	Production	Consumption	Ratio of Production to Consumption[a]	Ratio of Imports to Consumption[a]
Developed market countries	$109.7	$107.8	102.1	8.2
North America	34.1	34.6	99.5	2.7
Western Europe	40.4	36.5	111.1	20.3
Japan	33.5	34.6	98.1	2.1
Formerly Socialist countries	13.0	14.0	NA	NA
Developing countries	27.7	28.4	85.9	19.8
Latin America	11.9	9.0	92.0	10.6
North Africa	0.6	1.4	44.5	58.5
Other Africa	0.6	1.5	40.0	61.2
South and East Asia	7.4	8.4	89.8	15.1
China	5.3	5.4	100.5	3.7
Total	$150.3	$150.3	—	—

Source: Ballance (1992), Tables 2.1, 2.3, and 2.10.

[a]These ratios refer to 1989 and include intraregional trade.

has become more concentrated in the past decade. In 1988, the 25 largest companies represented 44% of the worldwide sales. This change is a reflection of the recent trend of mergers and acquisitions in the industry. In contrast to the concentration of the largest pharmaceutical manufacturers, however, most of the companies are small and have activities limited to a small number of markets. In the developing countries, there were only seven manufacturers in 1988 with sales exceeding $50 million, and only one with sales of more then $75 million.

Pharmaceutical Research and Development: An International View

Worldwide pharmaceutical R&D expenditures were estimated to be $27 billion in 1993. A recent survey noted that 49 leading international pharmaceutical manufacturers account for more than half of worldwide R&D and employ 93,000 R&D personnel (Center for Medicines Research 1993). Of these, nearly 40,000 are employed in the United States, where research expenditures increased from $1.5 billion in 1980 to $10.3 billion in 1993, representing an increase from 11.7% of sales in 1980 to 16.7% of sales in 1992 (The Boston Consulting Group 1993).

Bringing new drugs to market is expensive. DiMasi et al. estimate the cost to have been as high as $231 million in 1987 (DiMasi et al. 1991), and a recent Office of Technology Assessment (OTA) report estimated the be-

Table 5.2   World Ranking of Pharmaceutical Manufacturers, 1994

	Company	Nationality	Market Share (%)
1	Glaxo Wellcome	British	5.5
2	Merck	American	4.4
3	Hoechst-Marion Merrell Dow	German	4.4
4	American Home Products	American	3.5
5	Bristol-Myers Squibb	American	3.3
6	Roche-Syntex	Swiss	3.0
7	Pfizer	American	2.7
8	SmithKline Beecham	British	2.7
9	Lilly	American	2.4
10	Johnson & Johnson	American	2.4
Total			34.3

Source: *The Economist* (1995b).

fore-tax cost to be $259 million (the after-tax cost being $194 million) (Office of Technology Assessment 1993). Given the substantial investment required, firms allocate their research spending based on the expected market for their future products. As the demand is predominantly from the United States, Europe, and Japan, it is hardly surprising that the research agenda for the firms is directed toward alleviating morbidity-and-mortality-causing conditions in these countries. The leading causes of morbidity and mortality in the industrialized countries are chronic diseases and diseases often associated with lifestyle patterns. In contrast, the leading causes of morbidity and mortality in the developing countries remain communicable and perinatal diseases. Even when research work is conducted in the developing countries, their inhabitants frequently do not benefit from the end product. For example, the bulk of the research on the hepatitis vaccine was conducted in Africa, but the countries there are unlikely to receive the vaccine, for its cost exceeds the entire yearly per capita health expenditure in many African countries (Ijsselmuiden and Faden 1992).

A study of the new chemical entities (NCEs) released into the worldwide market from 1970 to 1992 found that the main therapeutic R&D areas of output by the three regions (United States, Europe, and Japan) were consistently concentrated in three disease areas: cardiovascular drugs (21%), central nervous system drugs (18%), and anti-infective agents (16%) (MacInnes et al. 1994).

European companies were marketing the largest proportion of NCEs. They were responsible for first marketing approximately 50% of the top 50 products in international sales in 1992 (MacInnes et al. 1994). However, their share of the worldwide market was declining between 1970 and 1992. This decline is attributed to escalating R&D costs and increasing price pressures by governments. These price pressures had the effect of further reducing R&D outlays and ultimately restricting sales. Although the European worldwide market share has been declining, Japanese companies have increased their share of NCEs. However, nearly two-thirds of these NCEs

Table 5.3   Leading Categories of R&D Projects WorldWide in 1988

Research Objective	Preclinical Stage[a]		Clinical Stage[b]		Drugs Launched in 1988		Total	
	Number	%	Number	%	Number	%	Number	%
Anti-infective	721	15.9	300	10.6	124	10.0	1145	13.3
Cardiovascular	509	11.3	395	14.0	170	13.8	1074	12.5
Neurological	442	9.8	373	13.2	156	12.6	971	11.3
Antineoplastic	554	12.3	323	11.5	59	4.8	936	10.9
Biotechnology[c]	620	13.7	190	6.7	32	2.6	842	9.8
Formulations[b]	213	4.7	273	9.7	118	9.6	604	7.0
Blood & clotting products	317	7.0	133	4.7	69	5.6	519	6.0
Alimentary products	223	4.9	185	6.6	109	8.8	517	6.0
Musculoskeletal products	215	4.8	153	5.4	94	7.6	462	5.4
Respiratory products	169	3.7	143	5.1	76	6.2	388	4.5
Top ten categories	3983	87.5	2468	87.6	1007	81.6	7458	86.7
Others	569	12.5	349	12.4	227	18.4	1145	13.3
Total	4552	100.0	2817	100.0	1234	100.0	8603	100.0

Source: Ballance (1992), Table 4.7.

[a]Includes chemical research and animal pharmacology experiments.

[b]Includes human pharmacology studies in medical research facilities.

[c]Refers to technological categories.

were marketed only in the Japanese home market. The proportion of NCEs marketed by US companies remained unchanged during this period (European Commission 1994). The decline in the European marketing success is especially marked in the area of biotechnology. A recent European Commission survey found that 65% of patents in biotechnology were American, 15% European, and 12% Japanese (European Commission 1994).

Research priorities have also been changing over time, as illustrated by the changing proportion of expenditures directed toward research into anti-infective and cardiovascular drugs. While the 1978 proportion of US pharmaceutical R&D expenditure for anti-infective research was 18.9% and 16.6% for cardiovascular drugs, the proportions in 1988 were 13.9% and 25.1%, respectively (Pharmaceutical Manufacturers Association 1990).

Table 5.3 shows the research directions of the worldwide pharmaceutical industry in 1988. The anti-infective, cardiovascular agents, neurological drugs, and antineoplastic drugs are clearly the most important. Table 5.4 shows the profiles of research expenditures for the United States in 1988 and 1989 by therapeutic class. The pattern of expenditures is similar to the worldwide trends.

A more recent snapshot of the types of research spending shows that increasing amounts are being spent on biotechnology, applications of the Human Genome Project, DNA diagnostics, gene therapy, and other high-technology areas. For example, in 1992, 33% of research projects in major

Table 5.4   US Pharmaceutical R&D Expenditures by Product Class, 1988–1989

	Percentage Share of R&D Dollars	
Product Class	1988	1989
Cardiovascular	25.1	23.0
Neoplasms, endocrine system, & metabolic diseases	18.5	15.2
Central nervous system & sense organs	14.6	15.4
Anti-infective	13.9	15.0
Respiratory	5.4	6.1
Gastrointestinal & genitourinary system	4.1	4.6
Biologicals	4.1	4.7
Dermatological	2.1	2.3
Diagnostic (in vivo)	0.7	2.0
Other human use drugs	7.8	8.0
Veterinary preparations	3.2	3.3
Veterinary biologicals	0.3	0.2
Vitamins	0.2	0.2
Total	100.0%	100.0%

Source: Pharmaceutical Manufacturers Association (1991), Table 2-2.

pharmaceutical companies were based on biotechnology compared with only 2% in 1980. While these are concomitant with the needs and markets of the developed world, they do not necessarily serve the needs of the developing countries, where the focus still remains on combating infective diseases. Discovering a drug has become an expensive and complex process dependent on technology and the availability of ample research money. The R&D orientations of major pharmaceutical companies are driven by the needs and economic demands of the developed countries for new drugs.

Multinational pharmaceutical firms have not entirely abandoned the health needs of the developing countries. For example, Roche has recently established a Tropical Medicine Unit, the aim of which is to produce affordable and innovative products to be used against tropical diseases, especially malaria, and Merck has donated its anti-onchocerciasis drug to the World Health Organization's Onchocerciasis Control Program in West Africa (Strutchler et al. 1993).

Whether in response to rising R&D costs or increased risk associated with developing a successful drug, drug firms throughout the world have consolidated, either through outright mergers or joint marketing agreements. Table 5.5 lists the ten largest global pharmaceutical mergers since 1988. The largest pharmaceutical company in the world was created by the acquisition by Glaxo of Wellcome, valued at over $14 billion. Not only are companies absorbing each other outright in this fashion, but they are also joining in marketing and research alliances. This is especially true in the biotechnology industry, where the large pharmaceutical firms frequently eschew outright mergers in favor of research agreements providing funds to the biotechnology firms in exchange for a share of the revenue or profit.

Table 5.5   Ten Largest Global Pharmaceutical Mergers, 1988–1995

Acquirer	Target	Size ($ billions)	Year
Glaxo Holdings	Wellcome	$14.2	1995
Bristol-Myers	Squibb	12.0	1989
American Home Products	American Cyanamid	9.5	1994
Beecham Group	SmithKline Beckman	7.9	1989
Hoechst	Marion Merrell Dow	7.1	1995
Dow Chemical	Marion Laboratories	6.2	1989
Upjohn	Pharmacia	6.0	1995
Roche	Syntex	5.3	1994
Eastman Kodak	Sterling Drug	5.1	1988
Sanofi	Sterling Drug (Europe)	4.5	1991

Source: "Why Europeans . . ." (1994).

These arrangements suggest that the generally small biotechnology firms have a unique structure or corporate culture that frequently allow them to lead the larger traditional pharmaceutical manufacturers in developing creative new products, contrary to the notion of economies of scale in R&D. The worldwide marketing reach of the big companies, however, is often a strength needed by the biotechnology firms. Many of these mergers or agreements are international in scope, blurring traditional identities of "nationality" of the resulting firms. For example, the Swiss firm Ciba-Geigy acquired a 49.9% stake in the US biotechnology company Chiron in 1994. Similar also was the acquisition of Syntex another US firm) by Roche (a Swiss firm) in 1994, at a cost of nearly $5 billion, and Roche's earlier acquisition of 60% of Genentech (United States) in 1990 for $2.1 billion.

Another approach is to merge product lines. An example of this is the recent decision of Rhone-Poulenc Rorer (itself an acquisition of an American firm by a French firm) and Germany's Hoechst AG to merge their blood-product divisions to form the world's biggest company in that field. Separately, Rhone-Poulenc is attempting to form a trans-Atlantic network of gene therapy companies.

Vertical integration has extended the target range of American pharmaceutical companies to include the acquisition of pharmaceutical benefit management companies: The purchase of Medco Containment Services by Merck for $6 billion in 1993, the 1994 acquisition of Diversified Pharmaceuticals by SmithKline for $2.3 billion, and the purchase of PCS Health Systems by Eli Lilly in 1994 for $4 billion are examples. As the United States moves inexorably toward managed care, pharmacy managers will wield increasing power in controlling drug prescription and use.

As a result of this merger activity, few American firms rank below number 25 in the world sales ratings. On the other hand, there are nearly 16 struggling European firms with yearly drug sales of less than $1 billion—most of them German, Italian, or French—which are possible takeover targets.

With multinational firms spanning many continents as a result of mergers, research has also begun to acquire an international flavor. For example, the research activities of Rhone-Poulenc Rorer, a firm jointly owned by the French state (62%) and private shareholders (38%), are spread between its centers at the Institute of Biotechnology at Vitry (France), a center at Dagenham (United Kingdom), Collegeville, Pennsylvania (United States), with Applied Immune Response (Santa Clara, CA, United States) and Chugai (Japan). Thus, while the company is French, its research activities are spread over three continents (Ward 1993). It is a partner with the Institute Pasteur Merieux (Paris) and is the world's largest producer of vaccines, with a 30% share of the global vaccine market. This share is almost as large as the combined market share of second-ranked Lederle and third-ranked Merck. Of interest to the developing countries is Rhone-Poulenc Rorer's research agenda, which includes developing a range of meningitis vaccines and more highly purified and effective whooping cough and cholera vaccines (Ward 1993).

Roche-Syntex, the result of the acquision of Syntex (United States) by Roche (Swiss) is ranked sixth largest in the world with a market share of 3%. It spent nearly $1 billion on pharmaceutical R&D in 1991, an amount equal to 23% of its pharmaceutical sales, a figure widely believed to be the highest in the pharmaceutical industry. Most of this can, however, be attributed to its US biotechnology subsidiary Genentech, which invested $212 million in R&D, equivalent to 40% of its 1991 total revenue of $515 million (Hodgson 1992). Roche's research centers are located on three continents— the Basel Institute of Immunology (Basel, Switzerland), the Roche Institute of Molecular Biology (Nutley, NJ), Welwyn Garden City (United Kingdom), and the Nippon Roche Research Center (Kamakura, Japan). It has a long-term research agreement with Harvard Medical School and with the Genetics Institute for AIDS Research. The Roche African Research Foundation is based in Abidjan (Ivory Coast) and conducts investigations into AIDS, malaria, and other tropical diseases and also tests compounds for anti-infective activity. It has manufacturing, finishing, and packaging facilities in South Carolina, France, Taiwan, and Switzerland (Hodgson 1992).

Table 5.6 shows the percentage of sales spent on R&D by European drug manufacturers. Many companies have expanded their collaborations with academic research centers. Glaxo, for example, has research collaborations with 80% of British universities. The British-based Wellcome Trust spends over $150 million on R&D globally, 30% of which is spent on basic research.

Within Scandinavia, the Swedish group Astra spends 19% of its sales revenue on R&D, with 85% going to clinical trails. In Denmark, research spending is controlled by foundations set up by the drug companies. Novo Nordisk, the world's largest manufacturer of insulin, spends 13% of its turnover on R&D (Hodgson 1992).

Among the Swiss companies, Sandoz has a research budget of nearly $1 billion. It has recently entered into a $3 million research agreement with the Scripps Clinic at the University of California, San Diego. It has invested

Table 5.6　European Pharmaceutical R&D Spending

Company	% Of Sales Spent on R&D	% Of R&D Spending on Academic Research
Astra	18.0	15.0
Bayer	7.0	na[b]
Boehringer Ingelheim	15.5	1.5
Ciba-Geigy	10.0	na
Fidia	25.0	na
Glaxo[a]	14.0	na
Henri Beaufour	20.0	30.0
Hoechst	14.0	10.0
Lundbeck	5.0	10.5
Novo Nordisk	15.6	1.0
Organon	13.0	18.0
Pfizer	14.5	na
Rhone-Poulenc	na	na
Roche	6.8	na
Roussel-UCLAF	20.0	na
Sandoz	14.0	na
Schering	15.0	na
SmithKline Beecham	9.1	na
Duphar	13.0	na
Synthelabo	20.0	na
Wellcome	14.0	30.0

Source: The European Pharmaceutical Outlook (1993).

[a]Since merged with Wellcome.

[b]Not available.

$100 million with the Dana Farber Cancer Institute in Boston and $75 million with the Neurosciences Institute in New York (Hodgson 1992).

The Japanese companies, although small compared to their western counterparts, are slowly making their mark on the worldwide R&D scene. While the global average of R&D spending is 11.5% of sales, spending on R&D has risen to 11% of sales in Japan from only 9% 6 years ago. Sankyo, one of the three largest pharmaceutical firms in Japan (the other two being Takeda and Yamanouchi) invented the anticholesterol agent pravastatin. This drug is the best-selling drug in Japan and is the second-largest seller for Bristol-Myers Squibb, which sells it worldwide outside Japan under the trade name of Pravachol. Yamanouchi makes the antiulcer drug famotidine (trade name Pepcid) for Merck, which is the fourth-biggest-selling drug for Merck (*The Economist* 1995b). Sankyo is about to launch the world's first treatment for late-onset diabetes, a drug which is projected to have a market of $333 million in Japan. And The Big Three in Japan (Takeda, Yamanouchi, and Sankyo) are thought to have, between them, seven new major drugs in the pipeline (*The Economist* 1995).

Germany's share of the world's new drug patents dropped from 16% of the world total in 1980–1985 to 8% in the years 1986–1990. The two big drug and chemical companies, Hoechst AG and BASF AG, have been moving research and production out of Germany. Two possible reasons for this are the German government's imposition of stringent environmental regulations on chemical firms and Germany's extremely strict controls on the reimbursement of drugs by its health care system ("Why Europeans . . ." 1994). The German government sets an annual expenditure target for pharmaceuticals. If this target is exceeded, the pharmaceutical companies have to reimburse the excess to the public health insurance funds. Partly as a response to these concerns, Hoechst AG merged with the American firm Marion Merrell Dow in 1995 in a transaction costing nearly $7.1 billion. In doing so, it created the world's third biggest pharmaceutical company with an estimated 4.4% of the world market share.

Canada and Australia have played only a minor world-wide role in the R&D process. Both countries have strict price setting mechanisms that may serve to hinder the flow of funds into pharmaceutical R&D. Canada's Patented Medicine Prices Review Board (PMRB) is charged with the responsibility of preventing manufacturers from charging "excessive" prices (Shulman 1994). The PMRB has established guidelines that determine an allowable introductory price for new drugs, as a function of prices of other drugs already available and prices of the drug in other countries. If prices are found to be "excessive," the patentee is allowed to lower its price and refund the excess revenues. If the firm refuses to comply, a public hearing is held. Ultimately, Board decisions are enforcable in the courts (Palmer 1994). Once drugs are introduced, their annual rate of price increase is limited to that of the CPI (Palmer 1994). Until recently, Canadian laws allowed generic manufacturers to obtain a compulsory license from the Commissioner of Patents, which permitted these firms to use a patented process to manufacture a drug in return for paying the patent holder a modest licensing fee. The manufacturers could then produce a generic version of the drug even though the product's patent was still in force (Cantor and Gross 1993). From 1965 to 1985, despite rapid growth in other countries, there was little increase in pharmaceutical research in Canada. In 1987, pharmaceutical R&D was less than 5% of sales (Lexchin 1992). The Canadian government revised its patent laws in 1987 and withdrew the special treatment provided to generic drug manufacturers, thus reducing the number of generic products that could reach the Canadian market. In return, the Canadian pharmaceutical firms pledged to double their ratio of pharmaceutical R&D to sales in Canada within 10 years (Scherer 1993).

Similarly, in Australia, the government has kept a tight rein on pharmaceutical costs through the Pharmaceutical Benefits Advisory Committee (PBAC). Prices for pharmaceuticals in Australia were 55% of the world prices in 1987; the low reimbursement rates are thought to be the cause of divestment of production facilities, reduction in exports, and the increased deficit resulting from the difference between imports and exports. The government launched a series of reforms in 1988 aimed at stimulating R&D by providing benefits to those companies that pledge to increase their share of R&D (Hirst 1992). Beginning in 1993 the PBAC required pharmaceutical firms to submit cost-effectiveness analyses along with their application for inclusion of a new drug in the national health insurance scheme. The PBAC has attempted to standardize these studies to make them comparable with one another. As an example, they must measure "marginal costs of obtaining additional health benefits with new drugs," and including indirect costs and benefits is discouraged (Henry 1992). Langley (1993) has expressed concern that the PBAC guidelines may be too rigid and inappropriate for the role of comparing drugs and setting reimbursement price.

China and India are two developing countries that have small research programs oriented toward traditional medicines for allopathic use. No other developing country has a significant R&D research agenda. The developing world is therefore dependent upon the large pharmaceutical firms in the wealthy countries for its supply of new and innovative drugs. The research agendas of these R&D firms are determined by the potential markets, which places the developing world at a natural disadvantage, given their populations' low purchasing power. Because investment capital in developing countries is so limited, the developing world, until recently, directed its pharmaceutical development programs toward copying the most useful western drugs and allowed domestic manufacturers to produce pirated versions of these drugs. With the advent of the 1995 World Trade Organization (WTO) treaty, this strategy is no longer feasible, for all signatories have to recognize international patents.

Worldwide Manufacturing and Sales

Research and development is concentrated in a few countries, but manufacturing has a more global base. Virtually all major pharmaceutical firms have subsidiaries worldwide that are involved in manufacturing and selling drugs. In many cases, drug manufacturing is limited to assembling the final product from imported raw materials. More than 90 countries have facilities to produce finished pharmaceutical products, but most of the industry consists of subsidiaries of multinational firms (Ballance et al. 1992).

The US pharmaceutical industry was one of the few industries cited by the General Accounting Office (GAO) for maintaining its competitiveness in the international market in the 1980s. It has consistently generated a trade surplus of more than $1 billion per year (US Congress, General Accounting Office 1992). Total sales of pharmaceutical products from US companies increased from $22.5 billion in 1980 to about $76.5 billion in 1992. In the United States, as in Japan, production and consumption are in balance. The United States produces 98% of its required pharmaceuticals, and imports account for only 2%.

The pharmaceutical sector is also one of the top performing sectors in the European Community (EC), accounting for more than 1% of its total GNP, and it grew at an annual rate of 6% between 1982 and 1992. Total pharmaceutical production was $110 billion in 1992, and employment was approximately half a million persons. The EC production of pharmaceuticals exceeds consumption by nearly 11%, and imports represent only 20% of consumption. The EC currently runs a pharmaceutical trade surplus of approximately $8 billion (European Commission 1994). Within Europe, production and processing plants for most drugs are located in the country where they are sold and many companies that produce drugs are small and local. In Germany, for example, 400 of the 600 pharmaceutical manufacturers are small (Burstall 1990). For the EC as a whole, local subsidiaries of multinational firms accounted for 40% of all 1986 sales (Burstall 1990).

The problems facing the European pharmaceutical industry are a reflection of the diverse nature of its member countries. While each of the EC member states adheres to the rules of the Munich Patent Convention, which provides for legal protection of the patented product or process for 20 years from the moment the patent is delivered, there are many exceptions to these rules. Prime examples are the small, family-run pharmaceutical companies in southern Italy which have prospered by producing copies of patented products and selling them at cheap prices. The recent passage of General Agreement on Tariffs and Trade (GATT) has also augmented patent protection and will adversely affect the small companies that thrived by producing cheap imitation products. The critical problem with regard to patents is that companies file for patents *before* the regulatory approval process is complete, effectively reducing the period of patent protection by nearly 50%. In 1992, the European Commission issued a directive establishing the Supplemental Protection Certificate, a mechanism that extends patent protection for 5 to 7 years beyond the normal patent term. The United States enacted similar legislation in 1984, the Patent Term Restoration Act, for the same purpose—to lengthen effective patent life to compensate for approval delays.

Another problem facing the EC is the strong regulatory environment in the health care sector, especially as it pertains to the reimbursement of pharmaceuticals. All European countries cover drugs through their national health insurance programs, and as single buyers these programs exert their monopsony power in negotiating prices for their products. France has one of the most closely regulated drug reimbursement policies. There are no French pharmaceutical firms in the top ten worldwide, and nearly half the French domestic market is held by foreign firms. Nor are French firms active in the worldwide export market, a fact attributed to the firms' focus on the domestic market and the francophone countries, which exhibit common cultural patterns of illness and treatment. A similar situation exists in Norway, where the authorities will refuse to license a new medicine if they do not consider that there is a proven need for it.

Germany, until recently, had one of the most liberal reimbursement policies with regard to pharmaceuticals. These high prices formed the cornerstone of the export success of German pharmaceutical firms worldwide. However, growing health care expenditures have forced Germany to rethink its policies and it has recently passed a law that caps pharmaceutical expenditures to a predetermined amount. The state's concern for containing health care expenditures overrides the concern about the international competitiveness of its pharmaceutical industry.

The Japanese market is the second largest in the world, and is estimated to be about $75 billion in size. It is characterized by a lack of big manufacturers such as those found in the United States and Europe. The firms are small and fragmented by comparison, and the largest firm, Takeda, is only one-fifth the size of Merck (see Thomas 1994). The market is relatively open and 25% is controlled by foreign companies. Another 20% consists of foreign drugs sold by Japanese companies (World Health Organization 1988b). Merck owns 50% of Banyu, one of the ten largest pharmaceutical firms in Japan.

The high rate of consumption of drugs by the Japanese is undoubtedly related to the fact that a significant portion of a physicians' income is derived from direct sales of drugs to patients. The Japanese market includes a high share of preventive, as opposed to curative, products (World Health Organization 1988). Vitamin pills ($2 billion) and brain tonics ($1.3 billion) are major segments of the market. Japanese firms do not export much compared to their American or European counterparts. Only 5% of their sales are abroad, in contrast to 60% of the American firms' and 80% for the Europeans (Harneijer et al. 1989).

The changes occurring in Japan's health care sector may have an influence on the future of its pharmaceutical industry. The Ministry of Health and Welfare has proposed more cost sharing for pharmaceuticals and has stopped reimbursing for some tonics altogether. It has also delinked physicians' salaries from the number of drugs they prescribe. Ironically, Japanese pharmaceutical prices are very low; some prices have fallen by more than 50% since the Ministry of Health and Welfare began price rollbacks in 1981. Yet, drug expenditures in Japan exceed those in the United States because of a strong preference for the latest products, a small generic market, and high per capita consumption (Ikegami et al. 1994).

The deleterious long-term effects of price controls are perhaps best exemplified by the case of Australia. In 1983, more than 75% of Australia's pharmaceutical products were manufactured locally from imported raw materials and almost 15% were produced using locally manufactured active ingredients. Now only morphine, codeine, and small quantities of other alkaloids are the active ingredients produced locally. In 1989 the Australian trade deficit for drugs was almost $400 million, up from only $45 million 10 years earlier (Comanor 1994).

In developing countries, local production of pharmaceutical products is variable and foreign imports play a major role in supplying the domestic market. Except for China, Mexico, India, Indonesia, Brazil, and Egypt, the pharmaceutical sector in most developing countries is heavily dependent on drugs from the multinational companies based in the United States, Europe, or Japan. Most production is domestic, and imports represent 20% of total consumption. "Production" in developing countries, however, often implies merely assembling the imported raw material (active ingredient) and the final packaging. According to the World Health Organization (WHO), over 49% of drug imports in Latin America, 58% in Asia, and 96% in Africa were from European pharmaceutical companies in 1984 (Comanor 1994). In the early 1980s the market share of multinational companies ranged from 30% in Egypt, 70% in India, 78% in Brazil, to almost 100% in many African countries (Comanor 1994). The importance of the private market varies from country to country, accounting for 30% of sales in Zimbabwe, 68% in Kenya, and 87% of the market in Bangladesh (World Health Organization 1988a).

The difference in drug consumption levels between the developed and the developing countries is striking. The ratio between aggregate spending between these two blocs is nearly 18 to 1 (*The Economist* 1995a). Even within the developing countries, there are significant differences in consumption. For example, while the average annual per capita consumption of pharmaceuticals in Latin America is $20.30, it is only $3.30 in sub-Saharan Africa. However, these differences are not as apparent when we compare consumption expressed as a percentage of the gross domestic product (GDP). The consumption of pharmaceuticals in developed market economies averages 0.95% of GDP but 0.67% of GDP in developing countries. However, it is interesting to note that both Latin America and China spend a higher percentage of GDP on pharmaceuticals than do the nations of western Europe (*The Economist* 1995b).

A worldwide comparison of pharmaceutical sales in 1985 ranked India as eighth with $1.78 billion in sales, Brazil 19th with sales of $1.41 billion, and Mexico 12th with $1.25 billion in sales. These countries accounted for nearly 5% of total worldwide sales in 1985 (Hirst 1992). The third world, it is estimated, will comprise 36% of the world market for pharmaceuticals by the year 2000.

Access to Appropriate Drugs in Developing Countries

Two problems in pharmaceutical policy are prevalent in developing countries. The first is reliance upon imported pharmaceuticals which are priced at world levels and require payment in scarce hard currency. The second is a lack of congruence between the health needs of the country and the drugs which are imported. The underlying reasons for these problems are best understood by considering the situation in several specific countries in Latin America, Africa, and the Middle East.

The World Health Organization (WHO) has developed an important role with regard to pharmaceutical use in the developing countries. Its World Health Assembly proposed in 1978 that the WHO establish a program on "essential drugs," defined as those that are "considered to be of the utmost importance and hence basic, indispensable, and necessary for the health needs of the population" (WHO 1988a). The WHO's Drug Action Program (DAP) was inaugurated in 1981 for the purpose of ensuring "the availability of a regular supply to all people, of a selected number of safe and effective drugs of acceptable quality at lowest cost" (London School of Hygiene 1989). The WHO (1988a) provides six criteria for selecting essential drugs, suggesting that the drugs be

- Clinically proven to be safe and effective
- Available in a stable, easily managed form
- Made with only one active ingredient
- Designed to meet clearly defined health care needs
- The less expensive of two comparable drugs
- Appropriate for a wide range of local conditions (World Health Organization 1988a).

The WHO maintains and periodically updates a Model List of essential drugs as an example for governments that wish to compile their own essential drugs lists and revise them to keep abreast of latest developments. This list currently includes 200 drugs considered essential for managing the most prevalent illnesses in developing countries. Today, over 110 countries have adopted the essential drug list in principle.

Whether countries should manufacture all or even most of these drugs or import them from major world manufacturers (most likely in the developed world) is not addressed by the WHO. This is an example of the classic "make or buy" decision faced continually by firms: Is it more efficient to produce one's own inputs, through vertical integration, or buy those inputs, presumably from firms specializing in producing those products. Obviously the answer must be determined empirically in each case and is likely to differ across inputs and over time.

In the case of a nation's pharmaceuticals there are the dual questions of price and access. If firms are passive price-takers, the prices are likely to be at (or near) world prices, well out of the reach of developing countries with per capita incomes less than 5 or 10% of those in developed countries. A country could bargain with drug companies more as a monoposonist (single buyer) and, if there is competition in the supply side, the low marginal cost structure of the industry suggests that firms may grant steep price discounts. This would be analogous to the discounts won by managed-care organizations in the United States prior to the price discrimination suit (see Chapter 4).

The second issue, access, may be more difficult. The problem is that for commercial reasons producers in the developed world have not chosen to invest in R&D to support pharmaceuticals for many conditions prevalent in developing countries. In other words, there is simply no supply of drugs in some clinical areas for developing countries to purchase.

What is a developing country to do? If the R&D firms in the developed countries have found that production of some drugs is a poor investment, it will be the same for developing countries. After all, capital for an investment project must produce yields consistent with worldwide rates. The only hope is to obtain outside subsidies, perhaps through multinational organizations, to encourage needed investment. This *still* does not address the question of whether investments should be made in by firms in developing countries or by established major pharmaceutical manufacturers. Developing countries may achieve substantial economies of scale in R&D and in manufacturing by collaborating, perhaps with specialization, whereby one country's drug sector produces vaccines for many poor countries, while another's produces antiparasitic drugs.

Many countries have developed a drug list similar to the WHO's Model as part of a broader pharmaceutical policy. The Philippines created a National Drug Policy in 1988, the cornerstone of which was the Generics Act. This Act "promotes, requires and ensures the production of an adequate supply, distribution, use and acceptance of drugs and medicines identified by their generic names" (Republic of the Philippines 1988). This Act is viewed by many as a statement by the government of the Philippines to the multinational firms that in their pursuit of new drug research and development, priority should be given to the national interest of the Philippine nation and the needs of its people.

A recent study estimated the proportion of all drugs offered for sale by the 20 largest European pharmaceutical manufacturers to six regions of the developing world that were essential drugs. Only 16% of a total of 3021 drugs were found to be essential. The proportion for each company ranged from less than 10%, by Boehringer Ingelhiem, Sanofi and E. Merck, to more than 30% for Wellcome and 39% for Astra (Hartog 1993). The majority of drugs sold were multivitamin combinations, minerals, and plant extracts, which the WHO does not consider essential medications. The findings were consonant with those of earlier studies which found that the pharmacologic properties of drugs manufactured by Swiss and German subsidiaries in countries of the developing world were inappropriate for their needs and that over half of these were combinations of two or more different active ingredients of dubious value (Hartog and Schulte-Sasse 1990).

In Indonesia, there are currently 285 drug manufacturers providing for 95% of the country's need for drugs. Raw materials for a dozen drugs are manufactured within the country. A drug shortage existed in the early 1970s, but Indonesia now has more than 13,500 drug formulations available on the market—perhaps in excess of the real need. Despite these production achievements, the per capita annual drug consumption is still only $2.50 (Darmansjah and Wardhini 1991).

Brazil is the world's ninth largest market for pharmaceuticals, worth approximately $1.9 billion in 1988. Despite the sector's high earnings, only 63 million Brazilians (48%) have access to medicines, leaving 52% of the population in 1986 out of the market. Brazilian per capita consumption of medicines in 1988 was $13 (World Health Organization 1988b). The Central Authority of Medicines (CEME) is a state-owned enterprise created in 1971 to rationalize the procurement of medicines for public hospitals and clinics and to coordinate Brazilian pharmaceutical policy.

The Brazilian drug industry is similar to that of the developed countries in terms of its abilities to formulate, package, and market pharmaceutical specialities. But it has failed to develop the advanced chemistry infrastructure necessary for the production of raw materials. According to CEME data, Brazil produces only 14% of the raw materials used in the preparation of drugs in the country. According to the Brazilian pharmaceutical industry association ABIFARMA, CEME bought 60% of its supplies from government-owned laboratories, 25% from domestically owned private companies, and 15% from foreign-owned private companies. The national laboratories have restricted themselves to transforming imported raw materials into their own brands of pharmaceuticals (Castelo et al. 1991).

Of the 470 drug companies in Brazil in 1985, 100 (21%) were subsidiaries of foreign companies. These subsidiaries accounted for 84% of the market sales. Thus the share of the 370 domestic companies was only 16%. The two largest domestic drug companies (Ache and Prodome) accounted for only 8.3% of total sales. It is estimated that antibiotics addressed 85% of the country's health problems, and yet only about 30% of the necessary raw materials for their production were produced in the country. The antibiotics produced domestically were older drugs whose production methods can be easily copied. Only one national company, the Brazilian Antibiotics Company (CIBRAN), is involved in the production of antibiotics; the other producers are affiliates of multinational firms. The import content of antibiotics has increased form 46 to 63% from 1976 to 1981 (Castelo et al. 1991).

There is thus no evidence that Brazil's domestic industries are any more responsive to health care needs than the multinationals. An overt policy of market protection for national companies in the absence of a clear national policy of investing in the development of manpower and technology produced little benefit for consumers, in terms of access, cost, and quality of drugs available. Brazil has not recognized pharmaceutical patents on products or processes since 1969, allowing its domestic industry to produce local versions of internationally patented products. Being a signatory to GATT and the WTO, Brazil is now forced to recognize such patents. The domestic industry has slowly extended its activities into more basic phases of drug production, but success in R&D will require a concerted effort of industry, government, and universities working together. A beginning has been made with the establishment of the Industrial Development Company (CODE-TEC), a collaborative effort between the Ministry of Health, Ministry of

Industry and Commerce, and the Department of Industrial Technology to develop research manpower and technology (Castelo et al. 1991).

In Panama's public sector, health care services are provided by the Ministry of Health and the Social Security Institute, the latter providing care for over 62% of the population. Pharmaceuticals are provided free of cost through the Social Security pharmacies to its beneficiaries. In 1988, its total pharmaceutical market was approximately $60 million and was equally divided between the private and the public sectors. Imports constitute nearly 80% of the market. There are a few national drug laboratories, but they are involved in assembling the final product from imported raw materials. There are nearly 388 drug products available in the market, of which half are combination drug products. Despite efforts to enhance prescribing of generics, 83% of prescriptions contain trade names. A fifth of the top 20 drugs prescribed were drugs of doubtful value. Many authorities state that drug prices in Panama may be three times higher than in neighboring countries. Drugs are often sold for unproven indications and many combinations are irrational and of unproven efficacy, and a majority of the new drug introductions did not offer a significant therapeutic benefit compared to the drugs already on the market. Many of the drugs sold by the subsidiaries of international firms are deficient compared to the same products manufactured and sold by the parent firms, with different active ingredients in the same brand product or lower strength of the active ingredient. In addition, many drugs sold by US or UK firms are not approved for sale in their respective home countries (Programa Regional de Desarrollo Científico y Tecnologico 1983).

Tanzania initiated its Essential Drugs Program (EDP) in 1983 with the hope that a rationalized, shortened list of essential drugs would be better than an open-ended list of drugs which could be used liberally by prescribers. Unfortunately, the execution of the EDP was bogged down in intragovernmental politics. While the EDP was implemented by units falling under the Ministry of Health, it was ignored by the publicly owned drug producers (Tanzania Pharmaceutical Industries and Keko Pharmaceutical Industries) and the importers and distributors (National Pharmaceutical Company—NAPCO). These importers fall under the jurisdiction of the Ministry of Trade and Industries and are concerned primarily with developing commerce, not health. There are other routes for drug procurement and distribution; and these contributed to the failure of the EDP policy. Many hospitals and dispensaries receive their drugs from the Central Medical Stores run by the Ministry of Health. Some voluntary agencies also receive drugs from the Central Medical Stores, while other voluntary agencies receive them from their benefactors abroad. In addition to the private sector production, NAPCO also procures and distributes drugs to the private sector (Munshi 1991). Lastly, the Danish aid agency, DANIDA, which is a major donor to Tanzania, also continues to supply drugs to the governmental sector.

One of the long-term goals of the EDP was to stimulate the drug manufacturing activities of the public sector. While the major local drug manufacturers are capable of manufacturing medicines like ampicillin, chloramphenicol, tetracycline, aspirin, diazepam, and other drugs in the EDP, capacity utilization of most plants is only 40%, with the Tanzania Pharmaceutical Industries plants running at only 25% of capacity. A major factor responsible for underutilization is the shortage of raw materials, which have to be bought in the world market with precious hard currency (Munshi 1991). Taken together, the absence of a coherent governmental policy and its inadequate implementation exemplify how a country's pharmaceutical sector growth can be severely stunted.

Nigeria spends only 1.5% of its budget on the health sector, and almost 90% of this is devoted to salaries of personnel and maintenance of existing structures. Nigeria's drug situation had been characterized, until recently, by an abundance of drugs that had no relation to the health needs of the population. Unfortunately, prescribed drugs were often unavailable in the government hospitals and dispensaries, forcing patients to buy drugs from the private sector at prices most of them could not afford. To address this issue a "National Drug Policy" was adopted which proposed a system of drug supply with total cost recovery from consumers. The government would purchase drugs cheaply in bulk and make them available for distribution at a nominal cost through public hospitals and dispensaries. While the private market can only sell drugs that are on the Essential Drugs List, this rule is not strictly enforced. The demand for drugs outside the public distribution system has made the business of drug distribution highly profitable (Salako 1991).

Another goal of Nigeria's National Drug Policy was to achieve self-sufficiency in drug manufacturing, with the aim of locally manufacturing 75% of all drugs consumed by the year 2000. Whether this is a rational objective is an open question.

Today less than 10% of drugs used in Nigeria are manufactured locally. At present little raw material is available in Nigeria. As in many other countries, most manufacturing consists of formulation of finished products from imported raw materials. A major reason for this is that the cost of manufacturing drugs locally is higher than importing them, because of the high cost of infrastructure erection and maintenance of existing facilities (Salako 1991).

The situation in many other countries is essentially similar. In Kenya, a study revealed that out of the 25 pharmaceutical manufacturers, 15 are subsidiaries of multinationals from Europe and America. Nearly 41% of total expenditures in the public health sector are spent on drug imports. As with Tanzania, extensive capacity underutilization exists; among 18 firms studied, mean capacity utilization was only 32% (Owino 1986).

In Yemen the problem of incongruence between the types of imported drugs and the nation's health needs is especially severe. Nearly 18% of expenditures on pharmaceutical imports went to vitamins and tonics. Only about 1% was spent on drugs to treat malaria, Bilharzia, and tuberculosis, the three most common disease in the country (Melrose 1982).

To summarize the picture of pharmaceuticals in developing countries, dependence on imported drugs is high. Furthermore, there is no ability to verify that imported drugs have been proven safe and effective in the exporting country (or another country with a credible drug review process similar to that of the US FDA). Furthermore, there is only a limited ability to assure that drugs imported by developing countries are of the same quality as those products consumed domestically in the exporting country.* Systems for procuring and distributing essential drugs are inadequate, as well. And lastly, drug prescribing practices, influenced perhaps by the multinational drug companies, tend to favor prescribing products that are not cost-effective (Wang'ombe and Mwambu 1987).

According to Wang'ombe and Mwambu (1987), policies that might be used to deal with these problems include the following:

1. Improving drug selection procedures and training personnel in the selection of the most useful drugs for national formularies
2. Using generic drugs instead of brand drugs whenever possible in these drug lists
3. Establishing a specialized agency for importing drugs
4. Establishing a national system of distributing drugs
5. Formulating guidelines that would encourage buying drugs in bulk in order to achieve economies of scale
6. Educating physicians and patients to improve drug prescription and consumption patterns
7. Encouraging domestic production of drugs if economically viable.

While these may seem obvious solutions, the experience of many developing countries suggests that despite the adoption of many of these goals, problems in implementation and execution continue to bedevil the pharmaceutical sector of these economies.

The Effect of the World Trade Organization Treaty

The recent passage of the World Trade Organization (WTO) treaty, especially its Agreement on Trade-Related Aspects of Intellectual Property Rights (TRIPS), commits each member country to provide a basic level of patent protection so as to shield patented products from competition for a total of 20 years (calculated from the date of patent filing). The magnitude

---

*This is, perhaps, a more complicated issue than it might appear. Suppose a manufacturer has just accepted returned shipments of expired drugs. Should these drugs be sold at a discount to developing countries? In some cases the drug might have full, or nearly full, potency for several months. And if the discount is substantial it might be more rational to *use* these drugs than to destroy them.

of the patent infringement problem is seen in US data: US drug manufacturers had an estimated $28.8 billion in overseas sales in 1994 but lost $1.5 billion in sales because of inadequate patent protection in just three countries—Argentina, Brazil, and India (Gardner 1994). It is expected that drug prices in many developing countries will rise, as they are prevented from manufacturing illegal copies of patented drugs. On the one hand, this may adversely affect the availability of drugs to poor countries whose populations will no longer have access to copied, "pirated" versions of patented drugs. On the other hand, pharmaceutical companies may now be willing to introduce their latest patented drugs into developing country markets now that illegal competition has been eliminated for the 20-year patent period. In response to the urging of developing countries, a "phase in" period of 10 years has been granted for implementation of TRIPS so as to allow them to ease into the new regulatory regime with minimal disruption to local pharmaceutical manufacturers.

References

Ballance R, Pogany J, and Forstner H, *The World's Pharmaceutical Industries*, Edward Elger Publishing, 1992.

The Boston Consulting Group, *The Changing Environment for US Pharmaceuticals*, April 1993.

Burstall ML, *1992 and the Regulation of the Pharmaceutical Industry*, London: Institute of Economic Affairs, Health and Welfare Unit, 1990.

Cantor JC and Gross DJ, *The Effects of a Drug Price Review Board: Lessons from the Canadian Experience*, Washington DC: US General Accounting Office, 1993.

Castelo A, Colombo AL, and Holbrook AM, "Production and marketing of drugs in Brazil," *Journal of Clinical Epidemiology* 44(suppl 2): 21S–28S, 1991.

Center for Medicines Research, *Trends in Worldwide Pharmaceutical R&D Expenditures for the 1990s*, Report No.CMR-93-1R, Charshalton, England: 1993.

Comanor WC, "Pharmaceutical research and the health needs of developing countries," Program in Pharmaceutical Economics and Policy Working Paper, UCLA, 1994.

Darmansjah I and Wardhini S, "The Indonesian drug advisory committee and the drug approval process," *Journal of Clinical Epidemiology* 44(suppl 2): 39S–43S, 1991.

DiMasi JA, Hansen RW, Grabowski H, and Lasagna L, "The cost of innovation in the pharmaceutical industry," *Journal of Health Economics* 10:107–142, 1991.

The Economist, April 22, 1995a.

The Economist, August 26, 1995b.

European Commission, *Communication to the Council of Ministers and the European Parliament on the Outlines of an Industrial Policy for the Pharmaceutical Sector in the EC*: Brussels, European Commission, March 2, 1994.

"The European Pharmaceutical Outlook", *Nature*, 361(6416): 756–8, February 25, 1993.

Gardner J, "Drug DME Firms Expect to get Benefits from GATT," *Modern Healthcare*, 24(49): 8, December 5, 1994.

Harneijer JW, Stefland P, Bannanberg W, Hardon A, and Walt G, *An Evaluation of WHO's Action Program on Essential Drugs*, Amsterdam: Royal Tropical Institute and London: The London School of Hygiene and Tropical Medicine, 1989.

Hartog R, "Essential and Non-essential Drugs Marketed by the 20 Largest European Pharmaceutical Companies in Developing Countries," *Social Science and Medicine*, 377(7): 897–904, October 1993.

Hartog R and Schulte-Sasse H, "German and Swiss Drug Supplies to the Third World," *Health Action International*, Amsterdam, 1990.

Henry D, "Economic Analysis as an aid to subsidisation decisions: the development of Australian guidelines for pharmaceuticals," *PharmacoEconomics* 1(1):54–67, 1992.

Hirst CA, "Government Initiatives in the Development of a Pharmaceutical Industry in Australia," *Clinical and Experimental Pharmacology and Physiology*, 19(1): 57–61, January 1992.

Hodgson J, "An Appetite for Technology: Hoffman-La Roche," *Biotechnology New York*, 10(8): 867–869, August 1992.

Ijsselmuiden CB and Faden RR, "Research and Informed Consent in Africa: Another Look," *NE JM*, 326(12): 830–834, 1992.

Ikegami N, Mitchell W, and Penner-Hahn J, "Pharmaceutical Prices, Quantitites, and Innovation: Comparing Japan with the US, *PharmacoEconomics* 6(5): 423–433, 1994.

Langley PC, "The role of pharmacoeconomic guidelines for formulary approval—the Australian experience,"*Clinical Therapeutics* 15(6):1154–1176, 1993.

Lexchin J, *Pharmaceuticals, Patents, and Politics: Canada and Bill C-22*, Ottawa, Ontario: Canadian Center for Policy Alternatives, February 1992.

London School of Hygiene and Tropical Medicine, *An Evaluation of WHO's Action Program on Essential Drugs*, Copenhagen: DANIDA, 1989.

MacInnes R, Lumley CE, and Walker SR, "New Chemical Entity Output of the International Pharmaceutical Industry from 1970 to 1992," *Clinical Pharmacology and Therapeutics* 56(3):339–349, September 1994.

Melrose D, "Double deprivation: public and private drug distribution from the perspective of the Third World Poor," *World Development* 11:181–186, 1982.

Munshi GK, "The development of the essential drugs program and implications for self-reliance in Tanzania," *Journal of Clinical Epidemiology*, 44(suppl 2):49S–55S, 1991.

Office of Technology Assessment, *Pharmaceutical R&D: Costs, Risks, and Rewards*, Report OTA-H-522, Washington DC: OTA, February 1993.

Owino PSW, "The pharmaceutical industry in Kenya: excess capacity, missed opportunities and planing failures," Paper presented at the Conference on Industrialization Strategy, Nairobi, August 4–8, 1986.

Palmer WN, "Access to affordable medicines: the role of the Canadian Patented Medicine Review Board," *Proceedings*, Annual Meeting of the International Society for Technological Assessment in Health Care (no. 133), 1994.

Pharmaceutical Manufacturers Association, *Facts at a Glance*, Washington, DC: PMA, 1990.

Pharmaceutical Manufacturers Association, Washington DC: PMA, 1991.

Programa Regional de Desarrollo Cientifico y Tecnologico (PRDCyT), Proyecto Especial

No. 4: Valoraciones Biofarmaceuticas (PEVAB), Inform Final, Washington, DC: Organization of American States, 1983.

Republic of the Philippines, "Republic Act No. 6675 (Generics Act of 1988)," Manila: Congress of the Philippines, 1988.

Salako L, "Drug Supply in Nigeria," *Journal of Clinical Epidemiology* 44(suppl 2): 15S–19S, 1991.

Scherer FM, "Pricing, profits, and technological progress in the pharmaceutical industry," *Journal of Economic Perspectives* 7(3):97–115, 1993.

Shulman SR, "The Canadian patented medicine review board: new rules and new status," *PharmacoEconomics* 6(suppl 1):71–79, 1994.

Strutchler D, Mittelholzer ML, and Handschin J, "Commitment of Roche in Malaria and other tropical diseases," *Tropical Medicine and Parasitology* 44(3):250–253, September 1993.

Thomas LG 3rd, "Pricing, regulation, and competitiveness: lessons for the US from the Japanese pharmaceutical industry,"*PharmacoEconomics* 6(suppl 1):67–70, 1994.

US Congress, General Accounting Office, *High Technology Competitiveness: Trends in U.S. and Foreign Performance*, Washington, DC: September, 1992.

Wang'ombe JK and Mwambu GM, "Economics of essential drugs schemes: the perspectives of the developing countries," *Social Science and Medicine* 25(6):625–630, 1987.

Ward M, "Rhone-Poulenc: from bioscience to markets. The how, why, and when of the world's seventh largest chemicals company," *Biotechnology New York* 11(7):798–801, July 1993.

"Why Europeans are being shorted on miracle drugs," *The Wall Street Journal*, April 18, 1994.

World Health Organization, *The Use of Essential Drugs*, Technical Report Series 770, Geneva: World Health Organization, 1988a.

World Health Organization, *The World Drug Situation*, Geneva: WHO, 1988b.

6

Pricing Pharmaceuticals in a World Environment

International comparisons of pharmaceutical prices are playing an increasing role in public policy concerning the pharmaceutical industry. Many countries, including Italy, Spain, Portugal, and Canada, refer to prices of drugs in other countries when setting allowable prices in their own country. United States congressional investigations have attempted to learn whether US drug prices are higher than those in other industrial countries.

Although earlier studies (e.g., Reekie 1984; Schut and Van Bergeijk 1986; Szuba 1986; US Department HHS 1990; Pharmacy Freedom Fund 1990) have indicated that prescription drug prices are generally higher in the United States than in foreign countries, these studies have been criticized for methodological shortcomings, leading some to discount their conclusions. In the early 1990s, Congress asked the General Accounting Office (GAO) to compare prices that manufacturers charge in the United States to those of drugs sold in Canada and the United Kingdom. The GAO found significant price differences at the manufacturer level between the United States and these other countries. In fact, all frequently dispensed prescription drugs included in their analyses were priced higher in the United States than they were in the United Kingdom and Canada. The GAO reports had an explosive effect on both the Congress and the pharmaceutical industry. Upon receiving the first report on the US–Canada comparison in early 1992, a hearing was immediately held before the subcommittee on Health and the Environment of the Committee on Energy and Commerce in the House of Representatives. Legislative bills targeted at regulating prescription drug prices were proposed at once, including the "Prescription Drug Prices Review Board Act of 1993" sponsored by Congressman Fortney Stark (D–CA).

But international price comparisons can be misleading, and serious flaws in previous cross-national comparisons of drug prices tend to overstate the relative cost of drugs in the United States. Moreover, critics of pharmaceutical price regulation, within and outside the pharmaceutical industry, have asserted that adoption of regulations that reduce drug prices in the United States would cripple pharmaceutical companies' ability to develop life-saving and life-improving drugs (Gross et al. 1994).

How should one compare drug prices in different countries? And with the right methodology, can we draw policy conclusions concerning the most appropriate regulatory response? These are the fundamental questions which should be considered within the context of pricing pharmaceuticals in the international perspective. To answer them, we first discuss the theoretical basis of international price variation, showing that demand conditions create an opportunity for producers to charge different prices to different groups of consumers. Next, we review the literature on international drug price variation, focusing especially on the GAO studies to see how accurately they have demonstrated price differences between the United States and other countries. We then suggest improvements in the methodology for measuring international price differences and ask whether uniform prices of pharmaceuticals would make all consumers better off.

Why Do Drug Prices Vary by Country?

Drug prices are expected to vary internationally because of differences in demand conditions in various countries. The first determinant of the price people in a country will be willing to pay for drugs is the country's income. The quantity of pharmaceuticals (and everything else) that people are willing to purchase typically rises with the level of income.* The amount by which the quantity demanded rises with income is defined as the income elasticity. Thus the demand curve for people in a wealthy country will be to the right of the demand curve for people in a poor country. In Figure 6.1, demand curves D_1 and D_2 describe the relationship between price and quantity demanded for drugs in two countries, a wealthy country, with demand curve D_1, and a poor country, with demand curve D_2. Each of the demand curves is associated with a marginal revenue curve, MR_1 and MR_2, showing the addition to total revenue as additional units of output are sold. The downward slope of the demand curve tells us that as one more unit is sold the addition to revenue is not merely the price of the last unit but must reflect

---

*Actually the demand for pharmaceuticals is not direct, but derived from the demand for health, as was discussed in Chapter 3. The demand for health implies a demand for all of the factors that produce health, including pharmaceuticals.

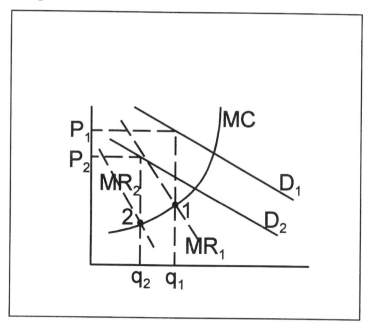

Figure 6.1 Demand for Pharmaceuticals Varies by Wealth

that *all* units have to be sold at this new (lower) price. MR is therefore lower than the demand curve at any price.

If a pharmaceutical manufacturer produces its product with marginal costs described by curve *MC*, it will maximize profits by producing at the level of output such that $MC=MR$ for each market. *MC* intersects the respective countries' marginal revenue curves, MR_1 and MR_2, at points 1 and 2, respectively. The price paid by consumers in the wealthy country will be p_1 for quantity q_1. Consumers in the poor country will pay price p_2 for quantity q_2, with $p_1>p_2$.

This is one explanation of why drug prices are observed to be lower in poor countries such as Mexico and China than in wealthy countries such as the United States and Switzerland. The same relationship will hold for virtually all consumer goods, including housing, food, and clothing, as long as the location of the demand curve is, at least partly, determined by income.

But there is a second reason why prices vary across markets, and this has to do not with the *location* of respective demand curve but with their *shape*, or more precisely, with the respective price sensitivity, or elasticity of demand. This is the realm of the theory of price discrimination and is based upon the profit-maximizing firm's desire to charge *each consumer* what each is willing to pay, and not merely what the last consumer pays.

The demand curve shows the price that will lead consumers to purchase a particular quantity. Normally, this implies that *all* consumers pay the same price—the price paid by the person buying the last unit of the good or service depicted by the demand curve. But some consumers are willing to pay a higher price than the price of that last unit. And typically *all* consumers are willing to pay a higher price for a smaller quantity, with a lower and lower price for successive units. Is there a way that sellers can somehow charge different consumers what they are *willing* to pay? The answer is, "Yes," sometimes. If different consumers are charged different amounts it is imperative that the various buyers not be able to bargain among themselves. For example, if business travelers absolutely *must* stay in hotels during the week, while vacation travelers are more flexible and can travel on weekends *or* weekdays, one would expect hotels to charge higher rates to business travelers. But could they succeed if vacationers could stand in the hotel lobby and sell their (discounted) reservations to the business travelers? No, the hotels could not successfully discriminate because the business travelers would rather buy these discounted room reservations from the vacationers at some price between their high rate and the vacationers' low rate. But of course this "arbitrage" is impossible; one cannot sell a Saturday reservation to someone arriving on a Tuesday! Thus, price discrimination occurs whenever a producer is able to sell the same product to different group of buyers, each with a different demand elasticity. Profit will be maximized when.

$$\frac{P_i}{P_j} = \frac{\eta_{Dj}}{\eta_{Di}}$$

Where $_i$ and $_j$ refer to two different markets, each with its own demand elasticity, η_D. The more price sensitive a market is (the higher its elasticity of demand), the lower its price. Many markets are characterized by groups of purchasers with different degrees of price sensitivity. Households, for example, can more readily defer long-distance telephone calls to off-peak time (evenings and weekends) than can businesses. In response to these different demand conditions, prices for businesses are often considerably higher than they are for households. The same is true for airline travel, where the differentiating characteristic is the purchaser's willingness to buy a ticket 14 or 21 days ahead or stay over on a Saturday night. It should be clear why airlines try to prohibit flyers from exchanging tickets and the associated coupons. In the case of pharmaceuticals, patients in wealthy countries will tend to be less price sensitive in their demand for pharmaceuticals. In part this results from people's preferences for medical care to maintain their quality of life, and in part it is because patients in wealthy countries are more likely to have insurance coverage to shield them from the full cost of drugs. Insurance coverage tends to lower consumer demand elasticity. For both reasons patients in wealthy countries will have a lower price sensitivity to drugs, being less willing to substitute less expensive drugs for more expensive drugs and also less willing to forgo use of drugs than patients in poorer countries.* We see, therefore, that both the position of the demand curve for pharmaceuticals and its shape (elasticity) will lead to higher prices for drugs in wealthy countries than in poor countries.

Comparisons of International Drug Prices

Prior to 1992 there were several studies that compared the prescription drug prices between the United States and other countries, including those by Reekie (1984), Schut and Van Bergeijk (1986), Szuba (1986), and the Pharmacy Freedom Fund (1990). Their findings were not conclusive regarding the pricing practices of manufacturers, for two reasons. First, while some studies measured pharmaceutical prices at the retail level, others looked only at wholesale prices. Therefore they could not distinguish between price differentials of pharmacists or wholesalers and those of drug manufacturers. Second, some of the studies (Reekie 1984; Schut and Van Bergeijk 1986) examined relatively small samples of drugs, limiting their generalizability.

To address the deficiencies of earlier price comparisons, the GAO began a series of price comparison studies in 1992. The GAO compared ex-manufacturer prices of identical prescription drug products sold by the same manufacturers in the United States, Canada, and the United Kingdom, a so-called "apple-to-apple" comparison. To do this the GAO selected the 200 drugs most frequently dispensed by US pharmacies, which represented 54% of all prescriptions dispensed in US drugstores during 1990. These drugs often came in multiple dosage forms, dosage strengths, and package sizes, each with its own price. The researchers therefore selected a single, commonly used US dosage form, strength, and size for each of the drugs in their sample for comparison. For their first comparison, of US and Canadian prices, the researchers were able to compare 121 of the 200 products by brand name, manufacturer, dosage strength, and dosage form in both countries.[†] The remaining 79 were not available in Canada in the exact form, strength, or size. These drugs included 39 of the 50 most commonly prescribed drugs in the United States. They then obtained US and Canadian prices for each specific drug product. They used the Wholesale Acquisition Cost (WAC) to represent the US actual manufacturers' prices and the Best Available Price (BAP) from the February 1991 Ontario Drug Benefit (ODB) Formulary to represent Canadian ex-factory prices. In addition to measuring

---

*Managed care in the United States has the effect of sharply increasing consumer price elasticity because of its ability to shift consumption from one drug to another (or even not to allow coverage for *any* drug) for large groups of patients because of price considerations. Managed care appears to have had significant effects in lowering prices for many health services (see Zwanziger and Melnick 1988).

[†]These products were not necessarily the top-selling products in Canada.

the 121 drug price comparisons, the GAO formed an aggregate using US quantity weights.

The researchers then attempted to identify the possible causes of price differentials by interviewing government officials, industry representatives, academic researchers, and pharmaceutical industry representatives in both the United States and Canada. Included in these interviews were officials from six drug manufacturers that sold 29% of the drugs in the study (US GAO 1992).

The principal findings of the study were the following:

> For the prescription drugs we examined, drug manufacturers charge whole-salers significantly more in the United States than the same manufacturers do in Canada. If a common US prescription of each drug included in our study was purchased at factory price in both countries, the entire basket of 121 pre-scriptions would cost 32 percent more in the United States than in Canada. Alternatively, when price differentials are computed drug by drug, the median price differential per package between the United States and Canada was 43 percent. (US GAO 1992)

The study found that the differentials were in large measure due to the cost-containment efforts of federal regulations and provincial drug benefit plans that pay for drugs for most Canadians. According to interviews with industry experts and drug company officials, the costs of research and de-velopment and marketing do not contribute to the price differences (US House of Representatives 1993).

In the GAO's US–UK comparison, only 77 of the 200 drugs could be matched between the two countries. As in the Canadian study, the research-ers found significant differences in the prices that manufacturers charged wholesalers for identical prescription drugs sold in retail pharmacies in the United States and the United Kingdom. A market basket of all 77 frequently dispensed drugs in their comparison cost wholesalers 60% more in the United States than that in United Kingdom.

The GAO studies, however, are subject to conceptual and methodolog-ical problems that limit the conclusions which can be drawn. First, both studies fail to account for generic substitution in any comprehensive way. More than one-third of the drugs analyzed by the GAO were available in generic form in the United States (Lane 1993). Furthermore, eight of the 10 drugs found by the GAO to have had the highest percentage differential have generic versions available in this country (Mossinghoff 1993). Generic drugs are priced substantially lower than the brand names, often 50% less (US House of Representatives 1993). A recent report (Neimeth 1993) in-dicated that the overall level of US pharmaceutical prices would be reduced by 12.2% if generic prices were included, And if one were to look at mul-tiple-source products alone, prices would be reduced even more dramati-cally—dropping by 45%.

Thus, while the comparison of relative prices for a particular branded drug may have been correct, the importance of the result is overstated if consumers substituted lower-priced generics for branded products more frequently in one country than in another. In fact, the use of generics is more widespread in the United States than elsewhere, especially after passage of the 1984 Drug Price Competition and Patent Term Restoration Act, which facilitated entry of generic drug products after patent expiration. So, merely comparing the prices of specific branded products gives a misleading picture of the relative costs to consumers of filling their doctors' prescriptions.

A second problem with the GAO approach is that it is based on wholesale prices, which do not account for the many discounts and rebates which are present in this industry. These discounts are usually negotiated between individual pharmaceutical manufacturers and their customers, including state Medicaid programs, managed-care programs, prescription drug insurance plans, large retail purchasers, and mail order pharmacies. The rebates for Medicaid programs during the period covered by the GAO studies, for example, were at least 12.5%. Now they are a minimum of 15.7%, which will total $6.4 billion over 5 years (Mossinghoff 1993). Even if these prices accurately described charges to individual pharmacies, there is no reason to believe that they reflect transaction prices to other classes of buyers, who in fact constitute a substantial segment of demand. This factor is important to the extent that discounting is more widespread in the United States than in Britain or Canada. In that case, the observed relative cost of pharmaceuticals in the United States is biased upward. Rather than comparing "apple to apple," the analysis actually compares "apples and avocados" as Congressman Alex McMillan (R-NC), a member of the Subcommittee on Health and the Environment, put it.

Third, the GAO price data is not fully comparable across countries. In the case of the US–Canada comparison, the GAO compared the best available price in Canada (from the Ontario Drug Benefit Formulary) with the published or "sticker price" for US products. The Ontario formulary lists prices paid by a large institutionalized buyer—the Ontario Drug Benefit Plan—that covers 40% of the drugs sold in the market (Mossinghoff 1993). The Canadian prices were therefore not representative of a manufacturer's prices in Canada but rather represented government reimbursement limits. The US Wholesale Acquisition Cost is a published list price without the application of rebates and discounts. The discrepancy between using the lowest discounted price in Canada and highest "sticker" price in the US strongly biases the GAO study toward concluding that Canadian prices are lower. For example, the GAO report lists Deltasone (used to treat adrenocortical deficiency states) 5-mg tablets as 82% more expensive in the United States, based on the 100-count package. Actually, Deltasone 5 mg is only sold in the 1000-count package in Canada. If one were to compare per tablet prices based on those two presentations, one would find US and Canadian prices of 0.012 cents per tablet and 0.013 cents per tablet, respectively. In other words, the Canadian price of this particular drug is slightly higher that its US counterpart.

Fourth, in explaining the cause of the price differentials between the United States and Canada or the United Kingdom, the GAO claimed that that "most of the differences in prescription drug prices between countries can not be attributed to differences in manufacturers' costs" (US GAO 1994). But they did not provide sufficient information to support their conclusion. They asserted that "this conclusion holds for differences in costs whether they are associated with research and development, marketing, production, or distribution" (US GAO 1994). They based these conclusions on their interviews with "pharmaceutical industry experts and some manufacturers." But in 1990, 8.8% of Canadian pharmaceutical sales was spent on R&D, while about 17% of sales was spent in the United States (US House of Representatives 1993). In other words, the United States devoted 50% more of its sales revenue to drug innovation than Canada did, on average. To maintain its competitive position in the world market, the US pharmaceutical industry continues to increase its investment in R&D. It has doubled its investment every 5 years since 1970, and an estimated $12.6 billion in innovation was spent in 1993 (Mossinghoff 1993). If one accepts a model in which drug prices are cost driven, differential costs of R&D cannot be ignored in explaining price differentials between the United States, with the world's most successful pharmaceutical industry in terms of drug innovation and production, and other countries like Canada where the pharmaceutical industry is relatively small.

Fifth, the GAO studies have also ignored other factors that contribute to price differentials, such as liability risk of pharmaceutical products. Manning (1994) extended the GAO US–Canada comparison by adding liability risk factors to the original model to identify the effect of the costs of these risks on the price differentials between the two countries.

The risks of a pharmaceutical product include adverse interaction, contraindications, overdose and treatment danger, mortality risk, frequency of life-threatening adverse reactions, pregnancy risk, and so on. These risks may result in substantial loss to drug manufacturers in countries like the United States where lawsuits are more frequent than in other countries such as the United Kingdom and Canada. Manning found strong and significant effects of liability risk in price differentials and suggested that roughly one-quarter of the observed variation in the price differential is attributable to anticipated liability cost. The best prediction of his model was that liability risk roughly doubles the average price differential and increases the median price differential by more than 80%. Therefore, he concluded that studies of international price comparisons that fail to account for differences in legal systems are lacking an important determinant of pricing behavior. Another way of looking at Manning's analysis involves conceiving of drug purchasers in the United States as purchasing a "different" product from that available in other countries. This difference is increased liability protection—or at least an increased likelihood of receiving compensation should a maloccurrence take place.*

The sixth and perhaps the most serious deficiency of the GAO studies was their failure to deal with different drug consumption patterns in United States, Canada, and the United Kingdom. Not only are different drugs frequently used for the same conditions in each country, but even the same drugs are taken in different forms and dosages (Payor 1988). Patterns of pharmaceutical consumption are determined to a significant degree by prices; consumers are more likely to purchase products which are less expensive than therapeutic alternatives that are more expensive. It has been noted that products that are very expensive are used less. Therefore, drugs with relatively high US prices are used less than they are in another country, and drugs with a lower relative price will be used more. Because consumption is inversely related to price, price comparisons overstate the effect on consumers. The GAO approach sidestepped the entire problem and considered a narrower question: Are wholesale prices higher in the United States than in the United Kingdom or Canada for the specific items that are major-selling American drugs? Note that this approach compares the prices of highly popular US products with those of less frequently prescribed products in other countries.

How to Measure Drug Prices Across Countries?

Perhaps no methodology can address all of the concerns discussed in the previous section, but there are some criteria that should be followed in order to maximize the value of the findings. First, in choosing drugs to be compared, products should be identical in at least two of the following three characteristics: chemical composition, brand name, and manufacturer. This matching will include some unbranded generics and is therefore broader than the same-manufacturer requirement used in other studies, but it still excludes branded generics and originator products licensed to other manufacturers and sold under different names. Alternatively, one could match products on the basis of Molecule/Therapeutic Category, comparing the weighted average price over all products with the same chemical composition in the same therapeutic category, regardless of manufacturer or brand.

Second, if one wants to compare the effect of price differentials on consumers, prices should be compared at the retail level rather than at the ex-manufacturer level. The difference between these two prices is the markup,

---

*This risk was made greater by a ruling by the California State Supreme Court that drug manufacturers have an even greater responsibility than before to inform patients of possible side effects of their products. The ruling said that manufacturers must make physicians aware of known or "reasonably scientifically knowable" risks or else they will face liability for injuries caused by those side effects" (see Dolan and Roan 1996).

or distribution margin, which includes the profits of both the dispensing pharmacy and the wholesaler if one is involved in distributing the product. In many discussions of the cost of pharmaceuticals, there is the implicit assumption that distribution margins are constant across products, with retail prices comprised of the wholesale price plus a fixed amount added to cover distribution costs. However, that picture is not accurate for the US economy. Steiner, particularly, has pointed to the "inverse association between the margins of manufacturers and [those of] retailers" (Steiner 1993). Salehi and Schweitzer (1985) found that the relationship also applies to pharmaceuticals. Branded pharmaceuticals, which typically embody a high manufacturing margin, have lower distribution margins than do generic products, which have relatively low margins at the manufacturing stage and have higher distribution margins. As a result, price differences between branded and generic products are greater at the manufacturing stage than they are at the retail stage. Manufacturer prices are therefore poor proxies for retail prices. In addition, wholesale or list prices are not indicators of transaction prices of prevailing discounts and rebates, especially in the United States. Moreover, prices should refer to the most popular package size for a drug, not the package size that manufacturers provide to wholesalers or retailers. These large manufacturer packages will be broken up when they are distributed to consumers and the prices are likely to overstate retail package prices.

Third and finally, both exchange rates and purchasing power parities (PPP) should be used to convert local prices to a common currency. PPP is an attempt to adjust official exchange rates for the average price level in different countries. For example, the official exchange rate may be 105 yen to the dollar. But travelers often note that prices appear significantally higher in Japan than in the United States. If prices were consistently 20% higher, that would imply that the official exchange rate should be adjusted by a factor of 1.20 (in this case multiplying the official rate of 105 by 1.20), yielding a purchasing power adjusted exchange rate of 1.26 yen per dollar.* Both results should be reported when exchange rates and PPPs yield significantly different estimates.

The methodology of recent work by Danzon and Kim (1993) is largely consistent with the above criteria and corrects for many of the deficiencies in the GAO and other studies. The study compares prices in nine countries for a single therapeutic category—cardiovascular drugs. Danzon and Kim found that price differences between countries depend greatly on the way in which the comparison is framed, particularly on which country's quantity

---

*PPP adjustment has its critics, however. Rogoff (1996) points out that a PPP adjustor, like any other price index, must weight items to form a "market basket." If the composition of market baskets varies across country, as it surely does, the PPP adjustor cannot accurately compare purchasing power in different countries. *The Economist* (1995) points this out by regularly publishing prices of Big Macs throughout the world. The magazine notes that these differentials, striking as they are, are neither representative of all commodities nor of great relevance to most consumers, either in the United States or in the respective foreign countries.

weights are used to construct the price index. Comparisons also differ depending on whether one compares prices per gram of active ingredient or prices per "standard unit" (e.g., per capsule or milliliter of liquid). By most measures, average US drug prices exceed those in most other countries, although for some products, US prices are lower. But equally important are the findings concerning the sensitivity of results to different samples and measures and the possible biases that can result.

> The results are sensitive to the measure of price. For example, prices in Japan appear 2 percent higher than in the US on a per-kilogram basis, but 32 percent lower on a per-standard-unit basis, because strength per pill is typically lower in Japan. The results can differ by 20 percentage points or more, depending on whether US quantity weights (Laspeyre index) or foreign quantity weights (Paasche index) are used. Use of the unweighted average of relative prices yields highly unstable results: the US appears 9 percent more expensive than Canada if Canada is the base; Canada appears 117 percent more expensive than the US if the US is the base. Only the Fisher index (geometric average of Laspeyre and Paasche indexes) yields conclusions that are invariant to which country is treated as the base. However, if US consumption patterns would remain largely unchanged even if we faced European prices, the Fisher index overstates the potential gain to US consumers from European prices. The results for hospitals differ considerably, with hospital prices in Japan, Sweden and the U.K. being considerably higher relative to the US than for retail pharmacy sales. (Danzon and Kim 1993)

These results indicate that differences in mix of products, dosage forms and strengths, and pharmacy type contribute significantly to the measure of price differences.

There are shortcomings, however, in the Danzon and Kim study. It did not include generic products, which lead to upward biased estimates of prices in the United States relative to most other countries. Also, it did not consider the effects of other factors on price differences across nations, such as production and liability costs, nor did it take the effects of government regulations into account. Still, its research methodology provides more valuable results than the GAO and other previous studies. None of these studies, however, addresses the question of why drug prices differ across countries. What factors should be considered in explaining price differentials?

Why Drug Price Differences Persist

The first consideration in explaining international drug price differences is differences in tastes and preferences that alter demand. Significant differences exist across cultures, for example, in choice of drugs as well as their dosage and form of administration (Payer 1988). Another important consideration is the physicians' economic incentive in determining drug demand and price. For example, in Japan, physicians tend to prescribe heavily at each office visit because of the high "doctor margin" in the health system that supplements reimbursed fees. This margin is the difference between official drug prices, set by Japan's Ministry of Health and Welfare, and the discounted price at which drug wholesalers sell their products to hospitals and doctors. US physicians do not have such an incentive and in the United States drugs only account for about 8% of health spending; in Japan, nearly 30% of the total health care bill is pharmaceuticals (Eisenstodt 1992).

Government regulation and third-party involvement also influence drug price and consumption volume. Governments in many other countries regulate prices either directly or indirectly, as described by Danzon and Kim:

> France and Italy directly regulate prices at launch and the subsequent rate of price increase. Germany, the Netherlands, Denmark and New Zealand operate reference price systems of reimbursement and thereby exert strong pressure on prices charged by manufacturers. The U.K. operates a system of profit regulation that constrains prices to yield no more than a target overall rate of return on capital in the U.K. The Canadian government monitors price levels at launch and rates of increase to assure that they are "reasonable." Although pricing is nominally free in the US, third party payers increasingly negotiate price discounts and operate formularies with generic and therapeutic substitution that have effects similar to reference pricing in other countries; volumes are also monitored. (Danzon and Kim 1993)

Policy Implications

Previous studies of international pharmaceutical price differentials have tended to overstate the US drug prices differentials. But even if US prices were higher than in other countries, the policy response is unclear. Are the high US prices necessary to maintain an incentive for pharmaceutical innovation and the US industry's competitive position in the international market? Direct regulation of drug prices runs the risk of harming the industry without necessarily lowering drug expenditures. While price control policies could provide cheaper medications and reduce health expenditures in the short run, removal of the incentive to invest in R&D may retard innovation and drive up health care cost in the long run. Alternatives to pharmaceuticals, such as hospitalization and surgery, are much more costly than medication. As Lane calculated,

> There are more than 900,000 hospitalizations per year in the US for heart failure, at an average cost of approximately $10,500 per hospitalization. Medicare pays for 80% of these hospitalizations, but does not pay for a relatively inexpensive drug which has been shown to reduce such hospitalizations by 30% over a 3 ½ year period. We estimate that if this drug could be made available to all heart failure patients it could save as much as $1.4 billion per year. (Lane 1993)

Therefore, a controlled price system for drugs may lead to an increase in total drug expenditures because use of less effective drugs may increase. The

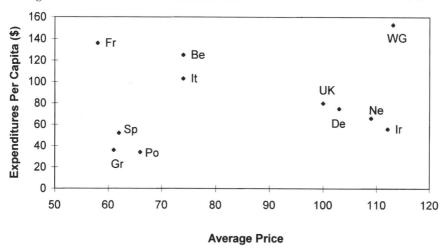

Figure 6.2 Pharmaceutical Expenditures and Prices in 11 European Countries, 1987. Source: Burstall ML, "European Policies Influencing Pharmaceutical Innovation," in Gelijns AC and Halm EA, ed., *The Changing Economics of Medical Technology*, Washington DC: National Academy Press, 1991.

French system of drug price controls produces some of the lowest drug prices in Europe, but pharmaceutical expenditures are extremely high in France—16% of total health expenditures, double the US proportion. This relationship is summarized in Figure 6.2 for eight European countries; France ranks eighth in general price level but second in total pharmaceutical expenditures. Another example is Canada, where government price controls over prescription drugs had little effect in containing total drug spending. Lowering US prices would erode the revenue base of pharmaceutical firms but may do little to reduce total expenditure (Dickson 1992). As the GAO reported,

> Prescription drugs compose a significant and increasing share of health care spending in Canada. In 1989, Canadians spent 3.9 billion Canadian dollars, or 6.0 percent of total health care expenditures, on prescription drugs. Expenditures on drugs have increased rapidly, growing at an inflation-adjusted annual rate of 10.6 percent between 1980 and 1989. (US GAO 1992)

As a result of the pharmaceutical industry's increasing long-term investment in research and development, it created 80,000 jobs in the United States between 1980 and 1991 while the overall manufacturing sector lost more than 1 million jobs (Mossinghoff 1993). It is one of the few high-technology industries in this country that has consistently maintained a positive balance of trade, and it has now accounted for over 62% of the new drugs introduced in the world market (Mossinghoff 1993). Price control policies may substantially reduce the industry's investment in R&D, which will greatly reduce its competitive capacity in global market. Again, Canada provides a useful lesson. The Canadian government's policies of price controls and compulsory licensing to generic manufacturers may have played a significant role in limiting Canada's innovative capacity in biomedical research and pharmaceutical product innovation (Neimeth 1993). As stated in the GAO report:

> In contrast to the United States, which has a large innovative drug industry, most of the innovative prescription drugs sold in Canada are supplied by foreign manufacturers. These manufacturers do little research and development in Canada. Canadian-owned drug manufacturers generally produce generic products that require little investment in research. As a result, R&D activities on prescription drugs, as a percentage of sales, are about half as high as in the United States: In 1990, 8.8 percent of pharmaceutical sales was spent on R&D in Canada, while approximately 17 percent of sales was spent in the United States. (US GAO 1992)

To the extent that US drug prices exceed those of other countries and the profits thereby generated stimulate additional R&D, a "free rider" problem appears with consumers throughout the world benefiting from R&D that is paid for, in effect, by US patients. From the perspective of any single foreign country, drug price controls may look attractive because each country's share in worldwide revenue is small, and a reduction would hardly alter the R&D investment plans of any company. However, to generalize from this and suggest that *all* countries that are net technology "importers" could benefit by forcing their prices down is an example of the fallacy of composition, in which a policy that would work for *one* member of a group would not work if it were applied to *all* members of the group. If non-US drug prices were significantly reduced, the effect on future R&D investment would be significant.

Lastly, lower prices in one market do not necessarily make consumers better off, and policy recommendations cannot be drawn from international price comparisons alone. International price differences exist in virtually every sector for a whole array of essential goods and services (Neithmeth 1993). These disparities reflect a variety of social, economic, historical, legal, and political conditions. Lower prices in a country may be attributed to its lower consumer demand, greater demand elasticity, lower labor costs, less sophisticated infrastructure producing such goods, or lower quality of goods produced. This last point characterizes many developing countries and countries of eastern Europe. These may not be the directions we would like public policy to direct us.

References

Danzon PM and Kim J, "International price comparisons for pharmaceuticals," Working Paper, Health Care systems Department, Wharton School, October, 1993.

Dickson M, "The pricing of pharmaceuticals: an international comparison," *Clinical Therapeutics* 14(4):604–10, 1992.

Dolan M and Roan S, "Court increases liability for side effects of drugs," *Los Angeles Times*, p. A1, August 31, 1996.

Eisenstodt G, "The doctor's margin," *Forbes*, November 23, 1992.

Gross DJ, Ratner J, Perez J, and Glavin SL, "International pharmaceutical spending controls: France, Germany Sweden, and the United Kingdom," *Health Care Financing Review* 15(3):127–140, 1994.

Lane RJ, "Testimony before the US House of Representatives, Subcommittee on Health and the Environment," February 22, 1993.

Manning RL, "Product liability and prescription drug prices in Canada and the United States," Working Draft, May 1994.

Mossinghoff GJ, "Statement before the US House of Representatives Subcommittee on Health and the Environment," February 22, 1993.

Neimeth R, "Testimony before the Subcommittee on Health and the Environment," February 22, 1993.

Payer L, *Medicine and Culture*, New York: Penguin Books, 1988.

Pharmacy Freedom Fund, *US citizens pay too much for prescriptions*, May 1990.

Reekie, DW, "Drug prices in the UK, USA, Europe and Australia," *Australian Economic Papers*, June 1984.

Rogoff K, "The purchasing power parity puzzle," *Journal of Economic Literature* 34(2): 647–668, 1996.

Salehi H and Schweitzer SO, "Economic aspects of drug substitution," *Health Care Financing Review* 5(3):59–68, Spring 1985.

Schut FT and Van Bergeijk PAG, "International price discrimination: the pharmaceutical industry," *World Development* 14:1141–1150, 1986.

Steiner RL, "The inverse association between the margins of manufacturers and retailers,"*Review of Industrial Organization* 8:717–740, 1993.

Szuba TJ, "International comparison of drug consumption: impact of prices," *Social Science and Medicine* 22:1019–1025, 1986.

US Department of Health and Human Services, Office of Inspector General, *Strategies to Reduce Medicaid Drug Expenditures*, 1990.

US General Accounting Office, *Prescription Drugs: Companies Typically Charge More in the United States than in Canada*," Report to the Chairman, US House of Representatives Subcommittee on Health and the Environment, Committee on Energy and Commerce, House of Representatives, September, 1992.

US General Accounting Office, *Prescription Drugs: Companies Typically Charge More in the United States than in the United Kingdom*," Report to the Chairman, Subcommittee on Health and the Environment, Committee on Energy and Commerce, House of Representatives, January, 1994.

US House of Representatives Subcommittee on Health and the Environment, *International Prescription Drug Prices*, Hearing Report, serial No. 103–18, US Government Printing Office: Washington, February 22, 1993.

Zwanziger J and Melnick GA, "The effects of hospital competition and Medicare PPS program on hospital cost behavior in California," *Journal of Health Economics* 7:301, 1988.

7

The Timing of Drug Approvals in the United States and Abroad

The timing of new drug approvals has important implications for a nation's overall health status, health expenditures, and social equity, and understanding the international diffusion of new pharmaceuticals is important, because the market for pharmaceuticals is so international, as was noted in Chapter 5. This trend toward multinational ownership of pharmaceutical firms and their worldwide R&D and sales efforts has accelerated with the formation of multinational trade blocs in both North America (the North American Free Trade Association—NAFTA) and Europe (the European Union—EU); in all likelihood similar blocs in Southeast Asia and South America will form.

The drug approval process in any country involves a balancing of conflicting social objectives: safety and access. Thus the approval process in any country will inevitably be criticized by those who would like to shift priorities one way or the other.

The United States has a widely respected but stringent review process overseen by the FDA. The FDA sets out guidelines for basic research and animal testing that must be met before human tests can begin. Once human tests are allowed, they take place in progressively larger phases so that dangerous products will be recognized before large numbers of subjects are exposed. The process has worked well, generally, but criticism of the delay has led to numerous reforms that seem to be effective in reducing the approval time.

There is also concern that the regulatory delays in the United States put

American patients at risk relative to those in other countries. A number of researchers have asked whether or not the United States suffers from a "drug lag." While some studies claim that there *is* such a lag, new research has found that *every* country experiences lags in approving important drugs, and the United States is relatively quick, compared to other major countries.

The Timing of Pharmaceutical Approvals and Health Policy

The timing of the approval of new pharmaceuticals in the United States is actually the result of two timing decisions—when the pharmacutical developer files a new drug's approval application and the length of the review process. Firms in any country would like reviews to be completed as quickly as possible in every market, and large markets are financially more important to firms than are small ones. But there are strategic considerations, because industry leaders know which countries have particularly stringent review processes, which have lenient ones, and which countries are dependent upon other countries to indicate an acceptable drug. Countries with a rigorous approval process require more lengthy testing and documentation, which slows down the preapplication testing process and, of course, delays the filing of the approval application. The two events, filing an approval application and approving a drug, are not entirely independent events: Firms will delay filing in a stringent country until absolutely all the evidence is in and can be presented. Firms may even wait intentionally until a drug has been in use successfully in another country before filing in the stringent country.

The approval of new pharmaceuticals by a country's regulatory authority involves a balancing of two conflicting objectives: assuring the population access to the latest therapeutic agents available while protecting patients from the risk of dangerous products. The two goals conflict because speeding access inevitably entails allowing approval of some drugs which turn out to be harmful. On the other hand, avoiding any drugs that might be dangerous would slow access to drugs which are later found to be safe and effective. This balancing is accomplished in the United States with a drug approval process that explicitly values both safety and efficacy. The process can be stopped at any point if findings suggest either lack of safety or efficacy. The FDA's recent interest in expanding postmarketing surveillance, which allows a new drug to be marketed while the medical community is alerted to watch for signs of harm caused by the drug, is an attempt to shift the balance toward access while accepting greater risk.

Underlying the approval dilemma is the existence of uncertainty as to a drug's true benefit and risk.

Ideally, each country will adopt those drugs whose benefit/risk profile is favorable relative to its preference for access and risk. But errors are inevitably made, and "bad" drugs are occasionally approved* and "good" drugs

---

*If one considers the approval process to be a screening "test," with a "positive" finding representing appearance of a problem and a "negative" test implying no problem, approval of a

sometimes are not. Errors of the former kind may result in recalls and with-drawals, while errors of the latter type result in frustration on the part of physicians and add fuel to the political desire to reduce the FDA's authority.

One would expect countries to be internally consistent in the speed of their approval process depending upon their relative preference for safety and access. Countries particularly risk averse, for example, would be expected to be slow in approving new drugs, waiting to learn of other countries' experiences. These countries would lag behind countries which tended to favor access. A nation's preference of safety over access may vary over time, but one would expect to observe consistent patterns of lags across countries, with some countries tending to lead in the approval "race," while others follow behind. The importance of a drug enters into the timing decision because of the expected benefit which such a drug may confer upon the population. Especially important drugs will be expected to produce greater benefit, for a given level of risk, than drugs which follow on, or mimic, others. The approval process may be inconsistent in the case of unimportant, "me, too," drugs. On the one hand, approval might come quickly because the more closely they are related to existing drugs, the less new risk they pose. On the other hand, the closer they are to existing drugs, the less benefit they will confer, and the less pressure there is to approve them rapidly. For important drugs, however, one would expect much more consistency in the relative approval times between countries, with corresponding leads or lags dependent upon countries' relative balance between acceptance of risk and benefit.

The Drug Approval Process in the United States

In the United States, upon completion of toxicological and safety testing in animals, drug companies are required to file an Investigational New Drug (IND) application with the FDA prior to any human testing. An IND ap-plication contains the drug sponsor's research plans, details of of manufac-turing processes, and the results of laboratory and animal tests-to-date. The "Clinical Section" contains a detailed description, or protocol, of the ini-tially planned clinical trials and a general overview of the studies that will follow. The "Manufacturing Section" describes the facilities, equipment, and techniques the sponsor will use to produce the drug (US Congress, OTA 1993).

Unless the FDA disapproves the IND application within a 30-day period, it is automatically approved and clinical tests can begin. For administrative purposes and as a means of prioritizing its work, the FDA rates each drug for which an IND is received according to the drug's novelty and the agency's subjective judgment of the drug's therapeutic potential. Until 1992,

bad drug is a false-negative result while denying a good drug is a false-positive. This analysis is more thoroughly developed in Intriligator (1996).

the FDA used a five-category rating system of therapeutic importance: "A" for important therapeutic gain; "B" for modest therapeutic gain; "C" for little or no therapeutic gain; "AA" for AIDS designation; and "V" for a designated orphan drug (described later in this chapter). Beginning in 1992 the rating scheme was changed to include only two categories, "P" (Priority) for the most important drugs, and "S" (Standard) for all other drugs.

Phase I Trials

Phase I studies are small trials, usually involving only healthy volunteers, conducted to assess safety, to see how the body absorbs and eliminates a drug, and to document the response it produces* Both clinicians, and statisticians are instrumental in deciding how many patients are necessary for the clinical tests, the length of time that each testing stage will require, the specific information that will have to be developed to prove efficacy for the compound, the likelihood that such information can be developed, and the overall and yearly expenditure estimates for the project (Wiggins 1981).

After the Phase I trials the drug company must decide whether to continue with the project. Based on information accumulated until this point, the company tries to determine whether the product is of sufficient quality to warrant the investment of the necessary resources to market the product. In addition, the company will try to estimate the manufacturing costs of the drug (Faust 1971). This will often be the first attempt to estimate these costs because it is the first stage in which an accurate description of the actual drug product is available.

Phase II Trials

In phase II trials the drug is administered to a larger number of individuals, usually up to several hundred subjects. Various doses of the drug are compared so that the large phase III trials can then test what has proven to be the most successful dosage. The groups selected consist of patients who the drug is intended to benefit. Under the 1962 FDA Amendments, substantial evidence of efficacy in the intended use of the drug is required before marketing approval can be granted. The FDA does not specify the trial design, but the design that is most likely to show a significant effect of the drug compares it to an inert substance, a placebo. Although studies comparing the experimental drug to other drugs on the market are possible, they entail more risk for the sponsor (for example, if the experimental drug is less effective than the other drug), and without a placebo control group, efficacy will *still* not be determined. This is why most FDA trials are limited to the experimental drug compared to a placebo. Most studies also are "blind" to reduce the likelihood of bias. A study is "single blind" if the patient does

*For cancer drugs, however, phase I trials involve cancer patients, not healthy individuals.

not know whether he or she is receiving the active drug or the placebo. A study is "double blind" if even the investigator does not know which patients are receiving the experimental drug. Most clinical trials are randomized double-blind experimental-placebo studies.

When successful, phase II trials usually provide the first significant evidence of efficacy. Additional safety data is also obtained during this phase and usually through concurrent animal studies.

During a phase II trial, corporate management will ponder detailed information consisting of the drug's expected manufacturing cost, price, expected sales at different prices, estimated length of time to reach market, and development costs likely to be incurred through the marketing stage (Wiggins 1981). This updated information is used to make better decisions about whether a drug should be a candidate for further testing or should be dropped.

Phase III Trials

The third, and final, premarketing clinical development phase involves large-scale controlled clinical trials of a drug's safety and effectiveness in hospital and outpatient settings at the dose and by the route which will subsequently be marketed. The larger sample sizes, ranging from several hundred to several thousand patients, increase the likelihood that actual benefits will be found to be statistically significant. Phase III studies gather precise information on the drug's effectiveness for specific indications, determine whether the drug produces a broader range and severity of adverse effects than those exhibited in the smaller study populations of phase I and phase II studies. This information forms the basis for deciding on the content of the product label and package insert if the drug is approved (US Congress, OTA 1993).

New Drug Application

The FDA has two subagencies which regulate and monitor the pharmaceutical research process: the Center for Drug Evaluation and Research (CDER) and the Center for Biologics Evaluation and Research (CBER). Drug sponsors seeking marketing approval for a new chemical, antibiotic, hormone, or enzyme drug product file a New Drug Application (NDA) with CDER. Biotechnological drug products and vaccines must file two applications with CBER, a product license application (PLA) covering the drug and an establishment license application (ELA) covering the facilities manufacturing the product.

The CDER has 60 days from the date a company submits an NDA to decide if it contains sufficient information for the agency to conduct a substantive review. The process of review is carried out by the Review Division and the results are given to the division director. If there are any disagreements concerning the strength of scientific evidence on the drug, the NDA moves up one level to the office director for more consideration. If disagreement continues, the director of CDER will review the application and proposed FDA decision (USDHHS 1990).

Once the agency reaches agreement, the Review Division director sends a letter to the company explaining the decision. The FDA's Approval Letter can either approve the product for market or declare that the agency would approve the drug once the company addresses concerns about its effectiveness or safety (called an "Approvable Letter"). Alternatively, the letter can state that the drug is "unapprovable" (US Congress, OTA 1993). The company has 10 days to respond to either an approvable or unapprovable letter, providing information regarding its attempt to correct the problem(s) stated in the FDA letter. If the sponsor does not respond within 10 days, the FDA automatically withdraws the NDA (21 C.F.R. sec 314.105). Most NDAs require at least one such amendment by the company, and a recent analysis by CDER revealed that for the 68 NDAs for new molecular entities submitted to the FDA in 1984 and 1985, the sponsoring companies had filed a combined total of 1,141 amendments (Uzzell and Meyer 1990).

By law the FDA must complete its review of an NDA within 180 days, although with each amendment, an additional 180 days are granted (21 C.F.R. sec 314.60). Even with the extensions, however, actual review time exceeds the statutory allowances. Data from the FDA indicates that the 23 NDAs for new molecular entities approved in 1990 took an average of 30 months to approve (USDHHS 1990).

The CBER review process for new products is similar to that of the CDER, although more emphasis is placed on the safety and quality of the processes and facilities used to produce a biological drug. Also in contrast to the CDER's NDA review process, there are no statutory limits on the amount of time CBER reviewers may take to complete their review of PLAs and ELAs (US Congress, OTA 1993).

Postapproval Research

Federal regulation requires manufacturers selling drugs in the United States to notify the FDA periodically about the performance of their products. This surveillance is designed to detect uncommon, yet serious, adverse reactions typically not revealed during premarketing testing. This is sometimes referred to as *phase IV*. Most postapproval studies are less than a year in length and involve relatively small numbers of subjects. In some cases postapproval monitoring is especially important because phase III trials were purposely made smaller or more brief than normal. This is done frequently in the case of HIV/AIDS drugs, for instance, because of the urgency of the medical problem. These additional studies usually include usage in children and drug interactions (US Congress, OTA 1993).

Recent Initiatives to Expedite Drug Approvals

The regulatory process described above is often criticized by the pharmaceutical industry as being unduly stringent and excessively lengthy, and it is commonly cited as a major cause of the increased costs associated with drug R&D. The time between an IND application and an NDA filing rose from 2.5 years in the 1960s to nearly 6 years by 1980. And the time from synthesis of a compound to an NDA approval rose from 8 to 15 years during the same period (DiMasi et al. 1994). Pressure to speed the FDA's review process also comes from organized patient groups, such as people with HIV/AIDS. They frequently point out that for rapidly progressing, terminal conditions the risk of an inadvertent approval of a "bad" drug has less significance, and the weighing of risks should favor access far more than it generally does.

In response, the White House Council on Competitiveness and the FDA proposed several initiatives aimed at reducing the time required to move a drug from clinical testing through marketing approval. Under these proposals: (1) drug sponsors could begin phase I clinical testing without receiving IND status from the FDA. Instead, Institutional Review Boards (IRBs) at hospitals or other medical institutions that administer the trials would review and monitor them; (2) the FDA could approve drugs for life-threatening diseases for which no alternative therapy exists on the basis of limited evidence of safety and efficacy. Sponsors could collect and provide the full complement of such evidence after the drug is approved; (3) the FDA could contract with outside experts in academia and other institutions to review pieces of NDAs in which the FDA expects little scientific controversy; (4) the FDA would look to foreign drug approval systems with sufficient high standards to warrant US approval on the basis of an approval in these other countries (Stanley 1981, US Congress, OTA 1993). Accelerated regulatory approval is intended to reduce the mean approval time by the FDA by 45%, to 5.5 years. Accelerated approval would put a greater emphasis on postmarketing surveillance while decreasing the time of phase III studies and the NDA process (McKercher 1992). Some of these proposals have been implemented.

The FDA has issued new rulings allowing for earlier access to INDs for patients with "life-threatening" or "serious" illnesses. In addition, the FDA is currently exploring the potential for some international "harmonization" of drug approval standards in talks with other countries (*Scrip World Pharmaceutical News* 1991). These and other efforts to streamline the review process appear to have had some success. The FDA approved 28 new molecular entities (NMEs) in 1995, an encouraging increase from its 22 approvals in 1994. The mean approval time for the approvals in 1994 was only 13 months, while for the 22 drugs approved in 1984 approval took nearly 20 months (Scherer 1996).

Another initiative approved by Congress in 1992 was the imposition of user fees to be paid by pharmaceutical sponsors for the review of their drug marketing applications (Public Law 102–571). This may allow the agency to increase resources devoted to approval review in order to shorten regulatory review times. Fees began at $100,000 for each NDA or PLA/ELA and are scheduled to rise to $233,000 over a 5-year period.

Is There a US Drug Lag?

Whether or not the United States lags behind other countries to an unacceptable degree is an important political issue, and concern that the United States consistently approves drugs later than other countries frequently leads to criticism of the FDA. Although the literature on delays in drug availability in the United States relative to other countries is large, it is unfortunately contradictory (Anderson 1992a). There is wide variation in methodology across studies and even definitions of measures of access to new pharmaceuticals differ from one study to another. Furthermore, the definition of which pharmaceuticals to include in the comparative studies lacks uniformity, and the sample of drugs in many of the studies is not well designed to answer the questions posed. The question of changing access over time has been a major policy focus of many international studies, but time periods vary across the studies, and many cover only a narrow span of time.

Most international studies have compared drug approvals in the United States to those in the United Kingdom. Wardell first asked whether the United States had a drug lag; he analyzed the approval of every drug eventually approved by the United States or the United Kingdom from 1962 to 1971 (Wardell 1973). He then updated the study to include drugs approved through 1976 (Wardell 1978). These studies found that drug approvals in the United States did lag behind those in the United Kingdom and that the situation had worsened in the later period. Wardell looked both at the failure of one country to (ever) approve a drug that the other had approved and at the delay in one country's approval relative to that of the other. Andersson has defined the former as the "absolute" drug lag and the latter as the "relative" drug lag (Andersson 1992a). Others have also found evidence to support Wardell's original finding of a US drug lag (Grabowski and Vernon 1977; Grabowski 1980; Berlin and Jonsson 1986; Kaitin 1989; Kaitin et al. 1989; Burstall 1991). Additionally, Grabowski and Vernon (1977) and Grabowski (1980) found the lag to be increasing over time. But the Grabowski study looked at all drugs introduced in the United States and the Grabowski and Vernon study looked only at drugs discovered in United States. Consideration of all drugs ever introduced merges both important and unimportant drugs and fails to distinguish between different lag patterns for the two types of products. But considering only US discoveries is overly restrictive for an industry as multinational as pharmaceuticals, where both research and marketing are international activities of all major firms, and many important drugs are developed by foreign drug companies.

Simmons suggested that the apparent US lag could be explained by the inclusion in the analysis of unimportant drugs, which were not as readily available in the United States (Simmons 1974). Coppinger *et al.* (1989) also criticized the finding of a US drug lag and showed that when discontinued drugs were omitted from the study, together with introductions of unimportant drugs and those that took place prior to 1977, the United States no longer appeared to have a drug lag relative to the United Kingdom. Parker (1989) found evidence of a drug lag in the United States but observed that it had declined over time. Parker's analysis, however, included all drugs that were introduced from 1970 to 1983, and measurement of lags based upon *all* drugs approved by a country might be biased upward because drugs that are related to existing products (so-called "me, too" drugs) may find earlier approval because much of the premarket testing has already been done. Andersson (1992b) looked at approval times in seven industrialized countries but considered all 553 drugs introduced in Sweden between 1960 and 1987. The study found that the United Kingdom and West Germany had been quicker in approving new drugs; the United States, Sweden, France, Italy, and Norway lagged. But because the study considers such a large number of products, including unimportant as well as important drugs, it is difficult to interpret the significance of the findings.

Several authors have attempted to restrict their analyses to important drugs, recognizing that limited access to drugs without substantial therapeutic impact does not impose the same kind of hardship upon patients as it would for more innovative drugs. DeHaen (1975) discusses "major" drugs but does not define the term. He analyzed the absolute drug lag for five countries over a short time period (1967–1973) and concluded that all countries show lags behind one another, and the United States is not alone in restricting access to new pharmaceuticals. In Parker's multinational study of drug approvals, he considered only drugs that were approved in at least three countries out of his 18-country sample, suggesting that approval by multiple countries validates a drug's importance (Parker 1984). This is also the approach taken by Berlin and Jonsson (1986) and by Andersson (1992b), who refer to "consensus" in their studies of absolute drug lag. But a drug's approval by many countries in a sample is not necessarily an indication that it is important. It may merely mean that there is consensus as to its safety and efficacy. In fact, if drug approvals *were* correlated with importance, studies of the absolute drug lag would be meaningless because drugs that were not eventually widely approved would be, by definition, unimportant! Hass (1983) approached the question of importance by considering top-selling drugs for inclusion in his study of drug approvals by 11 industrialized countries. But sales is an incomplete proxy for importance, because drugs that are not approved for marketing in major markets (such as the United States)

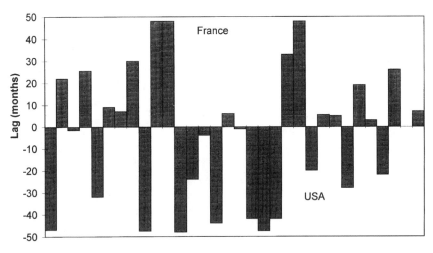

Figure 7.1 Approval Delays: France and the United States (in months). Source: Schweitzer, SO (1996).

will find their worldwide sales reduced, together with their apparent importance.

The analysis of the timing of drug approvals also illustrates important differences between the drug approval systems used in various countries. FDA approval identifies a drug as safe and effective and allows it to be marketed in the United States. But in other countries the process is more complex. In France, for example, the cost of prescribed drugs is reimbursed by the Social Security system and so the approval and marketing decisions are separated Weintraub (1982). The Commission d'autorisation de mise sur le marche (AMM) conducts the scientific review, analogous to that of the United States FDA. The approved drug's dossier then goes to the Commission de la Transparence, which conducts a joint clinical and economic assessment. The product will be covered by Social Security only after this commission has determined the price and level of reimbursement. Approval by the Commission de la Transparence, therefore, determines the date at which a new product can be effectively marketed.

Figure 7.1 shows the lag in approval (in months) for 32 drugs which were found to have been particularly important at the time of their introduction in both France and the United States by panels of physicians and pharmacists in each country (Schweitzer 1996). Bars above the line indicate an earlier French approval (a positive United States lag), while those below signify an earlier US approval (a negative US lag). The drugs are shown chronologically, in order of US approval.

The distribution of the lags appears strikingly random, with both countries having many—and frequently very long—lags. The United States approved 16 drugs first and France approved 15 first. There was one tie. Four of the American approvals occurred more than 48 months after the approval by France, and three of the French approvals were delayed as much. Furthermore, these delayed approvals for the United States were very long, with three lags greater than 90 months, and one of them greater than 100 months. The mean of the US lags was 42.2 months (SE = 34.2); it was only 25.4 months for France (SE = 22.0).

An approach for analysis of the timing of drug approvals is continued in work by Schweitzer et al. (1985), Grabowski (1988), and Grabowski et al. (1992) on differences within the US market. These papers studied lags in access to new pharmaceuticals for Medicaid recipients in states with drug formularies and found wide variation in access by state. They quantify the lag by constructing an index of a product's availability during an initial 4-year marketing period beginning after the drug is first approved by one state. This 4-year period is arbitrary but represents the idea that a drug's real contribution will be made during its first 4 years of use. After this time other drugs or treatments are likely to be introduced which will supplant it. This is a useful approach which may be "exported" to study of the United States international drug lag.

Additional analysis of approvals was done by considering the 4-year initial marketing period—the approach used previously to study access to new drugs in state Medicaid programs. The proportion of this 4-year period during which a new drug was available in each country is a meaningful measure of its accessibility in each lagging country because it emphasizes the period of time during which the drug was especially new and had the fewest competitors. The proportion of accessibility during this 48-month period for each drug is termed the Drug Availability Index (DAI) and ranges from 0.00 (implying that a drug was not approved within 4 years of its approval in the lead country) to 1.00 (for the leading country). Analysis of the DAI between the United States and France shows that France is slightly quicker in approving drugs than is the United States (Schweitzer 1996). The mean DAI for all drugs for France was 0.77 (SE = 0.33), and was 0.67 (SE = 0.41) for the United States. We note that the difference between each country's DAI is less pronounced than the difference between the mean lags measured in months because the DAI truncates the lags at 48 months. Neither of the differences is significant at the P = 0.05 level.

The frequency distributions of the lag times are similar for the United States and France, implying that each country has frequent and substantial approval lags. This observation is consistent with the observation made by DeHaen that all countries have drug lags.

A multiple regression analysis was performed to see if the US DAI could be explained by the simultaneous effect of each drug's therapeutic class (cardiac, digestive system, etc.), time, and the initial FDA rating of the drug's innovativeness given by the FDA at the beginning of the review process. One might expect the rating to predict speed of approval if the FDA were

Table 7.1   Average Monthly Approval
Lag by Country

Country	Lag (months)
Canada	65.35
France	42.62
Germany	72.24
Italy	69.22
Japan	64.00
Switzerland	28.35
United States	50.53
United Kingdom	61.53

to concentrate its resources on those drugs which held the promise of bringing especially large clinical benefits. The multivariate analysis explains a very
small proportion of the variation in US DAI, however, indicating that neither therapeutic classification, nor FDA designation, nor time explains the
US DAI with respect to France.

There is no consistent evidence that the drug approval process in the
United States is slower than that of France. Although the average lag for
US approvals, measured in months, is longer than it is for France, the proportion of time during the initial marketing period which new drugs are
available, measured by the Drug Availability Index, is not significantly higher
for the United States than for France. Furthermore, the data suggests that
the US approval process may have improved during the 1980s relative to
that of France, but the number of important drugs approved in this later
period is small, so the change is not statistically significant. Contrary to our
initial hypotheses, US approval was not quicker than that of France for drugs
that the FDA had designated as especially innovative, nor was it faster for
cardiovascular drugs, in spite of public attention to heart disease as this nation's leading cause of death. This finding is consistent with Andersson
(1992a), who also found approval times to be unrelated to a drug's therapeutic class or the FDA rating of therapeutic innovativeness.

A study of the timing of important new drug approvals by the G-7 countries plus Switzerland (those countries listed in Table 7.1) found similarly
large variation in approval times across country (Schweitzer et al. 1996). The
sample of drugs included in this study was somewhat expanded from the
earlier France–US comparison to include 34 drugs, based as before on con-
currence between the French and American panels of physicians and pharmacists. The average monthly lag for each country is shown in Table 7.1.

Switzerland had the fastest approvals, on average, followed by France and the United States, while Italy and Germany were the slowest of the countries studied. In spite of the apparently large differences between some of the countries, the variance of the lag was so large for each country that the differences were not generally statistically significant. Consistent with previous findings, the approval lags for all countries varied greatly. And equally importantly, all countries had long lags in approving many of the important drugs. Even in Switzerland, which had the overall earliest approvals, the average approval was over 2 years later than the approval by the first country in the sample. This analysis is not helpful understanding the speed of the drug approval process in countries with similar review mechanisms and criteria, for the wide variation in timing of drug approvals is left unexplained. The variation is especially surprising when one realizes that all the drugs studied are thought to have been important at the time the approval decisions were made.

There are many reasons why a country may lag behind another in approving new drugs. One reason is that pharmaceutical companies may be slow in filing for approval in a particular country. Often this is due to the strategy of waiting until additional data is available before starting an application process that is expected to be especially rigorous. If firms delay the application because of a perceived need to compile a more complete dossier in one country than is required in another, resulting lags are indicative of different societal preferences regarding access and risk between countries. Nonetheless, these lags ought to be consistent across drugs. The inconsistent pattern of lags evident from the various studies suggests that the approval process in many countries, including the United States, is not due to differences in social preferences, but is due to variation in the approval process itself.

This variation in delay for new important drug approvals is so large that it is possible that patients are frequently denied useful therapies. Whether this is the case depends upon the likelihood of decision errors (i.e., dangerous drugs being approved, or beneficial drugs being denied approval). A case study approach directed at these decision errors is undoubtedly a useful line of future inquiry.

One approach for improving the efficiency of the FDA might be for it to consider expanding its fast-track approval system, currently applied to HIV/AIDS drugs, to apply to all drugs thought to be therapeutically important, even if this implies greater delays for approvals of less important drugs. Of course, the success of this strategy is contingent upon improving the agency's ability to forecast drug importance.

References

Anderson F, "The drug lag issue: the debate seen from an international perspective," *International Journal of Health Services* 22:53–72, 1992a.

Andersson F, "The international diffusion of new drugs: a comparative study of seven industrialized countries," *Journal of Research in Pharmaceutical Economics* 4(2): 43–62, 1992b.

Berlin H and Jonsson B, "International dissemination of new drugs: a comparative study of six countries," *Managerial and Decision Economics* 7:235–242, 1986

Burstall ML, "Europe after 1992: implications for pharmaceuticals," *Health Affairs* 10(3): 157–171, Fall 1991

Coppinger PL, Peck CC, and Temple RJ, "Understanding comparisons of drug introductions between the United States and the United Kingdom," *Clinical Pharmacology and Therapeutics* 46: 139–145, 1989.

DeHaen P, "The drug lag—does it exist in Europe?" *Drug Intelligence and Clinical Pharmacy* 9: 144–150, 1975.

DiMasi JA, Seibring FM, and Lasagna L, "New drug development in the United States from 1963 to 1992," *Clinical Pharmacology and Therapeutics* 55: 15, June 1994.

Faust R, "Project selection in the pharmaceutical industry," *Research Management* 14: 46–55, 1971

Grabowski HG, "Regulation and the international diffusion of pharmaceuticals," in Helms RB (ed), *The International Supply of Medicines: Implications of U.S. Regulatory Reform*, Washington, DC; American Enterprise Institute for Public Policy Research, pp 5–36, 1980.

Grabowski HG, "Medicaid patients' access to new drugs," *Health Affairs* 7 (5): 102–114, 1988.

Grabowski HG, Schweitzer SO, and Shiota R, "The effect of medicaid formularies on the availability of new drugs," *PharmacoEconomics*, 1 (suppl): 32–40, 1992.

Grabowski HG and Vernon JM, "Innovation and invention—consumer protection regulation in ethical drugs," *American Economic Review* 67: 359–364, 1977

Hass AE Jr, "Where drug marketing patterns are similar," *Medical Marketing and Media* 18: 78–83, 1983.

Intriligator MD, "Drug evaluations: type I vs. type II errors," Paper presented before the UCLA Seminar in Pharmaceutical Economics and Policy, Working Paper #96–2, unpublished, 1996.

Kaitin K, "Reply to 'understanding comparisons of drug introductions between the United States and the United Kingdom," *Clinical Pharmacological Therapeutics* 46: 146–148, 1989

Kaitin K, Mathison N, and Worthington FK "The drug lag: an update of new drug introductions in the United States and in the United Kingdom, 1977 through 1987," *Clinical Pharmacology and Therapeutics* 4:121–138, 1989.

McKercher PL, "Issues in health policy: pharmaceutical research and development," *Clinical Therapeutics* 14(5): 760–764, 1992.

Parker JES, *The International Diffusion of Pharmaceuticals*, London: Macmillan, 1984.

Parker JES, "Who has a lag?" *Managerial and Decision Economics* 10: 299–309, 1989.

Scherer FM, *Industry Structure, Strategy, and Public Policy*, New York: HarperCollins, 1996.

Schweitzer SO, "An international comparison of timing of the approval of new drugs," in Heller O and Geisler E (eds.), *Managing Technology in Healthcare*, Boston: Kluwer, 1996.

Schweitzer SO, Salehi H, and Boling N, "The social drug lag," *Social Science and Medicine* 21(10): 1077–1082, 1985.

Schweitzer SO, Schweitzer ME, and Sourty-LeGuellec M-J, "Is there a United States drug lag? The timing of new pharmaceutical approvals in the G-7 countries and Switzerland," *Medical Care Research and Review* 53(2): 162–78 1996

Scrip World Pharmaceutical News, "FDA reforms include recognition of non-U.S. approvals," *Scrip World Pharmacetuical News* 1670: 19, 1991.

Simmons HE, "The drug regulatory system of the United States Food and Drug Administration: a defense of current requirements for safety and efficacy," *International Journal of Health Services* 4: 95–107, 1974.

Stanley GR, "Use of foreign data in a new drug application," *Food Drug Cosmetic Law Journal* 36:340–344, 1981.

US Congress, Office of Technology Assessment, *Pharmaceutical R&D: Costs, Risks, and Rewards*, Washington, DC: US Government Printing Office, 1993.

US Department of Health and Human Services, Public Health Services, Food and Drug Administration, *From Test Tube to Patient: New Drug Development in the U.S., and FDA Consumer Special Report*, DHHS Pub. No. (FDA) 90–3168, Washington, DC: US Government Printingk Office, 1990.

Uzzell JK and Meyer GF, "Learning lessons at the school of NDA submissions," *Pharmaceutical Executive* 10(6): 82–86, 1990.

Wardell WM, "Introduction of new therapeutic drugs in the United States and Great Britain: an international comparison," *Clinical Pharmacology and Therapeutics* 14:773–790, 1973.

Wardell WM, "The drug lag revisited: comparison by therapeutic area of patterns of drugs marketed in the United States and Great Britain from 1972 through 1976," *Clinical Pharmacology and Therapeutics* 1978. 24:499–524, 1978.

Weintraub M, "The French drug approval process," *Journal of Clinical Pharmacology* 22(5,6): 213–222, May–June 1982.

Wiggins SN, "Product quality regulation and new drug introductions: some new evidence from the 1970s," *The Review of Economics and Statistics* 63(4): 615–619, 1981.

IV

INTERVENTION IN THE PHARMACEUTICAL MARKET: PUBLIC AND PRIVATE

8

Pharmaceutical Regulation and Cost Containment

The US health care system is an amalgamation of public and private sectors. The public sector is responsible for determining which new drugs will be approved for use in the United States, but in recent years, both the public and private sectors have established programs to contain the cost of pharmaceuticals in an attempt to curtail rising health care costs. In many cases these programs affect the adoption of new products. The public sector has used a combination of fee restrictions and prospective reimbursement to contain costs for the Medicare, Medicaid, and Veterans Administration programs. The most powerful development in the private health care market has been the dramatic shift toward managed care, in which an enrolled population receives health care for a prepaid fee, and the organization uses administrative techniques to control utilization rates, cost, and quality of care. Both public and private health care sectors have used similar programs to contain costs of pharmaceuticals for their members. These include negotiated manufacturer discounts and rebates, the use of formularies to limit the types of drugs that a physician can prescribe and a pharmacist can dispense, the use of generic and therapeutic substitutions in place of more costly brand-name drugs, drug utilization review committees, and physician information and education programs. Increasingly, private health care organizations have begun to rely on pharmacy benefit management (PBM) programs, not only to implement cost-containment programs but also to educate physicians and monitor their prescribing patterns. Therefore, while marketing approval for new drugs must come from the Food and Drug Administration (FDA), it is largely through health delivery and financing programs in the public and private sectors that decisions are made as to whether or not a drug will be purchased.

This chapter begins with a brief history of the FDA's evolving role in the regulation of the pharmaceutical industry. The agency's powers have grown since its creation in 1938, occasionally in response to major drug-related catastrophies. Pharmaceutical manufacturers must present evidence to the FDA that their new drugs are both safe and effective in treating a particular disease or condition. However, drug companies are not required to prove that their drug is *better* than other similar drugs to obtain FDA approval, nor do they have to prove that the drug is more cost-effective than other similar drugs already on the market. Individual physicians are left to assess alternative therapies, and both public and private health care organizations develop their own programs to evaluate the relative merits of prescribed drugs as well as introduce cost containment mechanisms into their practices.

The chapter continues with a discussion of programs designed to control the cost of pharmaceuticals in both the public and private sectors. The most prevalent pharmaceutical cost-containment programs involve:

- Negotiating manufacturer discounts and rebates
- Using formularies to limit the types of drugs that a physician can prescribe and a pharmacist can dispense
- Using generic and therapeutic substitution in place of more costly brand-name drugs
- Creating drug utilization review committees
- Establishing physician information and education programs.

The final section in this chapter describes the evolution of managed care within the private health care industry. Increasingly, health care organizations have begun to rely on pharmacy benefit managers not only to implement these cost-containment strategies but also to establish disease-state management programs in which patients with chronic diseases are educated and monitored in the use of their medications and other therapies so as to improve quality of care while reducing drug program costs.

The Evolution of the FDA

Authority over access to medication has been hotly contested for more than 150 years. The American Medical Association (AMA) has consistently fought the "patent medicine" business throughout this period. Early on it divided drugs into "ethical" preparations of known composition advertised only to the profession and "patent" medicines of secret composition sold directly to the public. Although the AMA rejected as unethical any secret formula marketed directly to the public, it was powerless to enforce these views. In 1849 the association resolved to create a board to evaluate these tonics but proved unable to do so for lack of resources (Starr 1982).

According to Starr (1982), between 1900 and 1910 three factors enabled the medical profession to gain control of the flow of pharmaceutical information. First, journalists and other progressives joined physicians in a crusade for regulation of patent medicines as part of a more general assault on deceptive business practices. Second, as a result of its growing membership, the AMA finally acquired the financial resources to create its own regulatory apparatus and to mount a major effort against the nostrum makers. And, third, the drugmakers were forced to recognize that they were increasingly dependent on doctors to market their drugs because of the public's increased reliance on professional opinion regarding decisions about medications.

In 1905, after closing its journal (now called *JAMA*) to patent medicine advertisements, the AMA established a Council on Pharmacy and Chemistry to set standards for drugs, evaluate them, and lead the battle against nostrums. A year later, Congress passed the Pure Food and Drug Act of 1906. Although this Act marked the official beginning of federal drug regulation, it affected only the most flagrant of fakes. It did not require the disclosure of all contents, except in the case of narcotics, and it only banned statements on the label of a drug about its composition that were "false and fraudulent." This rule did not initially apply to claims about the effectiveness of drugs, nor to statements made in newspaper advertisements. After some initial caution, drugmakers discovered they could resume making bold claims, even intimating that their drugs now met a federal standard of purity and effectiveness (Starr 1982).

Neither federal regulation nor the AMA prevented proprietary drug companies from marketing drugs to the public; nor did they bar people from self-treatment. In 1912, the federal law was amended to cover fraudulent claims of effectiveness and was administratively extended in the 1920s to cover newspaper advertising as well as labels. Unfortunately, these regulatory efforts continued to be blunted by the patent medicine industry for the next two decades. In 1938, The Food, Drug, and Cosmetic (FD&C) Act was signed into law, after harsh public reaction to the death of 107 people who, unsuspectingly, drank a toxic solution marketed as Elixir Sulfanilamide (Silverman and Lee 1974). The Act created a new regulatory agency—the Food and Drug Administration (FDA).

Although the 1938 law did not incorporate all the new authority that proponents of the FDA had wanted, it did provide the agency with important new powers. The regulations against false advertising were stiffened, appropriate warnings had to be included in the labeling, excessively dangerous drugs were banned, enforcement procedures were strengthened, and penalties for violations were made more severe. Of particular importance, no new product could be put on the market until the manufacturer presented convincing evidence to the FDA that it was relatively safe.

The Food, Drug, and Cosmetic Act was next amended in 1962. Once again, it took a tragedy to increase the regulatory powers of the FDA. In 1958, a German firm, Chemie-Grunenthal, introduced a new drug, thalidomide, which quickly gained world acceptance as a particularly safe treatment for the "morning sickness" of pregnant women. But within a year, reports began emerging that over 50% of children born to mothers who had taken thalidomide early during their pregnancies were born with phocomelia, a strange deformity marked by seal-like flippers in place of arms and legs. At the end, it was estimated that the thalimomide tragedy afflicted some 10,000 babies in at least 20 different countries (Silverman and Lee 1974). The United States was spared widespread harm from thalidomide because the drug had not been approved before the birth abnormalities were discovered. But as a precautionary measure, the 1962 amendments further strengthened the safety requirements in the drug approval process (Nightingale 1981).

Another important amendment added in 1962 required a drug manufacturer to include proof of efficacy as a criterion for gaining market approval (OTA 1993). And within the last 30 years, several more amendments have been made to the FD&C Act, each time increasing the FDA's control over the manner in which pharmaceutical products are developed and used. Most of the recent amendments, however, have focused upon the approval process of new drugs, from the commencement of their testing on humans to the time the manufacturer files a New Drug Application (NDA) (see Chapter 7 for a complete description of the FDA approval process for new drugs).

The US Food and Drug Administration is recognized as one of the world's most important sources of consumer protection information regarding the safety and efficacy of new drugs. But the FDA does not control the high costs of prescription drugs, nor does it provide comparative information for consumers or physicians on alternative drugs available within a particular drug class. Once approved by the FDA, a new drug may legally be marketed for the conditions for which approval was granted. In years past, this meant that a successful drug could immediately gain large sales. But with drug coverage in some public and private health plans comes a second review in which each plan decides whether to cover the new drug or not. A negative determination means that even insured patients will have to pay for the drug directly, out of pocket. Thus, no description of the regulatory process applied to drugs is complete without an analysis of the effect health insurers have on access to and pricing of pharmaceuticals.

Cost-Containment Mechanisms

As mentioned previously, virtually every health care organization which reimburses for drugs, whether public or private, utilizes similar cost-containment strategies with regard to pharmaceuticals. Some programs were initiated in the public domain and then adopted by private organizations; others originated in the private sector.

Manufacturer Discounts

Large health plans, as major purchasers, can use their buying power to negotiate lower prices from drug manufacturers. This task is made easier when there are few differences between competing pharmaceuticals in a drug class. Then the health care plan will negotiate with the respective manufacturers and choose only one drug, based on price. In drug categories where comparison shopping is not possible, the organization may rely on cost-effectiveness data in choosing one drug over another (Taylor and Hagland 1993). For some plans, it might be more cost-effective to buy a more expensive drug that keeps patients out of the hospital than to purchase a less expensive drug that is associated with higher hospital utilization.

In addition to negotiating discounts directly with drug manufacturers, many organizations buy their pharmaceuticals from drug wholesalers. Wholesalers achieve cost savings through economies of scale of centralized operations, and today they account for about 70% of all sales by manufacturers (Pollard 1990). These savings are passed on to large purchasers through a network of rebates and value added services, particularly in drug product classes with several competitors and marginal therapeutic differences within the class.

Formularies

A formulary restricts the doctor's choice of drugs to drugs on a list (a "positive formulary") or to those not on a list of excluded drugs (a "negative formulary") when more than one therapeutically similar compound is available to treat a condition. In constructing formularies, health care organizations typically rely upon the recommendations of their own Pharmacy and Therapeutics (P&T) committees, made up of physicians and pharmacists. P&T members typically look at dosage requirements, side effects, and efficacy first, then at cost. If similar drugs are included on a formulary, they may be ranked, with dollar signs, from "most-effective, greatest cost-benefit" ($) to "least-effective, least cost-benefit" ($$$$$) (Mandelker 1995a). Drugs deemed too expensive or whose efficacy is not accepted by a P&T committee are left off the formulary, entirely.

Frequently the task of identifying the most economical product is not so simple, for even therapeutically similar drugs work differently for different patients. Some people tolerate drugs differently, producing different patterns of side effects. In other instances drugs which may work equally well for a particular condition present different risks for patients with comorbidities. And in some cases even a difference in administration makes drugs more or less attractive for various patients. Ranitidine (Zantac), for example, is similar in its effect upon gastric ulcers to cimetidine (Tagamet), but is taken only once a day rather than four times a day for the original Tagamet. For many patients the difference is not important, but studies have shown that compliance, and hence treatment effectiveness, of ranitidine is significantly higher among the elderly, who, for a variety of reasons, have more difficulty adhering to a medication schedule. In those cases, drugs which are *usually* similar, or even equivalent, may show important differences.

Many health care organizations face a difficult dilemma in implementing a formulary. In order to account for unusual situations, mechanisms are always available to allow a prescribing physician to override the formulary and enable a patient to obtain coverage for a nonlisted drug. But if these mechanisms were too easy, they would be employed too often, requiring the organization to pay for a more costly product when it was not necessary. On the other hand, if the exception mechanism is too rigorous, requiring large amounts of paperwork to justify the drug, some physicians may not bother, hoping that the patient will adjust to the formulary drug or will tolerate unfavorable side effects. Both of these eventualities entail a cost. One cost is the extra drug cost resulting from wrongly identifying a patient as requiring an expensive drug when he or she really does not. The other is the cost of other health services consumed by the patient who was given the less costly drug when the exceptional drug was warranted. The probability of the former type of error can only be reduced by more stringency in allowing exceptions to the formulary. More stringency, however, increases the probability of failing to identify a patient who *does* have an exceptional need and should have the off-formulary drug. It is clear that both errors are costly in both human and economic terms.

Despite their limitations, drug formularies have been adopted by a number of state Medicaid programs as well as by managed-care organizations in an attempt to control costs. The evidence, however, is that drug costs are not reduced through the use of drug formularies, as discussed in Chapter 3. This suggests that the costs of failing to identify patients who legitimately need an off-formulary drug tend to exceed the savings which arise by switching patients to a formulary drug when they would otherwise be receiving a more expensive alternative. Although expensive drugs are sometimes prescribed unnecessarily in a system without a formulary, the extra cost per patient may be modest. These necessary costs will be very large only if the frequency of this prescribing is very high and the cost differential between the more expensive and the less expensive alternatives is large. On the other hand, the extra costs associated with treating a patient for unnecessary side effects or for incomplete or delayed therapy caused by a suboptimal drug can be substantial, because even the cost of expensive drugs is far less than the cost of extra office visits or hospitalization.

A second rationale for drug formularies involves their ability to improve the quality of prescribing. Physicians are thought by some to be needlessly prescribing more expensive drugs when cheaper, equally good, alternatives are available. This may result from drug advertising and promotion activities which are purposely intended to promote the advantages of particular products, without providing comparative data on alternatives, as discussed in Chapter 2. If the purpose of formularies is to tell physicians which drugs ought *not* to be used routinely, and which *should* be, they are rather blunt instruments. Hillman has expressed concern that physicians are not as well informed in prescribing practice as they ought to be (Hillman 1991). But this is an issue that can be better addressed by physician education, a remedy closer to the heart of the problem. Better training for young physicians and better information for their older colleagues is a more direct solution to the problem than broad prohibitions against using certain drugs.

Generic and Therapeutic Substitution

Another approach used by health care organizations to reduce drug costs is to encourage the use of less expensive generic drugs, when such products are available. The savings associated with the use generic drugs are supported by site-specific comparisons of prescription costs in therapeutic categories with high versus low generic use. Weiner et al. (1991) reported that in a drug class comprised of only brand-name products (i.e., gastric-acid disorders), health maintenance organization (HMO) prescription costs were virtually identical to those of fee-for-service plans. However, in a class where generics were available (i.e., antianxiety drugs), the cost per prescription at the high-generic-use HMO was approximately 40% lower than at the fee-for-service site.

Some programs reduce drug costs by suggesting that their physicians rely on over-the-counter versions of brand-name drugs as a first step in therapy (Pollard 1990). In this scenario, subscribers buy the drug without a prescription, the patient does not need follow-up physician visits to authorize refills, and the plan does not have to pay for the drug under the prescription drug benefit.

Drug Utilization Review (DUR)

Utilization review of prescription drugs came of age in the latter half of the 1980s, enabling insurers, hospitals administrators, managed-care organizations, and drug claims processors to develop sophisticated drug utilization profiles of both physicians and patients (Vibbert 1989). DUR programs are usually carried out by independent firms that offer to control improper prescribing and dispensing patterns among physicians and pharmacists on behalf of health insurers. They attempt to serve dual goals of controlling pharmaceutical costs and improving the quality of drug therapy (Kralewski and Wertheimer 1994).

DUR programs have two interrelated components. The first deals with the types of reviews performed and the second relates to the nature of the interventions used when problems are uncovered (Brodie and Smith 1976). Tables 8.1 and 8.2 illustrate the levels of review and the types of intervention used in the DUR process, respectively.

The majority of reviews conducted by DUR programs focus on contract compliance, fraud and abuse, and drug-centered screens (levels 1–3 in Table 8.1). The most basic program simply compares the claims (which are submitted to the DUR firm after the prescription has been dispensed), to pre-arranged cost, volume, and refill agreements. These levels are geared toward recognizing abusive drug utilization patterns and overcharges (Kralewski and Wertheimer 1994). Review levels 4 and 5 focus on drug groups and deal with the inappropriate use of those drugs. These reviews concentrate on high-cost drugs, high-volume drugs, and controlled substances (ibid).

Most of these DUR programs have an in-house staff of pharmacists to screen patient profiles. In some cases, problems and recommendations are reviewed by a second pharmacist before action is taken. Many problems encountered are easily detected and therefore do not require sophisticated judgments. Some of the most frequent utilization problems dealt with are prolonged use of benzodiazepines (mild tranquilizers) past the time of acute need, wrong maintenance dosing of H_2 antagonists (antiulcer drugs) after the 6–8-week initial therapy period, and use of antibacterial drugs for viral infections (Kralewski and Wertheimer 1994).

The focus of various corrective actions varies according to the degree to which the program is willing to intervene in the drug therapy program. Kralewski and Wertheimer (1994) found that most DUR programs are restrained from taking aggressive corrective action when a problem is identified because of their contracts with the insurance plans. In fact, in many cases the data are simply sent to the insurance plan and there is little or no follow-up. When interventions take place, they frequently consist of a rather general letter sent to the physician noting that a patient is taking a potentially harmful drug combination or appears to be using abnormal quantities of controlled substances. But a very specific peer review panel recommendation accompanying the patient's drug use profile can be made. Thus, DUR programs have the potential to make significant contributions to both the improvement of the quality of drug therapy as well as the reduction of costs to the health care plan.

As a standing policy within a health care organization, DUR acts as a motivational factor encouraging physicians to keep up with the latest information on drug use and misuse. DUR programs seem to be effective in changing prescribing patterns. One comparison of pharmaceutical use in two health maintenance organizations showed that patient age and sex-adjusted use rates were approximately 6% lower in the plan which had instituted a DUR program (Weiner et al. 1991).

Table 8.1   Levels of Drug Utilization Review Performed by Private Sector Firms

---

Level 1—Contract Compliance

Reviews:

- Price charged is consistent with contractual agreement
- Volume dispensed is in compliance with contract
- Refills are timed in accordance with pre-established criteria
- Drug dispensed is in compliance with generic or formulary agreements

Level 2—Fraud and Abuse

Reviews:

- Randomly survey patients to determine if prescription was received
- Audit selected pharmacies to determine if the Rx was dispensed as billed
- Monitor high cost/volume drugs for inappropriate use or hoarding
- Monitor the use of controlled substances
- Monitor duplicate prescriptions

Level 3—Drug-Centered Screens

Reviews:

- Ongoing screens for drug/drug incompatibility
- Ongoing screens for inappropriate use of drug products such as steroids
- Special one time studies of specific drugs (i.e., the use of lovastatin (Mevacor) with/without prior authorization)
- Monitor the use of high-cost drugs

Level 4—Patient Drug Profile Reviews

Reviews:

- Create patient drug use profiles on those using multiple physicians and pharmacies or using a high-volume prescription
- Conduct in-house review of drug use profiles for:
    - drug incompatibility
    - wrong dose
    - wrong drug for diagnosis
    - drug-induced illness
    - overuse of drug(s), or
    - hoarding

Level 5—Patient Therapeutic Program Reviews

Reviews:

- Create patient drug use profiles on patients similar to those in level 4 but linked to diagnosis data
- Conduct peer reviews of patient profiles
- Conduct 6-month follow-up reviews of physicians on the quality of their drug therapy
- Conduct 6-month follow-up reviews of patients to determine if problem has been resolved

---

Source: Kralewski et al. (1994).

Table 8.2   Interventions Utilized by Private Sector Drug Utilization Review
Programs

Type 1—Adjust Payments to Pharmacy

Interventions:

- Reduce payment
- Deny claims

Type 2—Educate Pharmacists and Physicians

Interventions:

- Newsletters
- Conferences
- Counterdetailing

Type 3—Provide Patient-Specific Information to Physician and Pharmacist

Interventions:

- Form letter without profile
- Form letter with profile
- Personalized letter with profile

Type 4—Limit Patient Choice of Providers or Formulary

Interventions:

- Limit patient to one pharmacy
- Limit patient to one physician
- Develop limited drug formulary
- Develop incentives for use of less expensive drugs

Type 5—Discipline Pharmacist, Physician, or Member

Interventions:

- Drop patient from drug benefit program
- Drop pharmacist or physician from program
- Report pharmacist or physician to professional association
- Report pharmacist or physician to appropriate governmental agency

Source: Kralewski et al. (1994).

Disease State Management

Another program being instituted by some health insurers is Disease State
Management (DSM), which is an attempt to improve the quality of care
while reducing costs. DSM takes a systems approach to medical care and is
based on outcomes-oriented research. DSM identifies the course of treatment that is suggested by the medical literature to offer the best outcomes
and seeks to avoid treatments that are not shown to be effective. DSM protocols start at the first sign of a disease and take the form of decision trees,
indicating what diagnostic procedures should be undertaken and what should

be done under each outcome of those tests.* These decision tree branches are sometimes called "critical pathways." To the extent that cardiac bypass surgery is done on patients who would do just as well (or better) with angioplasty, or angioplasty is done on patients who would do just as well (or better) with drug therapy, DSM will improve the quality of care *and* lower costs.

Because DSM takes a system approach to medical care, some DSM protocols may increase reliance on drug therapy, thereby *increasing* pharmaceutical expenditures while *reducing* physician and inpatient care. Other protocols might attack problems of overmedication, such as general use of antibiotics for upper respiratory infections of viral origin. This protocol would improve health outcomes while *reducing* drug costs.

Drug Information and Education

Several health care organizations systematically provide physicians with information on drugs. This education has a variety of formats, including computer printouts of physicians' drug prescribing compared to their colleagues, bulletins and pharmacy newsletters prepared with data on drug costs and the availability of new generics, and medical group meetings (Zuvekas 1986). One example of physician education was a program at the St. Joseph's Medical Center in Phoenix, Arizona, where pharmacists held training sessions to educate the medical staff on their antibiotic cost control effort, resulting in a $235,000 reduction in antibiotic expenditures (Anderson 1993).

Hospital Programs

Pharmaceutical sales to hospitals made up about 23% of total US pharmaceutical sales in 1991, a decline from about 29% in 1983 (FDC 1992). This is seen in Figure 8.1 which shows the share of pharmaceutical sales by type of buyer. One reason for the decline in the hospital share of the overall pharmaceutical market is the major restructuring of the hospital payment system in the past decade. When Medicare adopted a prospective payment system (PPS) in 1983, paying by admission and not by cost, Medicare created incentives for hospitals to reduce the length of stay for Medicare patients and to reduce the cost of ancillary services, including drug costs. Even so, Medicare beneficiaries accounted for 45% of inpatient hospital days in 1989 and for 33% of the discharges (Graves and Kozak 1992).

As a result of declining hospital admissions, stays, and subsequent financial earnings, hospitals began to employ strict cost-containment programs, including well-controlled drug formulary systems. One study by the American Society of Hospital Pharmacists showed an increase in the use of hos-

*Some DSM protocols also deal with disease prevention.

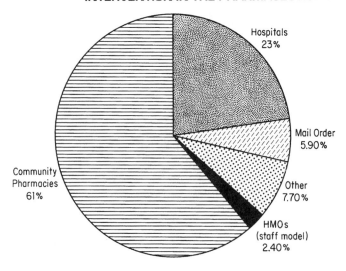

Figure 8.1   Pharmaceutical Sales in the United States by Provider Type

pital formularies from 54% in 1985 to 58% in 1989 (Crawford 1990). In addition, generic substitutions and physician monitoring were implemented.

A recent survey of hospital CEOs shows that nearly 60% of hospitals have a formal plan in place to control rising pharmaceutical costs (Anderson 1993). Today, hospital pharmacists are using more computers to dispense unit doses and to determine therapy costs using new software modules. Automated systems evaluate prescription choices and prices, even for drugs not currently part of a hospital's group purchasing contract (Hospitals Materials Management 1993).

St. Elizabeth's hospital in Boston tracks the number of clinical interventions by pharmacists, practices that improve care and save money. Each quarter, the number of interventions is tallied and staff pharmacists earn a bonus of up to 7% of salary (Hospitals Materials Management 1993). In addition, St. Elizabeth's designates one full-time "utilization review pharmacist" who deals full-time with quality and cost issues. It is estimated that this program alone has saved the hospital about $120,000 a year (Anderson 1993).

Another practice recently adopted by hospitals controls and limits the activities of salespeople from pharmaceutical companies. At Chelsea Community Hospital in Chelsea, Michigan, salespeople can only meet with the pharmacy director by appointment one morning a week, and no displays are allowed in the facility. St. Joseph's Hospital in Phoenix stipulates that salespeople can meet with physicians only to discuss drugs that are already part of the formulary. Sales calls to physicians, pharmacists, and the purchasing department must be prearranged. Displays are allowed only once a month in a central location (Anderson 1993).

One area in which future cost-containment efforts need to be improved is the maintainence of pharmacy inventories. Failure to maintain an adequate inventory forces hospitals to waste money by making costly, off-contract emergency purchases (Hospital Materials Management 1993).

Cost-Containment Programs in the Public Sector

Medicaid

Medicaid programs are administred by their respective states and combine federal and state funds to cover a wide range of inpatient and outpatient services to poor elderly, the permanently disabled, and recipients of Aid to Families with Dependent Children (AFDC). Pharmaceutical coverage for ambulatory drugs is an "optional" service under Medicaid, thereby giving states flexibility in deciding whether and how much to pay for outpatient prescription drugs. Nonetheless, only two states, Alaska and Wyoming, do not cover prescription drug costs (OTA 1993). In fiscal year 1987, Medicaid pharmaceutical expenditures in the United States approximated $3 billion, or 6.6% of total Medicaid program expenditures (HCFA 1988).

Typically, Medicaid enrollees receive their prescribed medications from retail pharmacies, which are reimbursed by the state Medicaid agency according to payment limits and established dispensing fees set by federal Medicaid regulations. To receive a prescribed medicine from a pharmacy, a Medicaid beneficiary usually presents a Medicaid card verifying his or her enrollment, along with the doctor's written prescription. A total of 22 states require Medicaid enrollees to share in the costs for their drugs (Soumerai and Ross-Degnan 1990). In these states the copayment ranges from $0.50 to $4.00 per perscription (ibid). Federal law prohibits states from requiring copayments from important groups of beneficiaries: children under 18, pregnant women, residents of long-term care and hospice institutions, some HMO enrollees, and recipients of emergency and family planning services (HCFA 1988).

State Medicaid programs reimburse the pharmacy a fixed dispensing fee and an additional amount to cover the acquisition cost to the pharmacy of the prescribed drug. The median dispensing fee in 1990 was $4.10 (Soumerai and Ross-Degnan 1990). But reimbursement of prescribed drug costs differs for single-source and multiple-source drugs. Until 1991, state Medicaid agencies were required to pay no more for a single-source drug than either the pharmacy's estimated acquisition cost plus a reasonable dispensing fee or the pharmacy's usual and customary charge to the general public (OTA 1993). State Medicaid agencies generally discounted the published average wholesale price for the drug by a fixed percent (ranging from 5 to 11%) to obtain the estimated acquisition cost (OTA 1993). Since published wholesale prices are generally higher than the actual wholesale prices paid to retailers, Medicaid essentially paid the manufacturer's price plus a retail markup for single-source drugs. For multiple-source drugs, the federal government required that in the aggregate, the state reimburse no more than 150% of the published price for the least costly product (OTA 1993). Until 1991, state Medicaid agencies had the authority to restrict the drugs that Medicaid covers. In 1990, about 22 states had restrictive formularies, which limited reimbursable drugs to a defined list. Another 28 states had "open formularies," under which all drugs were reimbursable except for those explicitly identified as ineligible (OTA 1993).

But in an effort to contain costs, the Omnibus Budget Reconciliation Act of 1990 (Public Law 101–508) required manufacturers selling prescription drugs to Medicaid patients to give states a rebate on their Medicaid purchases. In exchange, the law prohibited states from using formularies to restrict Medicaid patients' access to any FDA-approved drug in the manufacturer's drug line (ASHP 1991).

The required rebate on brand-name drugs has two main components. The first is the Basic Rebate, which requires the manufacturer to effectively discount the price of each drug it sells to Medicaid by a specified amount. The second component is an Additional Rebate, which requires the manufacturer to pay money to Medicaid whenever the price of its brand-name drugs increases more rapidly than price inflation. The Congressional Budget Office projected a total rebate for brand-name drugs to the federal government of $637 million in fiscal year 1992 (CBO 1992). Including the states' share brought this total to about $1.1 billion, or about 2% of the domestic manufacturers sales (OTA 1993).

An additional cost-containment feature of the OBRA 1990 legislation was a comprehensive drug use review (DUR) program for Medicaid recipients similar to that which was to have been established in the (repealed) Medicaid Catastrophic Coverage Act of 1988. As of 1993, states must provide for a DUR program for covered outpatient drugs that assures that prescriptions are appropriate, medically necessary, and not likely to produce adverse medical results (ASHP 1991).

State Pharmaceutical Assistance Programs (SPAPs)

During the past 15 years, 10 states have established SPAPs that extend pharmaceutical benefits to people 65 years of age and older who do not qualify for Medicaid but cannot afford to purchase private health insurance to supplement their Medicaid coverage. Four of these SPAPs also cover the permanently disabled. Together, these programs currently spend $500 million annually on prescription drugs (OTA 1993). Eligibility in a SPAP is limited by personal income ceilings determined by each state. They are typically between 100 and 200% of the federal poverty line. Virtually all of the programs have policies that require the use of generic substitutions. Those states without a generic substitution program require higher copayments from beneficiaries for prescriptions filled with a brand-name drug when a generic version is available (OTA 1993).

Medicare

The elderly are sicker and use more prescriptions than younger persons. In 1987, the elderly accounted for 13% of the population but purchased 34.2% of all prescriptions. More than 82% of older persons take at least one medication per year, and in 1987 they used, on average, 15.3 prescriptions (Reutzel 1993). Even so, Medicare does not generally cover outpatient drugs. An exception to the rule are drugs that only a physician or someone under a physician's supervision can administer. Many drugs given by injection or intravenously fall into this category, although, if the drug is usually self-injectable or self-administered, the carrier can deny coverage (OTA 1993).

Many private health insurance companies offer "Medigap" plans that supplement the hospital, medical, surgical, and pharmaceutical coverage of Medicare. These Medigap policies frequently cover deductibles and coinsurance required by Medicare. Although there were 22 million Medigap polices sold nationwide in 1993 (Schwartz 1995b), it is estimated that this number will drop drastically in coming years due to the growing number of managed-care organizations that offer comprehensive health care plans to the elderly at no additional cost to their Medicare coverage (a more detailed description of Medicare-HMOs is provided later in this chapter). One of the main attractions of most Medicare-HMOs is an extensive pharmaceutical benefit included in the plan, usually with a very low copayment. Private Medigap policies frequently require a deductible for drug costs, and they often limit the number of prescriptions a Medicare recipient may receive on a yearly basis.

Cost Containment in Managed Care

Probably the most significant area of change in the US health care system in recent years has been the development of managed care. Fundamentally, managed care can be defined as an organization that is responsible for the financing and delivery of health care to an enrolled population for a prepaid fee, using administrative techniques to control utilization rates, cost, and quality of care.

The first HMOs were started over 60 years ago, but development of large numbers of HMOs began in the 1970s in response to the HMO Act of 1973 (PL 93–222), which attempted to stimulate the growth of prepaid health care by providing start-up funding for HMOs. The law required that major employers offer their employees an opportunity to join a federally qualified HMO if there was one in their area. To become federally qualified, the HMO was required to provide a wide range of services, including physician services, other outpatient care, short-term mental health services, short-term rehabilitative care, substance abuse treatment, laboratory and radiology services, social services, immunizations and preventive health care, health education, arrangements for emergency care, and arrangements for out-of-area care.

Over the course of the last 20 years, HMOs have developed into four different models: staff, group, independent practice association, and network. The initial form of HMO that fit the federal prototype was the staff model. In this approach, typified by Group Health of Puget Sound, the organization hires its own medical staff to provide services to members. The medical staff is employed and paid a salary by the HMO. These HMOs typically own their own facilities. In 1993, there were 53 staff HMOs, with 4.8 million members (Muirhead 1994a). The group-model HMO contracts with an independent medical group to provide medical services to members. The best-known examples of the group-model HMO are the Kaiser Foundation Health Plans. Generally, group-model HMOs also own their facilities and equipment. In 1993, there were 68 group HMOs, accounting for 14 million enrollees (Muirhead 1994a). The independent practice association model–HMOs (IPA-HMOs) are affiliations of independent practitioners in the community who, in addition to their fee-for-service patients, contract to provide care for individuals enrolled in prepaid HMOs. These individual providers work out of their own offices. In 1993, there were 351 IPA-HMOs with 24 million members (Muirhead 1994a).

The network-model HMO contracts with several independent group practices hospitals, and pharmacies to provide medical services to members. In 1993, there were 68 network HMOs with 6.1 million members (Muirhead 1994a). All together, HMOs had approximately 49 million members in 1993, which was a 10% increase from the previous year and a 49% increase from 1990 (National Center for Health Statistics 1990; Muirhead 1994a). In California alone, 55% of those currently insured receive care through an HMO, as compared with 22% who maintain traditional indemnity insurance (Schachter 1995).

Traditionally, HMOs have proven their ability to achieve savings by reducing inpatient and specialty services as compared to fee-for-service providers (Luft 1981). However, as competition intensifies, and HMOs' market share increases, administrators are focusing on reducing costs of lower-priced items such as ancillary services and pharmaceuticals.

Pharmacy Benefits in HMOs

It is estimated that about 99% of all HMOs currently offer prescription drugs to their members (Muirhead 1994a), up from about 90% in 1986 (Zuvekas et al. 1986). In 1989, only about 25% of HMO plans covered prescription drugs within the basic benefit package, and 75% offered pharmaceuticals as a rider to the basic plan (Gold et al. 1989; Zuvekas 1986).

Since the early 1980s, the Health Care Financing Administration (HCFA), which administers Medicare, has been encouraging HMOs to provide Medicare coverage in return for fixed prepaid premiums. Recently, there has been a rapid increase in the number of Medicare beneficiaries who have enrolled in "Medicare-risk HMOs," where they receive all of their covered health care. In 1994, 161 HMOs offered some type of Medicare-risk contract, up from 153 in 1993 (Schwartz 1995a). As of the beginning of 1995, more than 2.3 million Medicare recipients had enrolled in HMOs, accounting for approximately 16% of the nation's total Medicare recipients (Jones 1994).

Typically, the Medicare-HMOs provide members full Medicare benefits plus additional services not normally covered under Medicare, including prescription drug coverage, preventive care, home health care, skilled nursing facility care beyond what Medicare pays, dental care, mental health coverage, and wellness and health education programs (Schwartz 1995b). An attractive feature of the Medicare-HMO is that there is little cost sharing for members and rarely any additional premium charged to beneficiaries beyond the Medicare Part B premium. Medicare pays the HMO a flat amount (capitation payment) for each subscriber equal to 95% of the average per capita Medicare expenditure in the region. Evidently this Medicare payment is sufficient to cover the cost of the services normally covered by Medicare plus the extra services. In fact, the profitability of these Medicare "risk contracts" indicates that the Medicare payment actually *exceeds* these costs (Jones 1994).

With increasing competition for Medicare enrollees and the incentives of per capita reimbursement, HMOs are challenged to maintain or lower their pharmaceutical costs. The importance of this area of coverage is seen in the fact that approximately 85% of the elderly use at least one prescription medicine during the year and that the per capita spending for prescription drugs by seniors was estimated to be nearly $500 in 1991, while spending by the top 11% exceeded $1,200 per person, or $100 per month (Long 1994). Considering that over 60% of all physician visits result in a prescription (National Center For Health Statistics 1987), and that HMOs spend over $5.3 billion on pharmaceuticals alone (Muirhead 1995), it is no surprise that there is growing interest in understanding HMO pharmacy benefits and their spillover effects on the rest of the health care system.

HMOs typically cover all prescription drugs with the exception of experimental drugs, over-the-counter drugs, and oral contraceptives. Formularies are used in most HMOs. Cost sharing is common, usually in the form of a deductible or a flat copayment per prescription. Zuvekas et al. (1986) reported that copayments ranged from $1.00 to $7.00 per prescription, with $3.00 being the most common. In addition, Muirhead (1994a) reported that about 16% of all HMOs impose a separate annual deductible on the benefit, which averaged $73 for individuals and $156 for families.

HMOs use three major models for administering drug benefits to their members: in-house pharmacies, direct contract pharmacies, and indirect con-

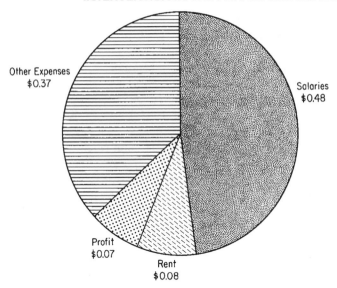

Figure 8.2 Where the Retail Prescription Dollar Goes

tract pharmacies through third-party payors. In-house pharmacies are owned and operated by the HMO and are located within its health centers. In group-and staff-model HMOs, the in-house pharmacy is used almost exclusively. It offers the potential for controlling cost, quality, and customer service and allows pharmacists to be available as a resource to the medical staff. However, an in-house pharmacy requires volume sufficient to support the fixed costs (Zuvekas et al. 1986).

Network and IPA plans do not have in-house pharmacies but rather contract for the services either directly with community pharmacies or indirectly through third-party payers. Reimbursement to the pharmacy may be negotiated on a fee-for-service or capitated basis for all drug benefits. Contracts usually require that special services be available to HMO members, such as home delivery, or 24-hour availability for emergencies. Currently, HMOs are contracting less with drugstore chains and more with independent pharmacies and mail order companies. There was a 6% decrease from 1992 to 1993 in the number of contracts between HMOs and chains, while there was a 44% increase in the use of mail order companies (Muirhead 1994a). As a result, retail pharmacies have realized the importance of controlling their own costs. Figure 8.2 shows the distribution of retail pharmacy costs, indicating that salaries is the area of largest potential cost savings.

Indirect contracting through third-party payers by HMOs function as major medical indemnity plans. The HMO reimburses members for drugs they purchase from any pharmacy, usually after a deductible is met. Members may be required to submit receipts to the HMO or file a claim form. Some plans even use outside third-party administrators to process drug claims. This type of plan is most likely to be used by IPA and network HMOs, especially when few members have drug coverage (Zuvekas 1986).

Some HMOs have adopted a combination of these models. The most common combination is in-house and contract pharmacies. An HMO may choose this combination when it has its own pharmacy but wants to enhance member convenience for marketing purposes.

HMO Cost-Containment Strategies

Most HMOs utilize the same techniques for restraining price and utilization of pharmacy products. In addition to patient cost sharing, HMOs bargain with pharmaceutical manufacturers for price discounts, develop drug formularies, require dispensing generic drugs and therapeutic substitutes when appropriate, maintain ongoing drug utilization review (DUR), provide drug information and education to physicians and patients, and utilize pharmacy benefit managers (PBMs).

The percentage of HMOs that use formularies climbed considerably recently from 49% in 1991 to 76% in 1993 (Muirhead 1994a). In addition, about 73% of all HMOs had generic substitution requirements, up slightly from 70% in 1992. As a result, generic drugs accounted for 39% of all HMO prescriptions in 1993 (Muirhead 1994a). The National Census Survey of HMO and IPA plans in 1988 reported similar figures for all HMO plans while noting that the proportion of IPAs using compulsory generic substitution was less than that for all HMOs (67 versus 73%, respectively) (Weiner et al. 1991).

About 62% of HMOs had drug utilization review (DUR) programs in 1993, up from 55% in 1992 (Muirhead 1994a). There is also a sharp increase in the use of pharmacy benefit managers (PBMs).

Pharmacy Benefit Managers (PBMs)

A PBM is an organization that is employed by managed-care organizations or others responsible for administering health insurance coverage to offer pharmaceutical services using efficient systems of prescription and dispensing oversight and cost-effective pharmaceuticals. Clients range from large employer groups who choose to self-insure to HMOs and other managed-care organizations. PBMs came of age in the 1980s, together with managed care, as big third-party payers reacted against the rapid growth in health care costs. Within the last few years, growth of managed pharmacy benefits has been rapid, as illustrated in Figure 8.3. It was estimated that, in 1995, PBMs would manage the pharmacy benefit for 28% of staff-and group-model HMOs 50% of mixed-model HMOs, and 61% of IPA-and network-model HMOs (Muirhead 1995). Initially, PBMs were hired to control phar-

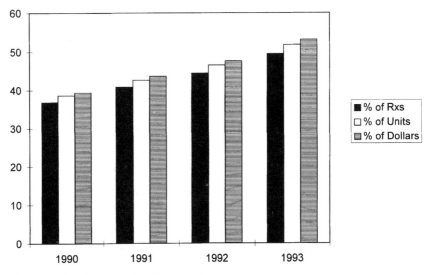

Figure 8.3 The Growth of Managed Pharmacy

maceutical costs by arranging networks of pharmacy providers, negotiating pharmacy dispensing fees, and bargaining for manufacturer rebates and discounts; they also managed formularies, claims processing, DUR, and physician and patient education (Muirhead 1994c; Glaser 1994). Recently, however, PBMs have come under intense competitive pressure to prove their value beyond the negotiated discounts and supervision services that any management organization can perform. With about 40 PBMs currently in operation (Mandelker 1995b), PBMs are searching for new ways to diversify their product line in order to entice new clients and maintain their current ones. One such service that PBMs have begun to offer clients is Disease State Management (DSM).

DSM, is an effort to reduce total health care costs by taking a systems view of medical treatment. It seeks to provide cost-effective care, often for chronic conditions, by emphasizing treatment protocols and changes in lifestyle habits of patients (Mandelker 1995c). The concept of DSM was adopted by some pharmaceutical manufacturers in 1992, when they realized that future sales and profits would be jeopardized by managed care and the possibility of national health care reform (Muirhead 1994b). They also realized that patient noncompliance was hurting sales, as well as reducing the quality of medical care.

A PBM offers DSM by first establishing clinical objectives for the disease state using existing medical literature and panels of medical experts. Next, an information system is established by which physician prescribing and patient compliance and outcomes are monitored. Lastly, an incentive structure is created to encourage compliance with the treatment protocol which is established. Two of the conditions that PBMs manage most frequently are asthma and diabetes. They are both highly prevalent and expensive to care for, especially if care is not well managed.

Disease state management relies heavily on the support of pharmacists. One PBM, Medco, pays community pharmacists to explain to asthma patients how to use their inhaler properly. In addition, participating pharmacists monitor the blood glucose levels of diabetics and consult with physicians about the appropriateness of a patient's drug therapy (Muirhead 1994b). Because of its systems approach, DSM must incorporate all the parties that contribute to the care of the patient in order for it to be successful. While the patient's physician receives copies of all communications to the patient, he or she is never involved directly in the program (Mandelker 1995c).

A related area in which PBMs are active is "outcomes" research. Outcomes research is the study of the efficacy of alternative therapeutic paths. If two patients suffering from the same illness were treated two different ways, which one would recover faster and would enjoy a higher quality of life? Increasingly, researchers are adding a pharmaceutical economics component to these studies by performing cost-effectiveness and cost/benefit evaluations of alternative drug therapies. Commonly referred to as "pharmacoeconomics," these studies evaluate cost differences between treatments and identify whether one path's higher cost is justified in terms of reductions in illness or death, improved quality of life, or reduced cost of other health services.

PBMs and drug manufacturers are playing an increasingly important role in conducting medical outcomes studies. Such a study can encompass all clinical and cost data, including medical claims, diagnostic testing costs, home therapy treatments, and drugs (Mandelker 1995d). Although outcomes are used in the preparation of formularies and the basis for drug utilization review committees, it is likely that one important end result of outcomes research will be improving physician prescribing patterns to improve health outcomes for the patient, as well as reduced costs for the health care organization.

The success of DSM programs depends on compliance by both physicians and patients with the protocols that are suggested. If physicians do not trust those protocols, or the incentives facing both physicians and patients do not sufficiently encourage compliance, change will not be effected. One threat to compliance, ironically, is the very fact that pharmaceutical companies have become involved with many of the PBMs and the DSM programs that are being implemented. There is a serious appearance of conflict of interest when a DSM protocol or PBM dispensing policy favors the products manufactured by the organization that has sponsored the protocol development or owns the PBM. This is an unfortunate situation because much of the underlying research is carefully done and is entirely valid. Over time, this sort of health services research will shift to more neutral organizations such as universities and independent research organizations.

References

American Society of Hospital Pharmacists, "Summary of the 1990 Medicaid drug rebate legislation," *American Journal of Hospital Pharmacists* 48: 114–117, 1991.

Anderson H, "UR pharmacists help MDs control drug costs," *Hospitals* 67(1):42, 1993.

Brodie D and Smith W, "A conceptual model for drug utilization review," *Hospitals* 50:143, 1976.

Congressional Budget Office, *Questions and Answers: Medicaid Prescription Drug Rebates*, Washington, DC: Congressional Budget Office, 1992.

Crawford S, "ASHP national survey of hospital-based pharmaceutical services, 1990," *American Journal of Hospital Pharmacy* 47:2655–2695, 1990.

FDC Reports: Prescription and OTC pharmaceuticals, "Mail order grew 37% to $2.9 billion in 1991 IMS survey; growth may slow soon," *FDC Reports: Prescription and OTC Pharmaceuticals*, 1992.

Glaser M, "PBMs emerging as key element in managed care," *Drug Topics* 138(11): 110–112, 1994.

Gold M, Joffe M, Kennedy T, and Tucker A, "Pharmacy benefits in HMOs," *Health Affairs* 8(3):182–190, 1989.

Graves E and Kozak L, *National Discharge Survey: Annual Summary, 1989*, DHHS No. (PHS) 92–1770. Hyattsville, MD: National Center for Health Statistics, 1992.

Health Care Financing Administration 2082 reports, *Pharmaceutical Benefits Under State Medical Assistance Programs*, Reston, VA: National Pharmaceutical Council, 1988.

Hillman A, "Managing the physician: rules versus incentives," *Health Affairs* 4:138–146, 1991.

Hospitals Materials Management, "Hospital pharmacists work to contain high drug costs," *Hospitals Materials Management* 18(7):1–15, 1993.

Jones D, "HMOs are seeking new ways to cover the elderly," *National Underwriter* 98(35):2–14, 1994.

Kralewski J and Wertheimer A, Ratner E, "Prescription drug utilization review in the private sector," *Health Care Management Review* 19(2):62–71, 1994.

Long S, "Prescription drugs and the elderly: issues and options," *Health Affairs* 2: 157–174, 1994.

Luft H, *HMOs: Dimensions of Performance*, New York: Wiley, 1981.

Mandelker J, "Formularies: balancing cost and quality," *Business and Health* 13(3 suppl):25–27, 1995a.

Mandelker J, "The expanding role of PBMs," *Business and Health* 13(3 suppl):6–10, 1995b.

Mandelker J, "Disease state management: identifying an Rx for savings," *Business and Health* 13(3 suppl):11–15, 1995c.

Mandelker J, "Outcomes: the science of prescribing," *Business and Health* 13(3 suppl): 28–30, 1995d.

Muirhead G, "HMOs are controlling more and more prescriptions," *Drug Topics* 138(21):72, 1994a.

Muirhead G, "The ABCs of PBMs," *Drug Topics* 138(17):67–68, 1994b.

Muirhead G, "California HMO forms its own PBM company," *Drug Topics* 138(17): 45–48, 1994c.

Muirhead G, "HMOs likely to expand use of pharmacy benefit programs," *Drug Topics* 139(1):40–42, 1995.

National Center for Health Statistics, *Highlights of Drug Utilization in Office Practice: National Ambulatory Care Survey 1985*, Hyattsville, MD: National Center for Health Statistics, 1987.

National Center for Health Statistics, *Health, United States, 1990* (DHHS publication No. [PHS] 91–1232), Washington, DC: US Government Printing Office, 1990.

Nightingale SL, "Drug regulation and policy formulation," *Milbank Memorial Fund Quarterly/Health and Society* 59(3):412–445, 1981.

Office of Technological Assessment, *Pharmaceutical R & D: Costs, Risks and Rewards*, Washington, DC: US Government Printing Office, 1993.

Pollard M, "Managed care and a changing pharmaceutical industry," *Health Affairs* 3:55–65, 1990.

Reutzel T, "The nature and consequences of policies intended to contain costs in outpatient drug insurance programs," *Clinical Therapeutics* 15(4):752–764, 1993.

Schachter J, "Insured people are satisfied with their medical care," *The Los Angeles Times*, August 28, 1995.

Schwartz M, "Medicare encouraging HMOs to enroll the elderly," *National Underwriter* 99(6):3–37, 1995a.

Schwartz M, "Surging medicare HMOs could dent Medigap sales," *National Underwriter* 99(8):3–30, 1995b.

Silverman M and Lee P, *Pills, Profits and Politics*, Berkeley, CA: University of California Press, 1974.

Soumerai S and Ross-Degnan D, "Experience of state drug benefit programs," *Health Affairs* 3:36–54, 1990.

Starr P, *The Social Transformation of American Medicine*, Cambridge, MA: Basic Books, 1982.

Taylor K and Hagland M, "A dose of pharmaco-economics: can health networks learn from the drug policies of managed care plans?" *Hospitals and Health Networks* 67(13):33–36, 1993.

Vibbert S, "Is utilization review paying off?" *Business and Health* 2:2–26, 1989.

Weiner J, Lyles A, Steinwachs, and Hall K, "Impact of managed care on prescription drug use," *Health Affairs* 2:140–147, 1991.

Zuvekas A, Fox P, Heinen L, and Pollard M, "Cost containment in HMO pharmacies," *GHAA Journal* Winter:22–34, 1986.

9

Patent Protection

To view the pharmaceutical industry merely as a producer of inputs into the health care sector would miss one of its essential activities—the generation of research and development knowledge. Indeed, this is the important characteristic distinguishing major pharmaceutical manufacturers from firms that only manufacture generic products. It is also the distinguishing difference between major drug firms in the United States, Europe, and Japan and those in other countries that merely reproduce products that are already marketed in countries with advanced pharmaceutical sectors. In Chapter 1 we looked in detail at the process of pharmaceutical R&D and in Chapter 5 we analyzed the pattern of R&D from the perspective of developed and developing countries. But we have not yet considered one of the essential mechanisms by which pharmaceutical R&D can be encouraged—the protection of intellectual property pertaining to new drugs by the patent system.

Patent protection is one of the primary factors determining the willingness of pharmaceutical manufacturers to invest in the development of a new drug. In the United States, market exclusivity can be legally protected for up to 20 years from date of filing by obtaining a patent from the federal government. Until ratification of the WTO treaty in 1995 the period had been 17 years from the date of issuance. Even with the delays imposed by the FDA's approval process, the monopoly granted by a patent allows drug companies to protect their FDA-approved products from competition from generic versions and may provide them with enough time to recoup their investment in R&D. Monopoly profits earned during the patent period lead competitors to develop and introduce immitative, or "me, too," drugs. These are new molecular entities that are similar, but not identical, in molecular structure and mechanism of action to the original new molecular entities.

The Boston Consulting group reports that in markets with multiple drug products, both initial launch price of new products and annual price increases of older drugs are substantially reduced. For example, in 1992 price increases for drugs in therapeutic areas with no new introductions were approximately 5.5%, while increases in therapeutic areas with more than one introduction were only one percent Boston Consulting Group 1993). And launch prices in therapeutic areas with average numbers of competing drugs already in the market were 14 percent below that of the leading product, but in the most competetive therapeutic classes the average discount was 36 percent (Boston Consulting Group 1993). As a result, the profitable life of a single drug on today's market is shortening.

Companies have a strong incentive to be the first to market a product for a given indication. There is anecdotal evidence that if virtually identical products are brought out as little as 3 to 6 months apart, the product that first appears will get the largest share of the market and maintain this advantage indefinitely (Wigggins 1981).

Without patent protection there would be no marketing exclusivity and competitors would immediately enter any market with a successful product, driving price down eventually to the marginal production costs, as discussed in Chapter 4. Future R&D would never take place because there would be no way for firms to earn a yield on those investments in developing intellectual property.

Patent laws, however, entail societal cost, for protection of intellectual property raises the cost of diffusion of knowledge and makes innovations prohibitively expensive for some who would benefit from its use. Patent protection can be seen as a tradeoff between present and future gains. At any point in time uninhibited diffusion of knowledge will confer short-term benefits to some. But their gain, if realized, will deprive those who originated the knowledge of the return on their intellectual investment and destroy any incentive for future such investments. Striking the right balance is an critical societal goal.

Patent Law

A patent is a legal protection that shelters an invention from being used, copied, or traded without permission of the patent holder for a certain period of time. The purpose of a patent is to encourage innovative activities by rewarding an inventor's intellectual achievement. Although patent laws can be traced back to ancient Greece, a useful starting point for understanding current patent issues is the Statue of Monopolies adopted in England in 1623. This act addressed patent concerns in a number of basic industries that remain relevant today, such as leather-working, glass-making, and manufactured goods.

In the United States, patent and copyright laws are derived from Article 1, Section 8, of the US Constitution, which provides that "The Congress shall have power ... To promote the Progress of Science and useful Arts, by securing for limited Times to Authors and Inventors the exclusive Right to their respective Writings and Discoveries."

This provision is the foundation of American patent statutes, Title 35 of the United States Code (USC), which was first enacted in 1790 and revised in 1793, 1836, and 1952, and the present Patent Act, enacted in 1952. The Patent Act is completely codified in Title 35 of the United States Code. It describes the legal requirements and practical steps for patent application, granting, use, and challenge that emanate from the statutory and judicial experience of the preceding century and a half (Miller and Davis 1990).

The Patent and Trademark Office (PTO), a bureau within the US Department of Commerce, is responsible for the administration of the patent system, including the issuing of patents and trademarks. Registration of copyrights is administered by the Library of Congress.

Patentability and Patent Categories

According to section 101 of title 35, an invention must be useful, new and nonobvious to be patentable. Each of these qualities is specifically defined.

"Useful" requires that the invention work for its intended purpose. It must have positive utility. Frivolous or immoral inventions are not patentable for they have no utility or negative utility.

"New" means that the invention must be different from what had been previously discovered or known. New methods of using old products may be patentable if all other statutory requirements have been met. Under section 102(a), a patent is unobtainable if the invention was known or used by others in this country or patented or described in a printed publication in this or a foreign country before the invention thereof by the applicant for the patent (CEB 1993).

By "nonobvious" section 103 explains "A patent may not be obtained ... if the differences between the subject matter sought to be patented and the prior art are such that the subject matter as a whole would have been obvious at the time the invention was made to a person having ordinary skill in the art to which said subject matter pertains." The determination of whether a patent is nonobvious, and therefore enforceable against an alleged infringer, is one of the most litigated issues in patent law. Usually, a three-step analysis has to be performed before the obviousness or nonobviousness of the subject matter is determined. The first step is to determine the scope and content of the prior state of knowledge, or "state of the art." Then the differences between the knowledge and the claims at issue have to be ascertained. Finally, the level of ordinary skill in the pertinent claim, described by the Patent Act, must be determined.

All patents in the United States can be classified into two major groups, utility patents and design patents (such as ornamental designs for articles of manufacture and certain types of plants). Since most patents, including pharmaceutical products, belong to the utility category, we discuss this category's subclassifications. Section 101 of the statute provides: "Whoever invents or discovers any new and useful process, machine, manufacture, or composition of matter, or any new and useful improvement thereof, may obtain a patent therefore, subject to the conditions and requirements of this title" (Miller and Davis 1990).

Thus there are essentially only two categories of patentable utility matters: products (machine, manufacture, or composition of matter) and processes. Products are physical entities such as machines and devices. Manufactures are any fabricated products that otherwise satisfy the requirements of patentability. A composition of matter is usually a new chemical invention, although it can be any composition of materials, not limited solely to chemicals (Miller and Davis 1990).

Processes are ways of getting somewhere else from where one starts, and they may be either a way of getting to something inventive or they may be an inventive way of getting to something already known (Miller and Davis 1990). Even if the drug itself is held not to be inventive, either because it not new or is merely an obvious derivative of a previously patented substance or has not yet been proved to be useful or effective in treating diseases, the inventors may seek to patent the way in which the drug is produced in the laboratory—the process, rather than the product.

How Are Patents Obtained?

Generally, a potential patentee must be prepared to demonstrate that the new process or product is new, useful, and nonobvious. This demonstration is made through the patent application. The first part of the application requires a specification describing how the invention works. The second consists of "claims," underlying the preceding specification. They are the actual patentable features of the invention. The "claims" are the asserted new, useful, and nonobvious advances beyond the prior state of the art of which the "invention" is a part (Miller and Davis 1990). The relation between the specification and the claims is that the claims point out what it is that is patentable about the specification.

For pharmaceutical inventions, an applicant can make four types of claims (OTA 1993):

1. A compound claim covers the chemical entity, including any and all formulations or uses of the chemical entity.
2. A composition claim covers a chemical entity formulated for use as a pharmaceutical. Such claims must frequently specify a particular form of administration (e.g., oral tablet or injectable drug).
3. A method-of-use claim covers the use of chemical compound or composition in a specified way. For example, the applicant may claim that a chemical

compound can strengthen the effect of an existing drug such as zidovudine (AZT) against AIDS when administered in a certain dose.

4. A process, or method-of-manufacture claim, covers the way in which a compound or composition is produced. These claims have been particularly important in recent years for drugs that rely on recombinant DNA technology.

For an application with a compound claim, there are tradeoffs in deciding how broad the claim should be. A broad claim may encompass thousands of compounds which share common structural characteristics that are thought to be responsible for providing a particular utility. The broader the claim, the greater its coverage and potential value. However, the broader the claim, the greater the chance that a patent already exists on some version of the compound, thereby defeating the novelty of the broad claim. If a patent already exists on a particular compound or composition, one can still apply for and receive a composition or method-of-use patent for new use even though the proposed use would infringe on the preexisting patent claim (OTA 1993).

The patent application is submitted to the PTO that will examine the application and conduct a search of past patents and of the related literature to ascertain whether the new invention is patentable and the claims are actually new, useful, and nonobvious.

The PTO denies patentability to some applications, but they can be resubmitted after revisions addressing specific requirements of the examiner. Usually, the process requires several submissions, denials, and resubmissions until the applicant and the examiner are in agreement (Miller and Davis 1990).

During the examination process, other patent applications making similar or identical claims may be filed, considered, and granted. An interference proceeding then will be commenced by the PTO with the objective of determining which application first conceived and reduced the patent to practice. This question of priority is decided during proceedings of the PTO Board of Interference.

What Protection Does a Patent Confer?

Once a patent is granted, it gives the patentee the exclusive right to make, use, or sell the invention to the absolute exclusion of others for the period of the patent. The owner has the complete right to determine who will have the right to use, make, or sell the patented item, and to a more limited extent, how or where it will be initially exploited (Miller and Davis 1990).

The patentee also has the right, under the Patent Act, to grant the patent privilege to others through licensing, contracting, or other means on a geographic basis. But there are antitrust implications in geographically limited licenses, and a patentee must not exceed the rights granted by the Patent Act to avoid committing an antitrust violation.

Duration of Patent Protection

The term of a patent depends on its type. Historically, a utility patent has a lifetime of 17 years from its date of issue. The international World Trade Organization (WTO) treaty enacted in 1995 extended the patent period for all signatory countries to 20 years from date of filing. This period is not extendable unless the product being patented is a drug, medical device, food additive, or color additive that has been subjected to regulatory review (CEB 1993). Because firms usually seek patent protection as soon as a potential drug compound is identified, a large portion of the patent period can be taken up by the sponsor's R&D activities and the US FDA's review of the NDA marketing application (OTA 1993). To attempt to restore the original intent of the Patent Act, Congress enacted the Orphan Drug Act of 1983 granting 7 years of exclusive marketing rights for new pharmaceutical products designed to treat rare conditions. As of May 1992, the PTO had issued 142 patent extensions, most often for a period of 2 years beyond the statutory 17-year exclusivity (OTA 1993). In addition, Congress passed the Drug Price Competition and Patent Term Restoration (DPCPTR) Act in 1984, which allowed the PTO to extend the patent term of drugs for up to 5 additional years when the patent term was eroded by regulatory review (see Grabowski and Vernon 1996).

Congress occasionally gives individual drugs additional patent extensions through special legislation. For example, in 1983, as part of the Federal Anti-Tampering Act, Congress extended two patent terms covering an anesthetic drug to compensate for delay in marketing approval while the firm conducted research at the request of the FDA that Congress deemed unnecessary (OTA 1993). In another case, Congress granted a patent term extension for the drug gemfibrozil to Warner-Lambert after it was shown to have a new use in combating high cholesterol.

The Office of Technology Assessment (OTA) has examined trends in effective patent lives for pharmaceutical innovations. The effective patent life is defined as the elapsed time between the FDA approval for marketing of a new drug and the expiration of the last patent that effectively protects the original compound from competition from bioequivalent generic products. The longer this period, the more years the firm has a monopoly over its product. The OTA measured effective patent life in two ways: the life of the patent protecting the product itself and the longest period of protection indicated by any patent covering a drug. According to the OTA's study report, the greatest threat to the effective patent life of a new compound is the delay between patent issuance and FDA's approval to market the product (OTA 1993).

The results of their analysis are shown in Figure 9.1 After declining steadily throughout the 1970s and the early 1980s, effective patent life re-

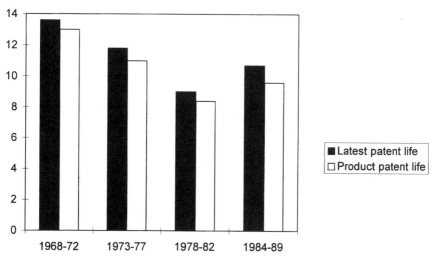

Figure 9.1 Effective Patent Life for Drugs Approved, 1968–89. Source: Office of Technology Assessment, 1993.

bounded somewhat in the years since 1984. Table 9.1 shows mean and median effective patent life for 113 drugs approved between 1985 and 1989. The table also shows the mean effective patent life by sales during the second year after the FDA granted marketing approval. Drugs with longer effective patents have higher early sales and, on average, 400 additional days of effective patent life are associated with an additional $100 million in sales (OTA 1993).

The estimated period of effective patent protection reflects only the period during which the original compound is formally protected from competition by a patent. The expiration of patent protection on the original compound may not mark the end of exclusive marketing, however. Some compounds may not experience generic competition for several years after the patent expires, either because of delays in FDA approval of generic copies or because the total market for the drug is too small to induce generic manufacturers to enter the market. Even more important, process patents that are issued after the original product patents sometimes may be effective in keeping generic products out of the market (OTA 1993).

Infringement of Patents

The patent law prohibits anybody without authority from making, using, or selling any patented invention within the United States during the term of the patent. As Title 35 section 271 states,

Table 9.1   Patent Life (Months) for New Chemical Entities Approved
1985–1989

	Longest Patent	*NCE Patent*
Effective patent life, total sample (n = 113)		
Mean	10.6	9.6
Median	10.7	10.0
Effective patent life, nonorphans (n = 94) (mean)	10.7	9.5
Effective patent life by sales in second year after introduction (mean)		
All drugs with sales data (69 drugs)	10.5	9.2
$0–10 million sales (43 drugs)	9.8	8.4
$10–$50 million (9 drugs)	10.6	8.4
$50–$100 million (8 drugs)	11.9	11.2
>$100 million (9 drugs)	13.1	11.7

Source: Office of Technology Assessment (1993).

Whoever actively induces infringement of a patent shall be liable as an infringer. Whoever sells a component of a patented machine, manufacture, combination or composition, or a material or apparatus for use in practicing a patented process, constituting a material part of the invention, knowing the same to be especially made or especially adapted for use in an infringement of such patent, and not a staple article of commodity of commerce suitable for substantial noninfringing use, shall be liable as a contributory infringer. (CEB 1993)

But as patent protection is territorial in nature, a US patent affords inventors protection only in the United States (Tancer 1993). So, a US inventor must seek comparable protection in each country in which he or she wants to use the patents. There is little or no protection for those who fail to do so, or who operate in a country that has either no patent laws or laws very different in scope or duration. Problems of protecting US patents in other countries have intensified in recent years. The International Trade Commission estimated 1991 losses to the pharmaceutical industry through patent piracy at $5 billion (Tancer 1993).

International Patent Treaties

Many countries have established their own patent systems following the basic framework of the British Statute of Monopolies in 1623 and patent laws of the United States (1790) and France (1791). The requirements for patentability and privileges for a patent recipient, however, are by no means consistent from one country to another. Many efforts have been made to harmonize the different patent systems worldwide. The following multinational conventions are major treaties to regulate formal and substantive patent matters between member states (Beier et al. 1985).

Paris Convention

The Paris Convention is the basic international convention covering all fields of intellectual property, including patents. Administered by the World Intellectual Property Organization (WIPO), the Convention has 94 member states, including the United States. Members must treat nationals of other member states equally with their own regarding the protection of intellectual property. It recognizes the date of first filing of a patent application in any member state as establishing a right of priority for a corresponding patent application in any other member state if the latter is filed within 12 months of the first filing (Beier et al. 1985). The United States had previously used a "first-to-invent" priority but is converting to the "first-to-file" system.

Patent Cooperation Treaty (PCT)

The PCT, together with the European Patent Convention, were enacted in June 1978. The PCT is also administered by WIPO and is set up on the basis of an "international application." Protection may be obtained at the option of the applicant in some or all of the member states, which presently comprise most Organization for Economic Cooperation and Development (OECD) countries and other countries having important patent activity (Beir et al. 1985).

European Patent Convention (EPC)

This Convention provides for a single patent application to be executed before the European Patent Office (EPO) designating any number of contracting states. The initial application may be made in any of the regional offices of the EPO but is in due course examined centrally by the EPO in Munich. The European patent does not mature into a single item of property but becomes a national entity in each designated state and emerges as a "bundle" of national patents—e.g., European patent (United Kingdom, European patent (France), etc.—which thereafter become independent objects of property (Beier et al. 1985).

Budapest Treaty

The Budapest Treaty was signed in 1980 and provides for the recognition of biological culture collections as International Depositary Authorities. Any new strain of microorganism can be deposited in one of these authorities for the purposes of applying for a patent application in any member state.

World Trade Organization (WTO)

The newly founded WTO was established to create a more formal agreement on trade-related aspects of intellectual property rights, Other objectives were to reduce distortions and impediments to international trade—taking into account the need to promote effective and adequate protection of intellectual property rights—and to ensure that measures and procedures to enforce intellectual property rights do not themselves become barriers to legitimate trade (Dennin 1995). This agreement is based largely on existing international conventions such as the Paris Convention. The WTO establishes a 20-year period of protection from the time of filing for the patent. As a member country, the United States is conforming to the new patent protection period, although this marks a departure from the previous 17-year patent period (dating from the date the patent was conferred).

Patent Procedures Under International Conventions

Normally, an applicant will make a patent application in one's home country and will file corresponding applications abroad at a later date. Foreign applications must be made separately in each country under the respective national laws. For EPC member states, the application may be sought either as separate national applications or in the form of a European application which also may claim Convention priority from the first application. Another procedure is to file an "international application" under the Patent Cooperation Treaty. An international application proceeds as a single application for certain preliminary investigations (formalities and novelty search, etc.) but must then divide into national applications in the designated states for substantive examination on its merits. Thus an international application ultimately results in separate national patents (Beier et al. 1985).

There are specific rules which apply to international patent applicants. For instance, patents applied for in various convention countries stand entirely independently so that invalidation in one convention country will not affect the survival of a patent in any other convention country, and the inventor has the right to be mentioned in the patent in all convention countries (Boehm 1967).

Shortcomings of the Patent System

Although the patent system has successfully encouraged innovations and stimulated firms to produce new knowledge and to sell or use it profitably, it has a number of disadvantages. The first is that new knowledge may not be used as widely as it could be, because the patentee, in order to maximize profit, will set a price sufficiently high such that some people who could make productive use of the patented item will be discouraged from doing so (Mansfield 1988). From the societal point of view, all people who can use the idea should be permitted to do so at a very low cost, equal to the marginal cost of their doing so. Another way of stating this is that the price of the information should be set equal to its marginal cost, which is often practically zero. Second, a patent with a long life may give competitors an incentive to make horizontal imitation: development of products that are close substitutes to a patented drug and yield little or no therapeutic gain. These imitative products are frequently alternative, but not necessary improved, methods of producing a drug that is manufactured with a patented process. According to Gallini (1992), the longer a drug's patent life, the more likely it is that rivals will make such imitations, or "me too" drugs. Extending patent life, therefore, may not provide the innovator with the anticipated increased incentives to engage in research or to patent the innovation. Gallini suggests that optimal patent lives are currently sufficiently short to discourage imitation. But Congress has tried to give pharmaceutical innovators longer protection periods by legislation like the Orphan Drug Act of 1983 and the Drug Price Competition and Patent Term Restoration Act of 1984, and the number of "me, too" drugs has increased as well (Gallini 1992).

It is important to recognize that the patent is not the only means for assuring market exclusivity for a product. The right to trademark a name also gives a form of market exclusivity. During the patent period physicians and patients learn to associate the brand name with the more scientific generic name. Thus, Motrin was the trade name of one of the most popular ibuprofen anelgesics, and Tylenol will always be thought of as the most popular form of acetominophen. And the popular antibiotics Bactrim and Septra are far easier to remember than their scientific name, cotrimoxazole. Even when a patent expires and other firms are allowed to market the same drug, they can only do so under the generic name. The trade name remains the property of the originator firm and enables the originator firm to retain some market share, either in the prescription market or in the OTC market, as discribed in Chapter 2.

Patents and Societal Choice

Patent protection represents a societal compromise between the objectives of encouraging innovation and investment in R&D and assuring society access to the fruits of this investment. Pharmaceutical patents are granted in the three areas of innovation: compound, composition, and process. A particular product may be covered by patents in any or all of these areas.

Although numerous international patent conventions exist, it is clear that nations continue to retain sovereign control over patents, and ultimately a patent applicant must apply for and be granted patent protection in each country in which they expect to market one's products.

The regulatory authority of the FDA over pharmaceuticals entails a sizable reduction in the effective patent period. In response to this reduction, Congress has lengthened the period of protection. While the legislation has been successful in encouraging development of more new drug products, it is not clear that investment in innovative research has increased. The side effect of encouraging development of imitative products is undoubtedly an effect of these attempts. These "me, too" drugs are seen by some as wasteful (Kessler 1994) because they add little clinically to the medical "armamentarium." They do have an important economic role, however, in moderating drug prices within drug classes.

References

Beier Crespi RS, and Straus J, *Biotechnology and Patent Protection: an International Review*, Washington DC: Organization for Economic Cooperation and Development, 1985.

Boehm R, *The British Patent System*, Cambridge: Cambridge University Press, 1967.

Boston Consulting Group, *The Changing Environment for U.S. Pharmaceuticals: The Role of Pharmaceutical Companies in a Systems Approach to Health Care*, New York: The Boston Consulting Group, 1993.

Dennin F, *Law and Practice of World Trade Organization*, New York: Oceana Publication, 1995.

Gallini T, "Patent policy and costly imitation," *RAND Journal of Economics* 23 (1): 52–63, Spring 1992.

Grabowski H and Vernon J, "Longer patents for increased generic competition in the US: the Waxman-Hatch act after one decade," *PharmacoEconomics* 10(suppl 2): 110–123, 1996.

Kessler D, Rose JL, Temple RJ Schapiro R, and Griffin JP, "Therapeutic class wars—drug promotion in a competitive marketplace," *The New England Journal of Medicine* 331:1350–1353, November 17, 1994.

Mansfield E, *Microeconomics: Theory and Applications*, 6th edition, New York: W. W. Norton, 1988.

Miller AR and Davis H, *Intellectual Property: Patents, Trademarks, and Copyrights*, St Paul, MN: West, 1990.

Office of Technology Assessment, *Pharmaceutical R&D: Costs, Risks and Rewards*, Washington DC.: Government Printing Office 1993.

Tancer RS, "Pharmaceutical patents and some international trade issues: Canada, the United States, and NAFTA," *Clinical Therapeutics* 15(6):1177–1984, 1993.

Wiggins SN, "The pharmaceutical R&D decision process," in: Helms RB (ed), *Drugs and Health: Issues and Policy Objectives*, Washington, DC: American Enterprise Institute, pp 55–83, 1981.

10

Evaluating New Drugs

Cost is only one determinant of a decision to purchase a good or service. The expected benefit to be derived from its purchase is another. As a result of new cost-containment incentives of managed-care plans, providers and insurers are subjecting new health services, and especially pharmaceuticals, to evaluation in which costs and benefits are explicitly compared. In this chapter we analyze the three methodologies that are frequently used to make these evaluations: cost-benefit analysis, cost-effectiveness analysis, and cost-utility analysis. We discuss the appropriate roles of each of these approaches and the uses to which they are being put, and we discuss programs in use in the United States and abroad for integrating these evaluations into health systems.

Optimizing Production of Health

The rationale for evaluating goods or services by comparing their cost to their expected benefits, however measured, derives directly from the theory of production, in which output is maximized for a level of expenditures by using a combination of inputs (goods and services) described by the point of tangency between a curve describing various quantities of each of two factor inputs that will produce the same level of output, the isoquant curve, and the cost line. The cost line describes the various combinations of these inputs that can be utilized at the same cost. The slope of this cost line is (the negative of) the relative factor prices. Figure 10.1 shows this relationship for two inputs, A and B. Curve Q_0 shows all combinations of A and B which produce the same level of output, and curve Q_1 shows all combinations which produce a different, higher, level of output. Cost line c_0 shows all combi-

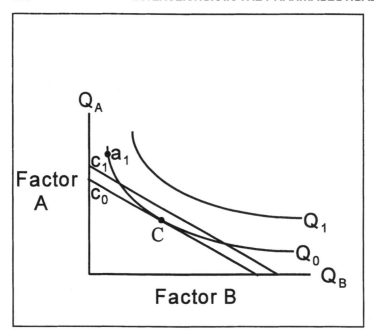

Figure 10.1 Maximizing Output Within Cost Limitations

nations of A and B that can be purchased with a particular level of cost. The slope of c_0 is determined, of course, by the relative prices of A and B. Any line above c_0, such as c_1, describes combinations which cost more than c_0, and any line below c_0 describes combinations whose cost will be less.

The point of tangency, C in the figure is special, representing the highest level of output that can be reached by using A and B consistent with cost c_0. Simultaneously, it represents the lowest level of expenditure needed to reach a particular output level Q_0. Any other point on the cost line, represents the same expenditure as c_0 but produces a lower level of output. Conversely, another point on the isoquant, such as point a_1 produces the same level of output as C, but at a higher cost. Only point C portrays a factor combination that achieves the highest level of output possible for a given cost—or, conversely, the lowest cost consistent with achieving a particular output level.

Alternative treatments, such as drug therapies, can be compared to one another with reference to the figure. A particular level of benefit, such as lives saved or cases of disability averted, is associated with producing a level of health, represented by Q_0, and all combinations of inputs which are needed to achieve that particular benefit are represented by the various points on the isoquant curve. While many therapeutic alternatives may pro-

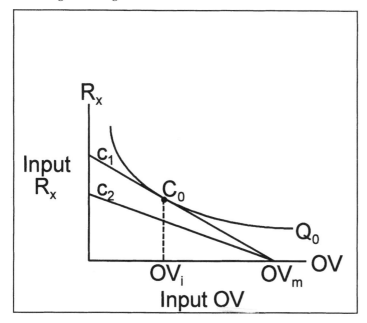

Figure 10.2 Choosing Among Drugs with Different Prices

duce the same level of benefit, only one does so at a lower cost than the others. This is the one described by point C.

All assessments that compare the cost of drugs to their efficacy derive from the model we have just considered. Using a suboptimal combination of treatments (for example, office visits and drugs) is analogous to our selecting a point on the budget line other than c_0, for one incurs the same costs but produces less health. Selecting the right *combinations* of inputs is critical to containing health costs while maintaining quality of care.

Another pharmaceutical economic assessment that frequently needs to be done selects the optimal drug from among alternatives in a drug class. Different drugs will produce different levels of health, holding other inputs constant. This could be represented by drawing a family of isoquants, one for each drug, depicting the level of health produced by a particular quantity of the drug (and other inputs). A drug that is less effective than another will have an isoquant lower than the other. In other words, selecting drugs that do the same thing, but require different intensities to be equally effective, is a technical issue—a matter of comparing isoquants.

A third possibility is to choose among drugs that produce the same levels of health, but at different cost, because one is more expensive than the other. All the drugs describe the same isoquant, but their budget lines differ, reflecting different prices. Figure 10.2 shows this situation, with the two axes representing quantities of pharmaceuticals and physician office visits as the two factors. Isoquant Q_0 shows the level of health that can be produced by equal quantities of the alternative products. But suppose product Rx_1 is the least costly. Its cost line is shown as c_1 and is tangent to Q_0 at point C_0. Drug Rx_2, however, is more costly, so its cost line, c_2, is rotated counterclockwise about the point OV_m, determined by the price of office visits. Line c_2 does not reach Q_0 at any level of use of Rx_2 and OV. At level of utilization OV_1, Rx_2 will only be able to produce a lower level of health, shown by an isoquant below curve Q_0.

An assessment that compares the cost of a treatment to the expected monetary value of its benefits is a cost-benefit analysis. But if the assessment measures the benefits in nonmonetary terms such as lives saved or years of life extended, the technique is a cost-effectiveness analysis. In the third technique, cost-utility analysis, the benefit of the intervention is measured by the amount of utility, or satisfaction, produced. An example of a cost-utility analysis is the attempt to measure the benefit directly by looking at the quality of life resulting from treatment. Approaches which attempt to measure improved quality of life measure the number of quality-adjusted life years (QALYs) or disability-adjusted life years (DALYs) produced by a program (see, for example, Kalish et al. 1995; World Bank 1993). We now consider some examples to illustrate how a comparison of costs and outcomes of alternative therapies might be performed.

Most of the analyses that compare a program's costs to its benefits, effectiveness, or utility consider the incremental or marginal changes rather than average levels, as noted by Eisenberg (1989). In other words one considers the consequences of increasing an already existing program, or utilizing a new drug. One therefore compares the *additional* program costs to its *additional* program outcomes. This is called marginal analysis. Marginal analysis is useful because most policy decisions are made incrementally, rather than program-wide. It is also important because marginal costs and benefits may differ from the average. Although one might want to know the average (or total) costs and benefits of cancer screening, it is usually more interesting to ask what would happen if we *increased* (or decreased) the amount of this screening by, say, $100 million.* To do the analysis one has to determine which patients would be screened with the additional money (or which patients would be dropped from current screening programs in the case of a marginal reduction). One would like to drop those patients who are most costly to screen, or for whom the case yield is particularly low. In the case of expansion, one would like to put one's resources where the efficiency is likely to be the highest. Ideally, a program is implemented from

---

*While most readers would have trouble thinking of $100 million as a "marginal" amount, to policy analysts in the Department of Health and Human Services, it is!

the beginning with the most efficient uses of resources first, followed by progressively rising costbenefit or cost-effectiveness ratios.

Cost-Benefit Analysis

Historically, cost-benefit analysis has been used to indicate whether public works projects such as dams or highways should be built. The ability of the approach to measure the social benefit of such programs is most useful. And extending the approach to health programs is possible because the ability to measure the burden of disease, including the economic burden of smoking- or alcohol-related disease, has been well developed (see, for example, Luce and Schweitzer 1978).

Suppose a disease can be treated by two regimens. The customary treatment entails use of a well-established drug accompanied by a relatively long hospital stay. The second treatment makes use of a newer, more powerful drug that shortens the hospital stay. A cost-benefit (*CB*) analysis of the new drug compares the cost differential of the drug to the cost savings (benefit) of the shorter hospital stay. Let us assume that the new drug costs $400, while the old drug costs $100. Suppose additionally that the new drug shortens the hospital stay by 2 days, from 5 to 3 days. If the hospital costs $1350 per day, the *CB* ratio of the new drug, *CB*, is the cost increase divided by the cost savings, or benefit:

$$CB = (\$400 - \$100)/2 \times \$1350 = 1/9$$

In other words, an expenditure of $1 on the new drug saves $9 in reduced hospital costs. Although this example appears simple and the results unequivocal, some decision makers may not realize the entire savings. A hospital facing prospective reimbursement would find the new treatment highly cost-beneficial, because the additional cost of the new drug is more than covered by the savings in hospital costs. An insurer paying for all of the treatment costs on a fee-for-service basis would also realize the full cost savings. The patient, on the other hand, may not be financially responsible for any of the health care costs of either therapy and would therefore be neutral between the two alternatives. And a hospital that is being paid on a fee-for-service basis may find that it is better off with the older therapy and longer hospital stay, especially if it has excess capacity and the earlier discharge simply produces more unfilled beds.

An extension of this analysis recognizes that a shorter recuperation entails a quicker return to normal activity for the patient. Counting increased wages makes the benefits to society even larger. But neither the hospital nor the insurer would notice the change. Only the patient's employer, and perhaps the patient, would. This shows that measuring the costs and benefits must always be done with reference to a particular perspective—the hospital, the insurer, or the patient, for example. Counting all financial impacts is termed the "societal" perspective, because society ultimately captures all the cost increases and savings. Cost-benefit analysis was originally developed to analyze infrastructure investments from an entire economy's (societal) perspective. But none of the individual stakeholders may realize all of these savings. In our example the hospital and the insurer are especially likely to benefit from the savings, depending upon the reimbursement system. They would therefore be expected to adopt the new technology. The patient, on the other hand, has little incentive to request the drug-intensive therapy if the costs of either treatment are reimbursed by the third party. The patient may even be indifferent to the indirect, time, cost savings if time off from work is covered by the employer's sick-leave benefit. The employer, however, has a stake in the decision in two ways. The first is that the costs of sick time (ignored in our first analysis) may be reduced by the new therapy. Additionally, the firm's future health insurance premium is dependent upon prior health care utilization. Therefore, adoption of a new technology may mean even more to the employer than to the insurer, for the insurer pays the additional cost of the old therapy in the short run but will pass it on to the employer in the longer run. Competition among insurers will be instrumental in speeding adoption of the cost-saving technology because as soon as one insurer requires the new treatment and passes the cost savings on to its clients in the form of reduced premiums, the other insurers will be induced to follow. Competition may not have such a dramatic effect on adoption of quality-enhancing services, however, because decision-makers have been slow to understand quality differences among health care organizations. Providers such as physicians and hospitals will be similarly reluctant to adopt new technologies if the savings accrue to patients rather than to them.

It is clear, therefore, that a cost-benefit calculation must be done with reference to particular stakeholders in the decision. One party may pay the higher costs but not necessarily receive the full benefits. This explains some apparent anomolies in which a cost-saving technology is not diffused as rapidly as one might expect. The explanation frequently lies in an analysis of the distribution of gains and losses among the decision-makers.

An example is the funding of smoking cessation programs. Numerous studies have demonstrated the excess health care costs associated with smoking, and yet health insurers have traditionally not paid for smoking cessation activities, and even HMOs did not offer these services until recently. Why is this? The answer is that many of the costs of smoking-related disease occur only later in the smoker's life, and the insurer of a young or middle-aged smoker knows that it is unlikely that the person will remain insured by the time ill effects such as emphysema or lung cancer present themselves. Either another employer's insurer will have to incur those costs or, if the person reaches age 65, it is Medicare which will bear the costs. The insurer is therefore faced with the choice of paying for smoking cessation programs for which it receives little benefit, or not covering them at all. The obvious remedy would be for Medicare to cover the costs of disease prevention programs for people of any age if the expected age of disease onset is at least 65. This would stimulate use of these prevention programs and thereby reduce the social costs of illness. But at present there is no mechanism by which Medicare can pay for health services consumed by younger patients, except for those with permanent disability.

A complete cost-benefit analysis must include not only the direct costs of medical care but also the indirect costs, which are comprised of the value of the patient's lost time performing normal activities. We considered this briefly in the previous example when we accounted for the reduced cost of time away from work associated with the newer drug therapy. Many new medical technologies achieve substantial benefits in terms of reduced indirect costs. Examples include arthroscopic and laproscopic surgical techniques, which allow the patient to resume normal function in a matter of days rather than weeks after surgery. Angioplasty for occluded coronary arteries is another invasive procedure which allows for a far quicker recovery than customary treatment: open heart surgery. Pharmaceuticals have achieved comparable benefits. Psychoactive drugs to treat depression and schizophrenia have been remarkably successful in allowing patients to lead near-normal lives at home and in the community rather than having to remain institutionalized. The burden of indirect costs is greater than that of direct costs for many diseases (Rice et al. 1985).

The indirect rewards of averted infections, strokes, and heart attacks are difficult to identify conceptually, let alone measure accurately. While the direct medical costs of diseases are straightforward, Rice and her colleagues have demonstrated that measuring the burden of premature death and disability must include the indirect, time, costs of the disease, as well. But there is little agreement on the appropriate measures of this dimension of the burden. The customary approach has been to measure the burden by lost wages, the "human capital" approach. The notion that people's lives are worth what the labor market pays people has clear logic to it, and it is consistent with economic reasoning that something's actual value is better assessed by the market's dispassionate determination than by people's perception. Thus the life of a successful professional is worth more than that of a schoolteacher. And it follows that the loss to society of premature death or disability will be greater in the former case than in the latter. But this calculation leaves many unsatisfied. Wage differentials are in part based upon historic patterns of gender and ethnic discrimination. Should adjustments be made in order to "correct" wages? Another major problem is that the loss brought about by the early death or disability of a retiree would have zero value under this approach, thereby eliminating estimated gains produced by drugs designed to treat diseases of the elderly. The human capital approach, while measuring one dimension of a person's worth to society, is incapable of capturing the whole picture.

A second approach to measuring the value of life goes beyond the labor market assessment and asks directly how people value various states of health. The technique assesses how much money individuals would be willing to pay to avoid a reduction in health status representing the consequences of a disease. If one could ascertain the appropriate amounts from individuals, such as by structured personal interviews, the values would represent the perceived burden of a disease leading to premature death or disability. The aggregate of these determinations of people's willingness to pay for health is proposed as one estimate of society's resources which ought to be spent on disease research or treatment. Donaldson et al. (1996) has applied this methodology to programs to reduce food-borne infection and, in another study (Donaldson et al. 1995), to antenatal screening for cystic fibrosis. And O'Brien et al. (1995) has used the approach to measure the value to individuals of improved therapy for depression. Nonetheless, the willingness-to-pay approach to measure the burden of illness has not been used extensively, perhaps because of the difficulty in developing an instrument that will accurately assess people's preferences for a wide variety of potential outcomes (for a more extensive discussion of willingness-to-pay, or "contingent valuation," see Drummond 1980).

A third approach is called "revealed preference" and analyzes existing spending decisions to discern how society currently values saved lives. Individuals and society continuously make decisions on spending money to save lives. Decisions made by individuals include decisions on adherance to preventive health practices such as influenza or tetanus immunizations. We also make daily decisions which balance health against other objectives. Examples include fast driving, excessive eating, smoking, or engaging in dangerous hobbies like mountain climbing or piloting small airplanes. But more frequently analysts have sought guidance on estimates of the value of life by looking at public decisions. Such programs include the decisions to install life-saving equipment at airports, on highways, or at work sites. Equally instructive are decisions which society makes *not* to spend resources for some of those programs because the interventions are "too expensive." One difficulty with this approach is its aggregate nature and another is the wide variation in expenditures that one observes. Consistency seems not to be the hallmark of either private or public decisions to save lives. For example, Table 10.1 shows the wide range of cost per life saved evident in existing nutrition intervention programs.

One last extension of cost-benefit analysis should be noted. This is the effect of time on the value of costs and benefits of illness and treatment. The time value of money implies that an amount of money in the present is worth more than the same amount in the future, not because of the effect of inflation on the value of money but because we all prefer money (or the things we can buy with money) now rather than later. Another explanation is that money is productive and having it in the present enables us to put it to work, such as by investing it or depositing it in a bank where it will accumulate interest over time. The importance of discounting can be great

Table 10.1   Cost-Effectiveness Ratios of Health Interventions

Program	Target Population	Cost per Death Averted, in dollars
Iron supplementation	Pregnant women	800
Iron supplementation	Entire population	2000
Iodine supplementation	Entire population	4650
Iodine of salt or water	Entire population	1000
Vitamin A supplementation	Children under 5	50
Vitamin A fortification	Entire population	154
Food supplementation	Children under 5	1942
Food supplementation	Pregnant women	733

Source: World Bank (1993).

if the time between expenditure on a program (say a smoking cessation intervention) and its benefit is long. For example, an expenditure of $1 today is equivalent to over $7 in 30 years at a discount rate of 7%. This puts a high burden of proof on many health programs because it is common for the benefits to be achieved many years after the treatment. If one asks society to give up current resources for the promise of returns at a later time, the time value of money dictates that those future benefits should be large enough to warrant deferring present consumption for future gain.

It is clear that present expenditure decisions based upon future benefits will be sensitive to the discount rate chosen. The lower the rate the greater will be the present value of those future benefits, and hence the more attractive these investments will appear. Choosing the appropriate rate is a matter of some disagreement among economists. The basic notion is that a rate should be chosen that mirrors interest rates or investment yields pertaining to *other* investments, for if the assumed rate is different from the "market" yield, the investment project is either overpaying or underpaying for its capital. Some do make the argument that interest rates for social investments ought to be below market rates so as to encourage those investments, but this is a difficult argument to defend because other investments that produce, say, jobs are also valuable to society. Choosing a discount rate is discussed in more detail by Luce and Elixhauser (1990).

Cost-Effectiveness Analysis

Frequently, calculation of the monetary value of outcomes is impractical. Under these circumstances, cost-effectiveness analysis is used. In cost-effectiveness analysis, outcomes are frequently measured in "real" rather than "monetary" terms. Suppose antibiotics *A* and *B* are both used to treat a particular infection. Drug *A* produces a cure in 80% of the patients taking it, but drug *B*, a recent entrant in the market, achieves a cure in 90% of the cases. Medically, drug *B* is the superior drug and would be expected to be noted as the "drug of choice" in treatment guidelines that look only at clinical effectiveness. But suppose drug *B* costs 30% more than drug *A*. Drug purchasers, whether they are consumers paying directly for pharmaceuticals or health plans that are purchasing drugs on behalf of an insured population, have limited resources available to pay for drugs. Alternative uses of those limited funds exist. The consumer can purchase other consumer goods which produce utility, such as food, housing, or entertainment. Institutional payers can pay for additional health services for their insured patients. The purchaser attempting to achieve a level of benefit at a minimum cost will need to compare the outcomes and the costs of the alternatives. In this example, the appropriate measure of outcome for the drugs is "cure for an infection." For every patient treated, drug A's expected benefit will be 0.8 cures, while drug B will achieve 0.9 cures. Let us assume that the cost of drug A is $10 per course of treatment, resulting in a cost per cure of $10/0.8, or $12.50. Drug B, on the other hand, achieves its 0.9 cure rate at a cost of $13 (30% higher than the cost of drug A). The cost per cure is therefore $13/0.9, or $14. Drug A is therefore less expensive per cure than drug B and will be the preferred choice for consumers or purchasers seeking to minimize the cost of treatment for the infection.

There are alternative approaches to this evaluation, and the decision of which to use is more complicated than may at first be evident. As is often the case, the question one asks should be determined by the sort of answer one is looking for!

For one thing, drugs produce widely differing effects, and consideration of alternative treatments must compare the appropriate outcomes. For example, a "clot-buster" drug given to heart attack patients in emergency rooms will be assessed according to the number of lives saved, while antibiotics (such as drugs A and B in the earlier example) and antidiarrheals are assessed according to the number of treatments or "cures" effected. Many drug therapies do not actually cure a disease but only control it. Antihypertensive or antihyperlipidemic agents do not cure their respective conditions, but contain them so that the sequela, such as stroke or atherosclerosis, are prevented.

Cost-effectiveness analysis is especially useful in comparing programs whose effects, or outcomes, are similar, such as saving lives, curing a disease, or preventing a recurrence. Not only can one compare treatments for the same condition, as we did in the comparison of drugs A and B, but one can even compare interventions that are totally unrelated—as long as they have the same kinds of outcomes. For example, one could compare the cost of saving a life through advanced cancer treatment with that of new sophisticated ambulances, or even new airport radar systems. Although the programs are totally different, and deal with different population groups, they have something in common—their ability to save lives. Similarly, one can compare programs that reduce disability, thereby producing disability-free days. One can compare the cost per disability-free days across programs that prevent debilitating disease, reduce arthritis pain, and produce faster recovery post surgery.

Although cost-effectiveness analysis can be used to compare programs producing a wide variety of outcomes, it cannot be used to compare programs with dissimilar outcomes. For example, cost-effectiveness analysis cannot be used to compare new life-saving ambulances with drugs that reduce the severity of arthritis. But comparing different approaches to the same problem, such as two different highway routes, or two different smoking cessation programs, is better left to cost-effectiveness analysis.

Cost-Utility Analysis

The inability of C-E analysis to deal simultaneously with different outcome measures is a serious weakness because many health programs have multiple outcomes. In response to this concern, cost-utility (C-U) analysis has received considerable scholarly and practical attention for over 20 years (see Luce and Elixhauser 1990). The idea behind C-U analysis is that degrees of disability can be quantified and compared across diseases and conditions.

There has been considerable disagreement among scholars concerning appropriate measurement techniques. The game-theoretic approach, based upon Von Neuman and Morgenstern (1953), elicits patient preferences and utilities indirectly by asking them to compare two illness scenarios or states by assigning probabilities to each that make the two occurrences equally preferable. A variation of this approach asks patients to equate the utility of two illness scenarios by placing each at different points in time.

Another way of measuring the value of function is to assign disability (or the converse, "ability") scores to health states. Full function for 1 year is counted as a full quality-adjusted life year (QALY), but disability reduces the QALY by some proportion, a. If this parameter represents the proportion of disability, $(1-a) = b$ represents the proportion of quality of life remaining ($0 \leqslant b \leqslant 1$). If $b = 1$, the full quality of life exists, but $b = 0$ implies a level of disability equivalent to death. This idea is useful in considering health programs because treatments frequently differ in the degree to which full health is achieved. In the case of end-stage renal disease (ESRD), for example, hemodialysis has been the life-saving therapy since the 1940s. The treatment, however, is highly intrusive of a patient's life, typically requiring three dialysis sessions per week, each lasting from 3 to 4 hours. Thus, dialysis is only a partial substitute for normal kidney function and therefore restores only a fraction of full QALY. Kidney transplantation, on the other hand, restores a patient to nearly full function. While both interventions save lives, transplantation achieves a higher quality of life, and a comparison of program costs and outcomes should acknowledge this.

But equating utility to some quantitative measure of disability or impairment is a big leap and may not be correct. Still worse is aggregating utility preferences across an entire population, necessary if one is to compare social preferences for one medical treatment or another.

Similarly, health programs can be compared by considering the time path

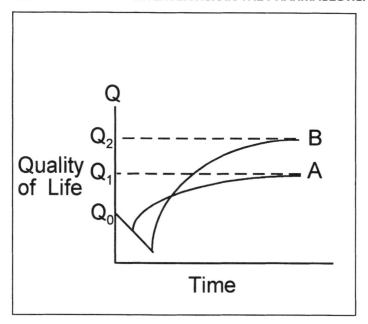

Figure 10.3 Quality of Life Over Time for Two Interventions

of recovery or achievement of function. Suppose, for example, that a more aggressive treatment achieves long-term outcomes superior to those achieved by the standard therapy but produces worse short-term effects. The quality of life over time for patients treated with the two therapies A and B is shown in Figure 10.3. The figure shows both patients starting off at the same level of quality of life, Q_0, representing moderate disability. Conservative treatment, A, produces moderate short-term pain, suffering, and disability, but the patient quickly improves to a quality of life of Q_1. Treatment B, on the other hand, produces more serious deterioration in quality of life during treatment, but the patient eventually recovers to Q_2 ($>Q_1$). Which treatment is better? By comparing the QALY profiles and discounting future benefits to their present value the two can be compared.

But as attractive as utility analysis is, important problems remain in its implementation. The most serious problem is the assignment of utility, or disability factors, to various health states. It is difficult to ascertain the proportion of ability represented by a particular state of health for any single patient. People differ in their perception of the severity of various limitations in normal activity and they adapt differently over time to their limitations.

Numerous approaches to measuring quality of life have been employed in the literature (see Luce and Elixhauser 1990). One uses the Activities of Daily Living (ADL) scale (Lawton and Brody 1969). The ADL scale consists of six dimensions of function, each measured with a Likert five-point scale.

The subjects are asked to rate their ability to function independently in dressing, bathing, toileting, eating, walking, and transferring from bed to chair. Responses to each of the questions range from 0 (cannot perform the function) to 4 (performs the function without difficulty). The ADL then sums all of the individual six scores to produce an overall functional ability score. The ADL is used frequently to measure the level of functional ability of individuals or groups. Its simplicity is a major feature, but a number of methodological concerns suggest that it is far from a perfect instrument. The first problem is lack of sensitivity to populations with generally good health. The ADL activities are so basic that only the quite frail have significant numbers of limitations. The second concern is that it may not be appropriate to weigh each of the limitations equally. A third problem is the ADL assumption that all scale increments are of equal value, so that, for example, a loss in function of two units in one scale is equivalent to losses of one unit in each of two different dimensions. Lastly, the ADL assumption that the average functional level for a group of individuals can be calculated as the sum of the functional scores for all members of the group divided by the number of individuals in the group is problematic. The assumption of equal utilities for each member of the community for each unit of the scale is a very strong assumption.

A variation on the QALY approach has been used by the World Bank in its 1993 *World Development Report* (World Bank 1993). In this study the burden of illness was measured for each country by estimating the extent of disability caused by illness and combining the resulting years of disability with the years of life lost due to premature death. This functional ability score is referred to as Disability-Adjusted Life Years (DALYs) (World Bank 1993). Another variation has been used by Culyer and his associates (see Culyer and Wagstaff 1995).

Policy Applications

The most frequently used approach to evaluate new drugs for policy purposes is cost-effectiveness. C-E analysis is especially well suited to the policy setting because health plans—both public and private—are frequently confronted with the question of whether or not to cover particular drugs, and if so, at what price.

The context of this question is usually the introduction of a new drug, with other drugs in the same therpauetic class already in the market. Health insurers rarely act as passive "price takers." Rather they exert their market power to bid down the price to the level that the plan feels the drug is worth. C-E analysis is frequently used to make this determination. In fact, knowing that insurers are now particularly concerned with the cost-effectiveness of drugs, many pharmaceutical manufacturers are developing large departments devoted to the study of the economic measurement of drug effectiveness.

In the United States the largest government health insurer, Medicare, does not reimburse for outpatient pharmaceuticals. Therefore there is no Medicare ambulatory drug reimbursement policy and so Medicare's direct role in assessing and using the cost-effectiveness of specific pharmaceuticals is small. However, Medicare pays hospitals prospectively through Diagnosis Related Groups (DRGs). Therefore hospitals decide internally on the most efficient course of treatment for each patient; Medicare does not pay for pharmaceuticals directly. State Medicaid programs, on the other hand, do reimburse for both inpatient and outpatient drugs. Rather than rely upon a pricing formula for pharmaceuticals, however, two other approaches are used in Medicaid programs: mandatory discounting and product selection through formularies.

Mandatory discounting of pharmaceutical prices was initiated with the 1990 Omnibus Budget Reconciliation Act (OBRA), which required drug companies to offer state Medicaid agencies the greatest discount they were giving to any other class of buyer. This program was discussed previously in Chapter 4. Pharmaceutical companies had traditionally granted deep discounts to Public Health Service hospitals, the Veterans Administration, local health department clinics, and some private providers such as university student health services. The intent of the legislation was clear—to force the pharmaceutical companies to give each Medicaid program the same large discounts already observed for these other providers of health care to poor, vulnerable populations. Unfortunately, the reality was somewhat different from the intent, as firms appear to have raised the discounted prices rather than lower the Medicaid prices (US Congress, General Accounting Office 1991).

The FDA is concerned with the efficacy of a new drug (as well as its safety), so clinical trials are usually designed to test the drug in question against a placebo (inert substance), as discussed in Chapter 7. If a positive effect is found relative to the placebo, the product is said to be "effective." Two questions should be asked about the results of such trials. First, is the study design a realistic representation of the actual circumstances which would surround use of the new drug by patients and their physicians (who were *not* associated with a clinical trial protocol)? Second are differences between the experimental and control subjects "meaningful," as opposed to being merely "statistically significant"? Often, study results are statistically significant but are nonetheless so small as not to be very important.

Some other countries attempt to measure the cost-effectiveness of drugs in order to determine coverage—both whether to reimburse for specific drugs and how much. The most prominent of these is Australia, which requires an assessment of the cost-effectiveness of all new drugs and compares each new drug with existing drugs within the same drug class. A new drug will be reimbursed at a higher rate than that of existing drugs in the therapeutic class only if the C-E analysis demonstrates its superior effectiveness.

France also attempts to set a reimbursement price for drugs based for upon their effectiveness relative to existing drugs. The French system is not as rigorous as that of Australia, however, and other considerations enter the decision process, such as the employment which would be created by a drug's manufacturing facility.

Canada also monitors drug prices for its 10 provincial health plans according to the demonstrated effectiveness of the products. Its Patented Medicine Prices Review Board was established in 1987 to prevent "excessive" prices of patented drugs. When new drugs enter a market that already has similar products, the Board sees that introductory prices of the new product do not lead to higher per day or per treatment costs than those of existing drugs. In the case of particularly innovative drugs, introductory prices cannot exceed the median price of the same product in seven other countries where the drug is already marketed. For older drugs, price increases can not exceed the rate of change in Canada's Consumer Price Index. The sanctions available to the Board, should prices be found to be excessive, include negative publicity and even removal of the drug's market exclusivity and allowing other manufacturers to produce generic versions of the patented drug through compulsory licensing (US Congress General Accounting Office 1993).

In the United States C-E analysis is not used at the national level by any of the government health insurers, as noted earlier. It is, however, used increasingly by private health care organizations, especially those that reimburse directly for pharmaceuticals, such as HMOs and other managed-care plans. In addition, providers such as hospitals that are paid prospectively and therefore internalize their costs also have an incentive to select cost-minimizing patterns of care. McFarland (1994) has described the use of cost-effectiveness analysis in comparing treatment programs for depression within a managed-care setting, and O'Brien (1995) has done the same for asthma.

The results of cost-effectiveness analysis in these managed-care plans less often determine allowable prices for competing products, as is the case in Canada, France, and Australia, and more often determine which product within each therapeutic class will be offered to subscribers through drug formularies. Formularies are increasingly used both by insurers and hospitals as a means of directing physician prescribing toward those products judged to be most cost-effective. Formularies work well in cases where a less cost-effective drug is unnecessary for a patient. In this case switching the patient to the most cost-effective product often produces significant cost savings. On the other hand, patients needing the more expensive drug, perhaps because they are less tolerant of the first drug's side effects, are likely to incur higher costs of care if they do not get the more expensive drug because the cost savings associated with the less expensive drug may be minor in comparison with increased use of other health care services such as physician visits and hospital days. Whether a formulary saves money is therefore an empirical question, determined by the characteristics of the covered patients, the relative costs of both pharmaceuticals and other health care services, and the strictness of the formulary itself. This question was discussed previously in Chapter 8. Studies attempting to measure the net cost-savings effect of drug formularies have found them to be far less effective than anticipated in containing overall health expenditures (Hefner 1980; Schweitzer and Shiota 1992; Sloan et al. 1993; Moore and Newman 1993, Horn et al. 1996).

A difficulty of introducing cost-effectiveness analysis for pharmaceuticals more widely is that economic studies are not routinely conducted as part of the FDA's drug approval process. The FDA's jurisdiction is restricted to the biomedical aspects of drugs, particularly a new drug's safety and efficacy. These studies are conducted for drugs individually, with efficacy measured as the effect of a drug compared to that of a placebo, frequently in double-blind randomized clinical trials. Hays et al. 1996 have noted the difficulty in extending the scope of randomized clinical trials to include cost-effectiveness analysis. Although these studies would be very useful to the health policy and medical communities, the increased size and complexities of the studies would impose a large burden on drug manufacturers were these studies to become part of the FDA's approval process. Perhaps for these reasons, the FDA has never required broader studies of drugs—neither including economic aspects nor looking at the comparative effectiveness of competing drugs. Both of these types of studies are therefore left to other investigators, generally academic, to conduct. It is these studies, and not the clinical trials conducted for the FDA, that form the basis of comparisons used by third-party payers.

Interpretation and Misinterpretation of Cost-Effectiveness Studies

Cost-effectiveness studies produce ratios expressing the cost of a particular health intervention relative to a measure of its outcome. As discussed previously, the ratios of a number of interventions can be compared and used to select the health intervention that will accomplish an objective at minimum cost, or alternatively, maximize outcome for a given expenditure. Frequently, the results of these comparisons are interpreted whether or not products are more or less expensive than other therapies.

It is relatively easy to identify medical interventions which are known to be ineffective. In fact, while the advance of medical science entails the discovery of new treatments, it also entails recognition that some previously utilized interventions have not been effective. On the other end of the effectiveness scale are treatments which are not only clearly effective, but for which there are no substitutes. But in the middle are a large number of treatments with varying degrees of effectiveness and costs. These treatments exhibit a virtual continuum of cost-effectiveness ratios. Positions on this continuum illustrate different values placed on health outcomes, and one would expect that individuals would choose different treatments based upon tastes, preferences, and incomes. Health plans, similarly, may select different treatments according to their willingness to pay for outcomes. Viewing treatment alternatives in this way may explain differences in treatments for different patients. One would expect all patients to have the identical treatment only in the cases where one treatment dominates all alternatives, either because other treatments are ineffective or because the difference in cost-effectiveness between alternatives is very large.

One of the difficulties of applying a single health plan to an entire community is that identical treatment choices are likely to be determined for everybody in the community, regardless of individual preferences or willingness to pay. Health coverage options offering different levels of cost-effective treatment to different individuals who are willing to pay for higher or lower levels of coverage will be more efficient in terms of permitting individuals to purchase the amount of health care that is consistent with their overall income and consumption decisions.

References

Culyer AJ and Wagstaff A, "QALYS versus HYE (healthy year equivalents): A reply to Gafni, Birch, and Mehrez (Comment), *Journal of Health Economics* 14(1): 39–45, 1995

Donaldson C, Mapp T, Ryan M, and Curtin K, "Estimating the economic benefits of avoiding food-borne risk: is 'willingness to pay' feasible?" *Epidemiology and Infection* 116(3):285–294, 1996.

Donaldson C, Shackley P, Abdalla M, and Miedzybrodzka Z, "Willingness to pay for antenatal carrier screening for cystic fibrosis," *Health Economics* 4(6):439–452, 1995.

Drummond MF, *Principles of Economic Appraisal in Health Care*, Oxford: Oxford University Press, 1980.

Eisenberg JM, "Clinical economics: a guide to the economic analysis of clinical practices," *JAMA* 262(20):2879–2886, 1989.

Hays RD, Sherbourne CD, and Bozette SA, "Pharmacoeconomics and quality of life research beyond the randomized clinical trial," in Spilker B (ed), *Quality of Life and Pharmacoeconomics in Clinical Trials*, 2nd edition, Philadelphia: Lippincott-Raven, 1996.

Hefner DL, *Cost-Effectiveness of a Restrictive Drug Formulary: Louisiana vs. Texas*, Washington, DC: National Pharmaceutical Council, 1980.

Horn SD, Sharkey PD, and Tracy DM "Intended and unintended consequences of HMO cost-containment strategies: results from the managed care outcomes project," *American Journal of Managed Care* 2:253–264, 1996.

Kalish SC, Gurwitz JH, Krumholz HM, and Avorn J, "A cost-effectiveness model of thrombolytic therapy for acute myocardial infarction," *Journal of General Internal Medicine* 10(6):321–330, 1995.

Lawton MP and Brody EM, "Assessment of older people: Self maintaining and instrumental activities of daily living," *Gerontologist* 9:179–86, 1969.

Luce BR and Elixhauser A, *Standards for the Socioeconomic Evaluation of Health Care Services*, Berlin: Springer-Verlag, 1990.

Luce BR and Schweitzer SO, "Smoking and alcoholism: a comparison of their economic consequences," *New England Journal of Medicine* 298:569–571, March 9, 1978.

McFarland BH, "Cost-effectiveness considerations for managed care systems: treating depression in primary care," *American Journal of Medicine* 97(6A):47S–57S, 1994.

Moore WJ and Newman R, "Drug formulary restrictions as a cost-containment policy in Medicaid programs," *Journal of Law and Economics* 36:71–114, 1993.

O'Brien KP, "Managed care and the treatment of asthma," *Journal of Asthma* 32(5): 325–334, 1995.

O'Brien BJ, Novosel S, Torrance G, and Streiner D, "Assessing the economic value of a new antidepressant: a willingness-to-pay approach," *PharmacoEconomics* 8(1):34–45, 1995.

Rice D, Hodgson T, and Kopstein A, "The economic cost of illness: a replication and update," *Health Care Financing Review* 7(1):61–80, Fall 1985.

Schweitzer SO and Shiota SR, "Access and cost implications of state limitations on medicaid reimbursement for pharmaceuticals," *Annual Review of Public Health* 13: 399–410, 1992.

Sloan FA, Gordon GS, and Cocks DL, "Hospital drug formularies and use of hospital services," *Medical Care* 31(10):851–867, October 1993.

US Congress, General Accounting Office, *Medicaid: Changes in Drug Prices Paid by VA and DOD Since Enactment of Rebate Provisions*, Washington, DC: General Accounting Office, 1991.

US Congress, General Accounting Office, *Prescription Drug Prices: Analysis of Canada's Patented Medicine Prices Review Board* Washington, DC: General Accounting Office, 1993.

Von Neumann J and Morgenstern O, *Theory of Games and Economic Behavior*, New York: Wiley, 1953.

World Bank, *World Development Report, 1993*, Washington, DC: World Bank, 1993.

11

Pharmaceuticals and Health Policy: A Look Ahead

The most important health policy issues that will concern health care providers, policy analysts, and the pharmaceutical sector in the foreseeable future will continue to be quality, pricing, and access. Of course one's vision of the future is clouded by uncertainty as to the direction that overall health policy for the nation will take. There is no way that the pharmaceutical sector can be separated from the way the entire health care system is organized, financed, and regulated. We organize our look into the future by considering seven particular areas: the structure of the pharmaceutical industry, health system reform, drug prices, patent protection, drug approvals, the effect of managed care on access to pharmaceuticals, and the evolving role of the FDA.

The Structure of the Pharmaceutical Industry

The pharmaceutical industry has undergone substantial consolidation in the past 15 years. This has been marked by mergers involving both domestic and foreign firms. These mergers have resulted in vertical and horizontal integration. In the former case, pharmaceutical firms have sought better control over the market for their products. The mergers between some of the largest pharmaceutical companies and major pharmaceutical benefits managers and wholesalers are examples of major R&D firms seeking better control of the wholesale pharmaceutical market. Other vertical mergers have taken place between R&D firms, including Pfizer, Johnson & Johnson, and Sandoz, and disease management organizations developing protocols that define appropriate use of drugs for insurers. Through these mergers the manufacturers seek better means of marketing their products to managed-care health plans.

Other mergers have been horizontal in nature, in which firms have sought to become bigger by acquiring another entity doing much the same thing with the expectation that economies of scale will reduce overall costs and increase efficiency. The largest horizontal merger was the acquisition of Wellcome by Glaxo.

While the largest mergers have involved R&D-oriented firms, liaisons between the major firms and the much smaller biotechnology firms may be of even greater importance in the future. Many of the Swiss drug companies have acquired major holdings in US biotech firms recently. Roche, for example, has interests in Genentech, Protein Design Labs, and Millennium. Ciby-Geigy has acquired part ownership of Chiron, and Sandoz owns an interest in Genetic Therapy and rights to inventions at the Scripps Research Institute and the Dana Farber Cancer Institute. Presently, few biotechnology firms have produced marketable products and still fewer have turned the corner financially to become profitable. But the opportunities for this sector are enormous and may ultimately dwarf the scope of the traditional chemical-oriented firms. But with the rewards have come risks far greater than anticipated. The number of research directions which show real promise has proved frustratingly small and many biotech firms have disappeared before reaching profitability. Another characteristic of the biotechnology industry is small scale and a reluctance among major firms with which biotech firms have merged to attempt to integrate their activities with the larger firm. The resulting structure of the merged firms frequently resembles a hub with a number of satellite enterprises operating around the periphery rather than a single, large, fully integrated enterprise.

Surprisingly, little concern about the antitrust implications of these mergers has been raised, even in response to mergers of major pharmaceutical firms. Perhaps this is because the activities of the constituent organizations are thought to be more complimentary to one another and not directly competing. If two firms that have different product portfolios (say, one emphasizing cardiac drugs and the other, antibiotics) the market concentration in any single drug class will not increase following a merger. Substantial room for capitalizing on economies of scale may still exist, especially in the areas of research, marketing, finance, and administration, and consumers are not made worse off by the merger. This certainly is the scenario that would be expected in the case of acquisitions of biotechnology firms. But even if this does describe past mergers in the industry, there is no assurance that continued consolidation would be similarly innocuous. In fact, one would expect that eventually the degree of complementarity among merging firms would lessen, and firms with competing products (or potentially competing products in the pipeline) would consider merging, with the result of fewer products competing with one another within a drug class. Vigilance against such anticompetitive developments will have to be exercised in the future.

Health System Reform

Comprehensive government-initiated reform of the US health system is unlikely for several years. But it is obviously wrong to conclude that the system will not evolve in major ways in response to nongovernmental issues and pressures. Managed care will continue to develop, with more and more consumers enrolled in health plans which receive fixed, capitated payment covering all needed services. These plans will increasingly contract with other providers and suppliers that, themselves, will be reimbursed on a capitated basis. With this increased responsibility for delivering care at a fixed price, providers will become even more cost conscious with respect to all health services, including pharmaceuticals. In fact, competition among health plans is a core philosophy of several recent national health insurance proposals, including the 1993 Clinton plan. Even if consumer choice expands to formally recognize a role for nonmanaged, "high option" care, price differentials will be such that most consumers will opt for the less expensive organization of care.

Presently little information is available to consumers or their employers concerning the quality of the care being purchased, either in the fee-for-service or the managed-care sectors. In the absence of this information it not surprising that the assumption is made that all providers are essentially equal, and price is the only criterion used to select health plans. Health care becomes a kind of commodity, with no differentiation between products or services. Plans or providers offering higher than average quality of care will, over time, be driven out of the marketplace because their higher quality is not appreciated and if it is offered at a higher price it will not be purchased.

It is possible that this situation will change if these higher-quality providers can begin to offer information to consumers that justifies their higher cost. Data on consumer satisfaction, access to specialists, and use of a broader array of pharmaceuticals might be persuasive for many consumers. Some plans might also begin offering subscribers the rights to second opinions by outside experts concerning treatment that is authorized. In former times, when patients were concerned about excess treatment, second-opinion programs were popular because patients wanted to know if they really needed aggressive treatment initially recommended by their physician. Today the opposite problem exists, with patients frequently thinking that they are receiving insufficient care. It is likely that some patients would like to have the option of obtaining an outside opinion, and would be willing to pay for the additional premium cost that such a service would entail. These options would lead to product differentiation in the health care market, enabling patients to select plans that better met their preferences in terms of quality and price.

Pharmaceutical firms will therefore continue to face a multitiered health care system, with many consumers demanding only the most cost-effective therapies, while others demand higher-quality treatment, even at a higher cost. This multitiered market will generate demand for a wide spectrum of products, ranging from inexpensive generic versions of older pharmaceutical products to costly new innovative drugs, and will even include more costly but only marginally better versions of presently patented drugs.

If the demand for pharmaceuticals will be multitiered, the marketing efforts of pharmaceutical firms will be similarly diversified. While most drugs will be sold through managed-care organizations with formularies, a share of the pharmaceutical market will enable individual physicians to be more selective in choosing drugs. Thus, while centralized marketing will grow, physician-directed marketing will continue to be important, especially in markets with lower penetration of managed-care plans.

The importance of cost-effectiveness of new drugs is related to the locus of drug decision-making in drug selection. Managed care will always demand products which give value for money, but it is likely that no single benchmark for cost-effectiveness will exist across all managed-care plans, and physicians representing patients in indemnity-type plans will focus especially on quality rather than price in choosing drug products. This implies that the pharmaceutical sector will continue to see demand for a wide variety of drugs: inexpensive generic products, more expensive generic products produced and marketed by major R&D firms, breakthrough innovative drugs, and less innovative "me, too" products that provide some additional benefit to some patients.

Drug Prices

More innovative drugs will continue to command higher prices than less innovative products, as has been the pattern in the past. Regardless of supply-side considerations, such as cost and risk, demand considerations will set drug prices, at least in the short run. This will direct pharmaceutical R&D investment decisions, of course, favoring breakthrough products over "me, too" products. As true as this is for the United States, where drug prices are substantially set by the market, it is even more the case in Europe, Canada, and Japan, where drug prices are set by national health insurance programs. In most countries in which drug costs are covered by comprehensive health insurance programs, prices are strictly regulated, with cost-effectiveness criteria used in setting prices. In these settings noninnovative products will be unsuccessful in achieving high launch prices, regardless of development costs. Major innovations, on the other hand, will find a more favorable climate for higher prices, again, regardless of R&D costs.

The major regulatory issues governing pharmaceuticals will continue to be related to access. The most important are patent protection, FDA approval, and the restrictions on access to information on drugs by physicians.

Patent Protection

The maximum period of patent protection for all products has been lengthened from 17 to 20 years by the 1995 World Trade Organization treaty. But actually lengthening of the patent period may not be as great as would appear because the inception of the patent has been moved up from the date of issuance to the date of filing. Whether or not the patent period is actually lengthened depends upon the length of the patent review process. Any lengthening further enhances the ability of drug firms to capitalize on their innovations, and delays the introduction of less expensive generic versions of formerly patented products. This has already had a dramatic effect on the patent status of products whose patents were scheduled to expire in 1995 and 1996. While patients in the United States are hurt by the delay in access to generic products, R&D firms gained by the WTO in two ways. Domestically, a lengthened period of market exclusivity is important in increasing the returns to investment in R&D. But the international implications of protection of patents and intellectual property are also important. Developing countries that have substantial pharmaceutical industries devoted to copying other countries' patented drugs for domestic consumption, such as India, are now forbidden from doing so. Major R&D producers now have two options if they want to enter these developing markets. The first is to enter these markets themselves, either directly or with marketing help of indigenous firms to market their products. But local prices will have to be far below those in developed countries in order to accommodate lower income levels in the developing countries. On the other hand, the major firms might allow foreign firms to continue to manufacture and market their drugs so long as a license fee is paid. This strategy would be especially appropriate if the innovative firms felt that the sizes of these foreign markets were small in economic terms, and that there was little anticipated gain in attempting to break into third-world markets.

Neither direct entry nor licensing can be successful unless the cheaper foreign products can be prevented from entering the primary markets—a process called "parallel imports." The extent of price discounting needed to market successfully in developing countries is substantial, so the threat of cheaper versions of the patented drugs reentering the primary markets of the United States, Europe and Japan is serious. Treaties banning parallel imports generally work well, but they cause consternation among patients in the primary markets. US consumers, for example, are miffed at hearing how low drug prices are in Mexico. But major R&D firms could not survive if worldwide prices were based upon the lowest prices anywhere in the world. Treaties banning parallel imports are especially difficult to enforce when they create trade barriers between countries in existing trade blocs, such as the US and Mexico, or the wealthier EU members and Greece, Portugal, and Spain. As important as patent protection is in granting marketing exclusivity, it must be remembered that technology evolves quickly in this industry, and competitive products are frequently introduced even during an originating drug's patent period. The effect of these drugs depends largely upon their qualities relative to the older product. If a product represents a substantial improvement in efficacy, side-effect profile, or convenience, it will be more successful in taking away market share. But if it is not appreciably different from the earlier drug, its ability to compete will not be very great, and certainly there will be no opportunity to charge a higher price.

Drug Approvals

The speed of regulatory drug approval has been a highly visible concern of critics of the FDA, and studies in the 1970s indicated that regulatory delays were impeding access to new drugs by US physicians and their patients and creating a "drug lag." More recent studies have called these findings into question, however, suggesting that during the 1980s the FDA was, in fact, relatively quick compared to other major countries in approving new drugs. And more recently the FDA has streamlined its approval process and has substantially shortened the time for approval. In part this has been possible due to increased resources brought into the agency through user fees paid by NDA applicant companies.

Of course, the actual timing of a drug's approval depends on when the approval application is submitted as well as the length of the review process, itself. Unfortunately, little is known about the determinants of when drug manufacturers initiate the review process in a given country—either the date of initiation or the strategy of deciding which country's approval to seek first. It is surely a function of the attractiveness of the market and the perceived rigor of the review process. An important trend is the consolidation among the review agencies, such as has taken place in the European Union. No doubt other trade blocs, including NAFTA, will eventually follow suit in establishing a common drug approval mechanism adhered to by all member states.

Managed Care and Restricted Access to Pharmaceuticals

A particularly subtle trend in pharmaceutical access is the imposition of a second regulatory process controlling access to pharmaceuticals for members of managed-care plans. Ironically, this brings United States policy more into conformance with most foreign health systems, in which a separate agency is interposed between the scientific review agency (comparable to our FDA) and the consumer. This other agency decides which products will be reimbursed by the patient's health plan. Health-plan drug product selection has important implications for physicians, patients, and pharmaceutical manufacturers.

For physicians, an important dimension of autonomy has been removed through managed care. Although physicians are still free to prescribe any approved drug, patients will be unhappy if the chosen drug is not covered by the health plan. And this problem becomes increasingly serious as the prices of newly introduced drugs continue to rise. Physicians in managed-care programs are usually allowed to prescribe nonformulary drugs and to have them reimbursed, but there is always enough bureaucratic difficulty in doing so such that physicians are implicitly discouraged from prescribing these nonformulary products. There may be explicit penalties for more liberal prescribing, too, if the managed-care plan engages in physician practice profiling in which practice patterns, including specialist referrals, procedures, and prescriptions are tracked. Many plans do this to identify physicians who are high-cost providers—that is, those who tend to refer more frequently to specialists, perform expensive procedures, or prescribe more expensive drugs. Controlling health plan costs depends upon the plan's success in reducing the cost profile of participating physicians, so efforts will be made to identify these physicians and then change their behavior.

For patients, restricting drug choice may impose distinct burdens; potentially less effective drugs may be authorized, or those with worse side-effect profiles or reduced convenience. Patients will ultimately have to make individual assessments from the alternatives available as to health plan cost and access to quality services: Some plans will stress cost savings over access to the latest or most costly services and others will stress access at a higher premium cost.

For pharmaceutical manufacturers the trend toward managed care affects nearly all aspects of their business, especially R&D and marketing. Under managed care, allowable prices for new drugs will increasingly be related to the effectiveness of the products; many plans will perform an explicit cost-effectiveness analysis on each new product. Therefore, products which are unlikely to offer clear therapeutic advantages over existing products are less likely to be developed unless they can be profitably marketed at a low price.

Managed care also affects drug prices because of the ability of large purchasers, such as HMOs, to negotiate large discounts with manufacturers. These discounts appear whether the purchaser buys the drugs directly for its own pharmacies or on behalf of community pharmacies (usually chains of pharmacies) that contract with the managed-care organization. Other community pharmacies have fought these discounts granted to their competitors, claiming that they were discriminatory. They reflect, however, the purchasing power of the managed-care organization and the ability of these organizations to shift purchasing from one drug within a particular therapeutic category to another on the basis of price. Independent pharmacies do not have that same market power. The unaffiliated pharmacies have been embroiled in a large suit in federal court against the pharmaceutical industry, the results of which might jeopardize the entire policy of "tiered pricing." A final resolution of the case is probably many years off. If tiered pricing becomes illegal, what will be the response of the pharmaceutical industry? It is, of course, more likely that discounted prices will rise than that high (undiscounted) prices will fall, so overall drug prices would be expected to rise.

The rate of increase in drug prices is already highly scrutinized, and major R&D manufacturers agreed in the early 1990s to hold price increases to the rate of increase of the Consumer Price Index. Manufacturers now know that profit from a new drug has to be based on its launch price and not future price increases.

The FDA

The FDA's critical role in the pharmaceutical sector is being challenged from several directions. Seen narrowly, the FDA controls access to pharmaceuticals through its NDA application review process. Drugs are either approved for marketing after demonstrating safety and efficacy or they are not. Seen more broadly, however, the agency's regulatory scope is much larger, for it controls access to information, as well.

The FDA's jurisdiction includes oversight authority on drug labeling and advertising. One policy which has irritated both physicians and pharmaceutical manufacturers is the agency prohibition on distribution by manufacturers of information pertaining to the use of its drugs for purposes other than those approved. "Off-label" use is common throughout the medical community and such prescribing always entails an assumption of risk by the prescribing physician. But pharmaceutical manufacturers may not discuss or even disclose such use with physicians, let alone promote it. The FDA therefore has a significant role in controlling the diffusion of knowledge in the pharmaceutical industry. Recently, critics have questioned the appropriateness of this role, suggesting that the agency should be more lenient in allowing the distribution of information concerning off-label use, as long as appropriate caveats are included warning physicians of the approval status of the drug and its use.

Other critics of the FDA question whether the FDA should classify drugs as to whether or not they are "safe and effective" or should instead use a more continuous rating scale, including information such as *how* safe, *how* effective, and for *whom*. It may be that drugs not found to be safe and effective in general, *are* so under certain circumstances, and perhaps physicians should be given this information and be allowed to prescribed accordingly. Dichotomous characterization of drugs for use under widely varying circumstances may not be the best public policy approach for the FDA.

At the heart of the issue is the nature of the regulatory process that attempts to protect consumers. Two models of regulation were suggested many years ago by Milton Friedman, who discussed the differences between licensure and certification of professionals. According to the licensure approach standards are set for those who engage in an activity (or for services or products). Those meeting the standards are allowed to be offered to consumers and those failing to do so are not. The decision is a dichotomous one, and there is no room for ambiguity. Many examples of this approach are seen. Food safety laws allow the sale of fresh meat and fish meeting standards for cleanliness, while banning diseased or otherwise contaminated products. In many states fruit not meeting specified minimum size is not allowed to be sold and is discarded. Many professions are licensed, usually by state professional boards, including architects, attorneys, and engineers. In the health sector, licensed professions include physicians, dentists, nurses, and pharmacists. And other occupations are similarly regulated, including building contractors, tree surgeons, and even beauticians. These licensure laws assure that practitioners have passed examinations demonstrating minimal skill levels. But they also assure that nobody who has not met these standards is allowed to practice the profession or trade. Consumers are therefore protected, but at the expense of freedom to choose less-qualified products or providers.

A more flexible approach relies upon certification, rather than licensure. Under certification, a wide variety of qualities of service and product are allowed to be marketed given the condition that consumers are informed of the quality standards attained. Board certification for physician specialists is the best-known example of this form of regulation in the health sector. Although only licensed physicians may practice medicine in any state, any physician may practice a specialty. But only those physicians passing the specialty board examinations may call themselves "board certified" in that specialty. Consumers therefore have a choice of physicians to treat their particular condition—either board-certified specialists or not. Frequently those choices are made on behalf of patients by health plans or hospitals. It is common, for example, for academic medical centers to grant hospital privileges only to board-certified physicians (or those younger physicians who are on their way toward becoming board certified). The advantage of the certification model in medicine is that consumers (or their health plans acting as the patient's agent) are free to choose from a broader array of practitioners, often demonstrating a variety of lines of demarcation between them. In the case of pharmaceuticals, the range of alternatives available to physicians would expand if the FDA rated, rather than approved, drugs. A criticism of this approach, of course, is that physicians might make mistakes given the new array of products available. While true, it is likely that patients are paying a high price for the present level of protection in terms of restrictions on the drugs they can use. If the concern is really that physicians need to be better informed about pharmaceuticals, a more direct approach would be professional continuing education on the subject. Patients will be best served by having the broadest choice of pharmaceuticals available and the best-educated physicians choosing among them.

Conclusion

The future of the pharmaceutical sector will be determined by a number of forces outside of the sector itself. The most important, of course, will be the pattern of health system reform. In the absence of comprehensive government-led reform, market-driven reforms such as managed care will continue. These will impose cost-effectiveness criteria on the industry but perhaps expand consumer choice in terms of product selection.

The most important regulatory issue concerning the sector will be the jurisdiction of the FDA and whether Congress mandates it to expand options and information available to patients and their physicians. If so, the medical community will then have the responsibility of assuring that physicians can make informed choices which really will be in patients' best interests.

Index